The Prisoner's Philosophy

THE
Prisoner's Philosophy

Life and Death in Boethius's
Consolation

Joel C. Relihan

with a contribution on the medieval Boethius by
William E. Heise

University of Notre Dame Press
Notre Dame, Indiana

University of Notre Dame Press
Notre Dame, Indiana 46556
www.undpress.nd.edu
All Rights Reserved

Hardback edition published in 2017

Library of Congress Cataloging in-Publication Data

Relihan, Joel C.
The prisoner's philosophy : life and death in Boethius's Consolation /
Joel C. Relihan ; with a contribution on the medieval Boethius by William Heise.
p.   cm.
Includes bibliographical references (p.   ) and index.
ISBN-13: 978-0-268-04024-6 (pbk. : alk. paper)
ISBN-13: 978-0-268-16030-2 (hardback
1. Boethius, d. 524. De consolatione philosophiae.
I. Heise, William (William E.) II. Title.
B659.D473R45   2006
100—dc22
2006028978

∞ *The paper in this book meets the guidelines for permanence and durability of the Committee
on Production Guidelines for Book Longevity of the Council on Library Resources.*

Clarae Gratiaeque

filiabus optimis

Contents

Preface

The concluding chapter of my *Ancient Menippean Satire* (Johns Hopkins 1993) offered in brief compass an interpretation of *Consolation of Philosophy* as a Menippean satire, and deferred to a later time and another book a full exposition of the argument. After a lapse of many years, the present volume fulfills that promise. I do not repeat that analysis here, though I do allude to some of its particulars and stand by its main conclusions: that *Consolation* is a Christian work that dramatizes not the truths of philosophy as a whole but the limits of pagan philosophy in particular; that it belongs to the history of an ironic genre of Platonic inspiration that shows the scholar at play; and that the culmination of this history is to be found in the Christian Platonism of the twelfth century.

What I had intended as a sequel has become an opportunity to reexamine my methods, to refine my definitions, and to defend my practices of interpretation. My thinking on the nature of the ironies of the text, and on the specific relations between pagan philosophy and Christian belief that are expressed within it, has changed and, I hope, matured over these intervening years: my comparison of Boethius and the emperor Julian (2005) shows that I take Bakhtin less seriously and autobiography more seriously than I have in the past; and what is traditionally labelled satiric has its place in *Consolation* alongside that of Menippean satire. These developments have informed my translation of *Consolation*; its second printing (Hackett 2004), with revisions drawn from early reviews, is used here throughout. The introduction to that translation is not a miniature version of this study but rather presents a number of plot lines for the curious reader of *Consolation* to follow; but even as the production of the translation focused my own ideas for this work, the translation itself with its own, different critical apparatus may be used by the reader of this volume as a complementary, not a redundant, resource.

Both response and resistance to a dozen years of scholarly activity have proved fruitful. A number of works appeared immediately after the publication of *Ancient Menippean Satire:* Peter Dronke, *Verse with Prose from Petronius to Dante* (1994); Bernhard Pabst, *Prosimetrum: Tradition und Wandel einer Literaturform zwischen Spätantike und Spätmittelalter* (1994); W. Scott Blanchard, *Scholar's Bedlam: Menippean Satire in the Renaissance* (1995); Gian Biagio Conte, *The Hidden Author: An Interpretation of Petronius'* Satyrica (1996); the dissertation of Bradford Gregory Hays, *Fulgentius the Mythographer* (1996); and Jon Haarberg, *Parody and* The Praise of Folly (1998). Similarly, the years just prior to this study have seen another flurry of important publications: theoretical matters have been made clearer by Carter Kaplan, *Critical Synoptics: Menippean Satire and the Analysis of Intellectual Mythology* (2000); Kirk Freudenberg, ed., *The Cambridge Companion to Roman Satire* (2005); and Howard Weinbrot, *Menippean Satire Reconsidered: From Antiquity to the Eighteenth Century* (2005), which the author graciously allowed me to see in prepublication form. Marenbon's authoritative *Boethius* in Oxford's Great Medieval Thinkers series (2003) and the special Boethian issue of the *American Catholic Philosophical Quarterly,* edited by Siobhan Nash-Marshall (78.2; spring 2004), were enthusiastically read.

Classicists and medievalists may be surprised to discover how popular the term Menippean satire has become in discussions of modern literature, and how many works have been claimed to fall under its influence, among them *Tristram Shandy, Moby Dick,* and *Gravity's Rainbow.* Such contemporary critical approaches to the genre offer welcome insight into the intellectual enterprise of *Consolation,* but Boethius rarely finds a place in them. In fact, it is now possible to write of Menippean satire without any reference to antiquity at all, as in M. Keith Booker, *Flann O'Brien, Bakhtin, and Menippean Satire* (1995). On the other hand, Weinbrot 2005, whose understanding of both ancient and early modern literature and Menippean satire is profound, acknowledges Boethius but does not see *Consolation* as Menippean at all; and even those critics who admit that its genre has some importance for the interpretation of *Consolation* have been generally unwilling to see the text in the context of the history of a classical genre.

Granted, *Consolation* is awkwardly poised between the usual traditions and divisions of Western literature, but the fundamental problem is the general lack of recognition that *Consolation* is critical of the intellectual synthesis that it both presents and undermines, that it is both philosophical and ironic. I wish to place *Consolation* in the genre's vital center, which I understand more in terms of the parody of encyclopedic knowledge than in the exaltation of polyphony; my debts to Northrop Frye's anatomy are ultimately greater than those to Bakhtin. The questions that need to be raised and answered about *Consolation* have to do with plot and intertextuality, with irony and the presentation of wisdom, with literary history and a many-branched reception. Modernists must be called to take Boethius into account; classicists must be urged not to allow their knowledge of late antiquity and its philosophical and religious traditions to determine the interpretation of the text, but to let an understanding of the Menippean *Consolation* modify their understanding of late antique culture.

Over the strenuous objections of Pabst (1994) I insist that it is not a retrojection of modern aesthetics or deconstructive theory that leads me to these conclusions. Rather, my motivations are a close attention to the details of the plot; a willingness to consider a broad range of works as parallels; and an acceptance of the ironic reception of the text from the time of its writing into modern times. I see three fundamental stories intertwined in *Consolation*: an ironic retelling of *Crito,* with a prisoner who refuses to leave his prison precisely because he is a philosopher; a philosophically intense adaptation of Lucian's *Jupiter Confutatus,* with its presentation of a questioner who deflates the otherworldly authority figure by means of embarrassing questions about the relation of free will and divine foreknowledge; and a sober reduction of Job to a quiet dialogue in which the wounded innocent ultimately learns wisdom in silence. *Consolation* is a Menippean satire not merely because of the mixture of disparate literary influences that lie behind it, or because of its mixture of prose and verse, or for its mixture of fantasy and morality. More important than these formal considerations is the book's status as a problematic encyclopedia, its deliberate dramatization of the act of writing about systematic knowledge and its calling into question the value of that knowledge. There are many benefits to be gained here, not least that *Consolation* is more philosophically satisfying, or at least more Platonic, for a problematic, rather than a happy, ending. In the presentation that follows I will not merely make the claim that *Consolation* conforms to the definition and fits into the history of the genre that I have detailed in *Ancient Menippean Satire*; I will build from the ground up and develop a revised version of the interpretation of the text that helped in the creation of that definition and that history.

I used to take the Christian presence in *Consolation* more as a latent thing, as the path not taken, as the way out of Philosophy's labyrinth that is hinted at but never achieved. But, emboldened by the work of others, I now see it much more actively at work—the prayer advocated at the end is not the philosophical path to God that Philosophy had earlier intended the prisoner to travel, but a different, Christian path that the prisoner chooses, offered grudgingly by a Philosophy forced to admit that her intended approach does not quite satisfy or console this particular patient, a Philosophy who wanted to lead but who ultimately only can point him to his true home. Boethius is truer to Plato by not being as optimistic as Augustine: there is no logical path, and certainly no trivial or quadrivial path, that leads from the world of human logic and perception to the divine realm. What is most remarkable about *Consolation*, in its relation to Platonic and Christian worlds, is that the author tries so hard to resist apocalypse, and that the narrator is neither an Er nor a Scipio nor a St. John nor a Plotinus. After all of its intellectual heavy weather, *Consolation* is about humble access to God through prayer, not revelation.

I have been presenting various incarnations of this reading of *Consolation* over many years to more and less receptive audiences. I am pleased to have as a partner in this enterprise a former student, William Heise, who will address more fully than I can some medieval readings and uses of an ironic *Consolation*. But, if I pause now to remember and acknowledge some other debts to sympathetic colleagues over these many years, I do not imply that they are in agreement with me or responsible for my errors. Among many, I single out Charles Wright, of the University of Illinois at Urbana-Champaign, who enlisted me to teach an English graduate seminar, "Boethius and the Twelfth Century Renaissance," in the spring of 1990; James O'Donnell of the University of Pennsylvania, a source of constant encouragement, not least through the e-seminar on Boethius over which he presided in the fall of 1994 and in which I was allowed to participate; Danuta Shanzer, now also of the University of Illinois, generous with her criticisms and with her advice in matters concerning Boethius and Alan of Lille; Jon Haarberg and Howard Weinbrot, both for electronic conversation and for a peek at their works in prepublication form. To the patience of my editor at Notre Dame, Barbara Hanrahan, I will be forever grateful. To my family, which has also waited patiently for the completion of this book, I owe my greatest debt.

Texts, Translations, Terminology, Dramatis Personae

In presenting new approaches to and new interpretations of a well-known work, this study imagines an audience of amateur and professional classicists, medievalists, philosophers, theologians, and literary critics already familiar with Boethius's *Consolation* but willing to look at it in the context of less familiar literary works. I hope to avoid Boethian boilerplate. The thorough commentary of Gruber (1978; a second edition is promised for 2006) and the partial commentary of Sharples (1991), the general studies of Boethius by Courcelle (1967), Chadwick (1981), and Marenbon (2003), and the influential interpretive essays of Lerer (1985) and Curley (1986, 1987) are crucial jumping-off points. For the Latin text, I rely on Bieler's second edition (1984) and generally avoid textual matters, though I have consulted the new text of Moreschini (2000). I have not thought it necessary to offer anything like a complete bibliography of works on *Consolation*, even if such a thing were possible; the bibliographies of Gruber (1997 and 1998; a third volume has yet to appear) and Kaylor (1992) are highly recommended. The translation of Boethius's *Consolation of Philosophy* that is excerpted throughout this volume is reprinted from the corrected second printing (2004) of my translation of the entire work, published in 2001 by Hackett Publishing Company. It is reprinted here by permission of the publisher. Its "Suggestions for Further Reading" (xxvi–xxvii) may also be consulted.

I do not encumber the apparatus with lists of editions of standard classical authors and the like. For ease of reference, particular editions of works of Boethius and others will be found in the bibliography under the editors' names; journal titles are not abbreviated. All Latin and Greek quotations in the text are translated, and, with only a few exceptions, all noted, all translations are my own; the most significant exception is my use of the Douay-Rheims Bible. I have also supplied some of the Latin translations of texts in William Heise's chapter; notes that I have added to his essay I enclose in square brackets.

In citations of the text of *Consolation,* passages from the poems (traditionally, *metra*) have a special designation: 3.m.9.1–3 refers to the first three lines in the ninth poem of the third book. Passages in prose have no such special abbreviation: 1.3.4 refers to the fourth sentence in the third prose section of the first book. No attempt has been made to refer to the line numbers of Bieler's edition, though such practice may be found in some other current studies of *Consolation.* The subtitles found in translations (meter 3, prose 2, etc.) are only modern conveniences, which I have avoided. The accent marks that accompany some of my translations from the poems indicate the rhythm of the original and are taken from my translation; for brief poetic citations I have not included them.

I have also avoided calling Philosophy by the titles "Dame" or "Lady," which to my ear only conjure up the conventions of courtly love. She has no title, and if one were to be supplied, "Muse" would be entirely more appropriate. I satisfy myself with the capital letter; when I refer to lower-case philosophy I never place it first in a sentence. More difficult is naming the other participant in this dialogue, who also has no title. To call him simply "I" would cut this Gordian knot but would encourage too great an assimilation of character and reader. My solution is more complex. "Boethius" is the name of the author, and of the historical reality to which the text undoubtedly points; "the narrator" is used when I speak of the character whose voice we occasionally hear when we think of the one who went on from his dialogue with Philosophy to write down their words, after the fact. But in reference to the actual dialogue I prefer two other terms: "the prisoner" is used to describe this character from his own point of view, the political victim; "the exile" is used to describe him from Philosophy's point of view, the one who needs to be recalled home. I do not claim that these terms are purely objective and free from interpretation, but I have tried to use them consistently, and I hope that they will be found to be useful.

Chapter One

The Ironic *Consolation* and Its Reception

Boethius's *Consolation* is typically taken as a serious philosophical work, even by those who admit to its Menippean affiliations. This is not unreasonable, as its sophisticated philosophical content reflects Boethius's mature thought on crucial topics and proved fundamental to the medieval schools.[1] The legend of his martyrdom makes it uncharitable to suggest that his last words did not literally satisfy his soul; and as most readers do not have patience for the book's details, it seems much safer to confound philosophy and pedantry and attribute its perceived dullness to high-mindedness. Critics of modern Menippean satire do not imagine that *Consolation* is relevant to the genre and its history. Now I have long read *Consolation* as an ironic text—literally, its words meaning other than what they seem to mean—and I have found the greatest support in this approach not from classicists, who are rarely fascinated by or engaged with the text, but from Northrop Frye and from various more modern medievalists, who are willing to believe that if Chaucer liked it, there must be something more to it. Payne's *Chaucer and Menippean Satire* is my predecessor here; though the readings of Chaucer presented in it have not found wide acceptance, and though my view of the nature of the genre is quite different, Payne rightly emphasizes the ironies of Boethius's text as crucial ingredients in its literary influence.

But the conclusions about the nature of *Consolation* that I put forward in *Ancient Menippean Satire* I achieved primarily through a study of it in relation to antecedent classical and late classical Menippean satires, not to later works and traditions. An ironic interpretation seemed indicated, as I could read the end of *Consolation* only as a description of a dialogue reaching an impasse, and this reading came to make sense in the light of a classical tradition (stretching from Menippus and Varro through Seneca and Petronius on to Lucian, Julian, and Martianus Capella) in which scholars and satirists take to task the theories and constructs that in others of their works had satisfied them. A constant theme in the genre is that those who presume to oberve the world from some superior vantage point, whether as moral critics (satirists) or intellectual critics (philosophers), cannot understand what they see, because human life and thought, inherently irrational, cannot be made to fit the logical categories of such observers; consequently, theorists are the butt of the humor of a Menippean satire. The observer's confident pronouncements, belied by the facts, force the reader to interpret them as commentary more on the observer than on what is observed—we hear what the embarrassed critic does not. Surprise endings tend to debunk the preceding discussions; what is advocated (typically between the lines, because the antidogmatic genre is allergic to preaching) is an antitheoretical common sense; the genre is Christianized as the common sense of Menippus's Cynicism is recast as Christian piety in late antiquity, not only in Boethius, but in Ennodius as well.

Again, this definition and history was not arrived at *a priori* but by the consideration of the details of interpretation of individual texts. It was the *Mythologies* of Fulgentius that started me on the road to Menippean satire: its tale of a narrator whose mythological studies are changed after his argument with his Muse starts along an Ovidian path;[2] the resulting library of mythical interpretations, expounded to the narrator by Calliope, a mythical character who will allegorize herself away in the middle of these debunking rationalizations, belonged to a quite different tradition.[3] The purpose of the Menippean compilation is to embarrass our mythographer and his theories about the end of the age of myth, demonstrate the comic and literary vitality of the myths that he seeks to reduce to mere morals, and show the limitations of the knowledge contained within his presumptuous encyclopedia.

Of course, Martianus Capella's *Marriage* is an obvious sticking point in the history of the genre when it is viewed this way: why such a vast effort to create an encyclopedia whose point is that the truth lies beyond its compilations?[4] But I think that this is the surface meaning of these texts; I refuse to take as protestations of modesty such passages as the end of Martianus's *Marriage*, in which Satyra, the Muse of work, abandons it in disgust as a hodge-podge without a clear didactic point (9.997–1000).[5] These works helped me to see some of the realities of the plot of *Consolation*: that the debate between the prisoner and Philosophy is a debate between an author and his Muse; that there is a struggle for control of the work and its interpretation; and that Philosophy is frustrated by the narrator's questions, never gets to talk about what she wants in the later books, and is forced to abandon many of her goals. The resulting book is not what its Muse intended. It was, then, an ironic reading of *Consolation* that helped to formulate what I thought were the characteristics, the nature, and the history of the genre of Menippean satire as a whole; I was able to discern a pattern of development in which *Consolation* occupied a place intermediate between the genre's Cynic origins and its twelfth-century transformation.[6]

That *Consolation*, so understood, can be seen as occupying a specific place in a lengthy literary history is one sort of argument for the interpretation that I offered in my previous study. But what I seek to do now is to make my assertion of a Menippean reading of *Consolation* more plausible, and to bolster an argument made in conjunction with antecedent Menippean traditions, by an intensive appeal to the details of the plot and structure of *Consolation*, to the other traditions and texts that I see at work in it, and by considering later authors who saw in *Consolation* either failure in its serious and surface goals or success in its ironic and subtextual ones. Payne offers a suggestive reading of *Consolation* that may help in the interpretation of Chaucer, but I will be pursuing those later texts that would support the argument that *Consolation* presents a Philosophy whose teachings do not satisfy or are not the ones that she wanted to teach. Both of these attempts, to relate the details of *Consolation* to parallels in texts outside of its genre and to recover a specifically ironic reception of *Consolation*, will be offered as further arguments for the interpretation that I propose.

For I do not think that *Consolation* is merely truth-testing (as Dronke labels it), or even that it celebrates the inalienable right of human beings to be free from the straitjacket of rational thought (*pace* Payne). Marenbon is content to say that *Consolation* explores the limitations of Philosophy as a conscious goal.[7] I would go further; I find myself more in the company of critics of Menippean satire in the Enlightenment and in the modern world, who argue that the genre insists on the essential disconnectedness of facts and rejects the mythical modes of reasoning that look for theories to explain events (Kaplan 2000, inspired by Wittgenstein), or that it uses at least two voices to oppose a threatening or false orthodoxy (Weinbrot 2005). But in considering *Consolation*, I am much more specific: the Philosophy that would give the prisoner wings and a chance to fly out of prison (4.1.9) is never allowed to do so, because the prisoner grounds her by his demand for an accounting of his own life and of earthly life in general. In books 4 and 5 the narrator closes Philosophy's open door out of the prison. When the prisoner compels Philosophy to admit that divine foreknowledge of human events does impose a sort of necessity on human action and free will, we see that the prisoner's own philosophical nature and interests, at odds with the journey to his true home that the personified Love of Wisdom freely offers, does not allow him the particular freedom that is Philosophy's gift. Acting as a philosopher, the prisoner deprives himself of Philosophy's undeniably great gift of a heavenly vision; he is forced to be satisfied with God's contemplation of the earth, rather than the earth's contemplation of God. In this collision of desires a *via media* is glimpsed, the common sense that is the path not taken in Menippean satires, and here this is Christian faith. Philosophy, who had chided the prisoner for looking down to the ground at the beginning of *Consolation*, abandons her effort to make him look up to heaven and so looks down with him as the Menippean observer, a *catascopus;* the world that she and the narrator see does not make sense to them through their own eyes, but would through the eyes of God.[8] The prisoner prays, using Philosophy's expertise only to establish a groundwork for prayer, and it is quite doubtful that this is the flight home that Philosophy had in mind.

I submit the following as the crucial "hard data" that any interpretation of *Consolation* must deal with, the four unfulfilled promises of the text. First, as it is styled a consolation, we expect a treatment of death and of the soul, but, despite a few promising passages in which Philosophy seems to be on the verge of satisfying our desires, she never does. The title is therefore playful and paradoxical, raising, but ultimately frustrating, certain serious expectations.[9] Second, Philosophy tells the narrator that she will help

him remember who he really is (1.6.14 ff.; cf. also 1.2.6), for this forgetfulness, intimately bound up with his forgetfulness of her, is the true cause of
his illness. The call to Socratic self-realization does not lead to any explicit
definition of the nature of a human being in general, or of the narrator in
particular; at least, not within the bounds of the text.[10] Third, Philosophy
promises to lead the narrator to his true homeland (4.1.9 and the subsequent
4.m.1; 5.1.4): she never does. There is nothing like a Platonic myth in *Consolation*, no vision of heavenly harmonies or guided tour of the universe, no
peek into the abyss, no apocalypse, no release from the prison. Fourth, and
finally, Philosophy never administers the harsher remedies that she promises. The prisoner says that he is ready for them at 3.1.2, but the last use of
the image of the medicinal draft is at 4.6.57, when she offers a poem whose
sweetness will ready him for further discussion. But the harsh remedy al-
luded to is surely Socrates' cup of hemlock,[11] and the prisoner does not die,
possibly because he does not want to go where Philosophy would take him.
He will not die, but live. One expedient is to claim that at the dialogue's end
the prisoner is ready for what has not yet been accomplished, and that he has
been properly prepared to die, to learn who he is, and to enter Philosophy's
homeland. This may well be true. But then preparation consists of a pattern
of absences, omissions, and frustrations of expectation that must be viewed
as central to the interpretation of a dialogue which, on its face, ends up far
from where it began and concludes with arguments that it misunderstands.
The prisoner, rejecting the journey to heaven, remains on the earth.[12]

Reception: Historical and Idiosyncratic Considerations

That Philosophy does not succeed in her desire to lead the exile to his death
and thus to his true home, that there is a struggle for control of the argument, that Philosophy's concluding arguments represent the tempering of
her system by the prisoner's (I will argue, Christian) desires—this interpretation seems not to have been advanced before. Modern readings, typically
favorably impressed by the Christian philosopher's unexpected rejection of
Christianity and revelation in an hour of need, are more concerned to define
those competing claims of reason and experience within the text whose
reconciliation is symbolized by its integration of prose and verse, of poetry
and philosophy. I claim that the Christian sentiment, expressed in biblical

allusions at crucial junctures, liturgical language, and emotional and devotional stance, emerges as a sign of the system to be preferred when neither Philosophy nor experience can make sense of the prisoner's place in the world.[13] It is fair, then, to raise the question of where my reading comes from, which sees this work as an autobiographical account of a philosopher's growing dissatisfaction with some of his own prior beliefs, and which ends in the acceptance of a different set of values, in effect, a deconversion.[14] In *Ancient Menippean Satire* I proposed a definition of the genre that spoke more of self-parody and the parody of encyclopedic knowledge than of Bakhtinian polyphony; within the history of the genre I saw a change from the parody of the social critic (in Rome, the satirist) to the parody of the intellectual critic; Varro, with his feet in both worlds, inspires the encyclopedic fantasies of late antiquity; Boethius, along with Fulgentius and Ennodius, effectively Christianizes this genre. But to claim that Martianus Capella's *Marriage of Philology and Mercury* aims to make fun of its encyclopedic content and favor the mystical ascent to the truth that is not found in books—this may seem too counterintuitive, or simply too modern.[15] Are these views the product of my own historical location, a reflex perhaps of modern deconstructionist theory, or a retrojection of twentieth-century aesthetics?[16] Is this reading of Boethius a naïve and quixotic attempt to recover an original meaning, the author's intent? Or, worse, as my views on *Consolation* have changed over the years, is it merely a desperate compulsion of evidence to fit a theory?

Just as I would not reproduce my earlier work on Menippean satire as probative of my reading of *Consolation*, so too I would not claim that I have merely synthesized the work of others. Yet among modern critics I would identify three as inspirational, even if I do not accept their ultimate conclusions. Payne finds in the dialogue the prisoner's constant struggle to escape from the intellectual straitjackets that Philosophy would impose on him, but finds no such specifically Christian escape.[17] Lerer hears in the silence with which the work ends the language of prayer, but also the acceptance of Philosophy's ability to direct his thoughts and his prayers.[18] Dronke helps to define one of *Consolation*'s major lines of influence in the development of medieval autobiography; but, although he speaks of the undermining, relativizing, and truth-testing of the Menippean genre, the multiple "I"s of a Menippean text, and the truth that arises in the interplay of minds, he does not claim for the end of *Consolation* a new truth but the prisoner's gaining of a "radiant strength."[19]

For the *fides quaerens intellectum* in these matters, we may invoke reception for considerations of method that will allow us to sail between the Scylla and the Charybdis of assertion and complaisance. But reception is itself a curious thing. We are denied access to a text's original meaning, if there ever was such a thing, and are constrained to view it through the filters of subsequent use and interpretation as text becomes icon. Yet we still exercise our right to reject (perhaps only to try to reject) certain influential views, as texts may inspire utterly contradictory lines of influence, as in fact *Consolation* has. After all, the positivist interpretations of the last hundred years are the first to be swept away in order to let reception have its say about classical literature. And there are further complications, as the rightly rejected theoretical approaches of ages past (the medieval allegorization of Vergil, for example, or the moralizing of Ovid) may be approached for insight, and at the fuzzy edges of hermeneutic principle is heuristic reality: texts are inexhaustible, and readers are well advised to listen to what other readers have to say about them.[20]

Reception theory is certainly right to encourage a sort of humility in the face of history, but humility is not method: there is no particular logic by which individual readers unconsciously assemble the inevitable filters or consult the particular elements of the great chain of reception. By our own patterns of reading we create our own models against which we evaluate what we read next.[21] Ancients and moderns would probably agree that reading and interpretation are matters of the reader's self-discovery.[22] We are not perfect microcosms of literary history; reception theory may encourage us to pat ourselves on the back for our mastery of Great Books in Sequence, whether we have read them or not; but we must remember our normal desire to read our books from back to front, and our traditions from front to back, and to skip about as the spirit moves us.

Further, once we are consciously aware as critics of reception's role in the reading and interpretation of texts, the rules are changed, and unconscious influences may be less powerful than conscious desires. We may have very different explicit motivations when we try to constitute the particular chain of reception at whose end we would stand. This strikes me as resembling the essential Catholic-Protestant debate: whether authoritative texts are to be understood in the light of an ongoing revelation, or whether they are to be stripped of the accretions of a fallible tradition. In practice, there are no pure forms of either, and both, in their theoretical, pure forms, are very much alike because they equally refuse to stand still: both continuing revelation and continuing rejection of yesterday's readings threaten to produce that on-going revolution that cynics would say is the true religion that organized religion tries to suppress. I draw the analogy because literary criticism, like literary creation, is an arena in which inspiration has an undeniable role. The processes of both are numinous.[23]

I was once very carefully told that I should never say that I had "figured out" the meaning of a work; rather, I should examine my conscience to discover what personal and historical forces made my particular interpretation inevitable. The first half of this statement is fair, but surely the second is ridiculous; if nothing else, natural contrariness should make me dissatisfied with such an analysis of my own motives. We may, and should, labor mightily to discover the historical prejudices of others, but I would maintain that our own can never be completely known to us. Inspiration leads us as readers and critics to conclusions that we must think essential to the work in question and lends us a rhetoric that is the tool that lets us try to persuade others of them. For persuasion is at the heart of the enterprise: my opinions *per se* should be of interest to no one, but, if I may continue my analogy, my desire to win converts to my opinion is. Certainly the least persuasive forms of argument are "I read the work this way because my teacher told me to," or "Current history requires this interpretation." If we think that our readings are purely idiosyncratic, meditations upon our own prejudices and not upon the text, or if we think that they are mere historical artifacts, fashioned by accident and circumstance, we ought to keep quiet. There is no compelling reason for burdening others with our private thoughts; as critics we must all believe at some level that what we think makes at least some pretense to wider application.

I cannot say therefore by what specific theory I insist that the details of the plot of *Consolation* need careful attention, and that prevailing interpretations seem to ignore crucial details which, when taken into account, would change those interpretations. I suppose that there is something of New Criticism in this (if the term has any relevance left);[24] I admit that "common sense" is a tyrannical label for an attempt to deal with all of the phenomena of a text. But it is not necessary to engage in hand-wringing over the necessity of interpretation, nor is it proper to label assertion as arrogance, a pejorative term for an inevitability. What I would offer is a protestation of honesty, showing to the best of my ability the steps and stages by which I reached my conclusions, and how my reading of *Consolation* affected my explicitly stated theories about the nature and history of the genre of Menippean satire. I am willing to call this an argument, in all of the senses of the term.

The Scholar at Play

In other words, I claim that in reading *Consolation*, as in reading the other late classical Menippean satires, most modern readers have simply missed the joke. The text is both over-familiar and under-read; it is the modern reception of the text, and the expectations raised in readers because of this reception, that must be countered. One has to agree with reception theory here and admit that it is practically impossible to come to *Consolation* for the first time, though I hope to demonstrate in what follows just what such an encounter might be like. And so I do think that I have "figured it out," though I am uncertain of the relative proportions of revelation and analytical discovery. But I am not the first; I am not proposing a complete "paradigm shift"; not all people at all times have missed this joke; we may speak of a "Menippean reception" of *Consolation*. I have argued that Menippean satire takes its inspiration from Plato and that in the course of its history it returns to its origins in the twelfth century, in increasingly philosophical discussions of whether humans and human reason can find a logical place in the fabric of the physical universe.[25] The fact that rational theories cannot explain irrational human beings is originally the entrée for attacking the silliness of philosophy; in time it becomes the argument for the existence of a transcendent reality. Boethius is not at the end of any tradition; the often-repeated phrase "last of the Romans, first of the Schoolmen" asserts this reality in one way, but the history of Menippean satire shows it in quite another.[26] In the history of the genre that I detailed in *Ancient Menippean Satire*, the genre that has its origins in Plato finds its comic fulfillment in Alan of Lille and its sublime transformation in Bernardus Silvestris. It is the twelfth century that proceeds from Boethius's text into prosimetric accounts of the inadequacy of Philosophy, and thus of the necessity of Theology, to explain the place of human beings in creation. Boethius is intermediate in his use of prose and verse—he does not write a medieval prosimetrum, though he does influence its development. So too in techniques of dialogue: Boethius' *Consolation* exists along a trajectory that leads from the Socratic dialogue to the medieval consolatory dialogue and the instructional dialogue, but is not equivalent with any of them.[27] Many of the extraordinary characteristics of *Consolation* can be made to appear more reasonable when they are located within the history of a developing, unfolding genre.

It is easier to claim that we should read in the light of reception than to prove that we inevitably do; but it is certainly true that *Consolation*, which has exerted its influence in many different genres and in many different ways, suffers in modern times from being largely removed from the arena of creative imitation. In the Middle Ages, when it was endlessly imitated, authors saw within it many more things than we see now, including its comic and ironic potential (see chapter 9). For example, we know of an eleventh-century musical production of *Consolation*, in which a similarity between the poems and the Psalms must surely have been exploited;[28] we also know of a Burgundian commentary on *Consolation*, into which obscene stories were interpolated as glosses.[29] The twelfth century uses *Consolation* to construct myths that describe the end of Christian Platonism and the inability of the mind to comprehend the universe, but the relations between Philosophy and the prisoner are also the inspiration for Abelard's depiction of Heloise, for the debate between Reason and the Lover in *Romance of the Rose*, for the sublimation of Dante's grief for the dead Beatrice in *La Vita Nuova*.[30]

Modern readers and critics circumscribe and limit the possibilities of *Consolation* because it is a work that seems to have ceased to engage the imagination of modern authors. This trend begins in the Renaissance, as Humanist literature seems to bypass *Consolation* altogether, though its influence may be detected in a few of that era's Menippean satires.[31] In fact, contemporary interpretations seem more pious than the most adulatory ones of the Middle Ages.[32] The *Consolation*'s prisoner who, at the point of death, is forced to wrestle with eternal questions and to locate his soul in eternity, continues to work his influence, perhaps even in *Darkness at Noon*.[33] The Boethius who wrestles with philosophy and politics lies behind one of the characters in Iain Pears' brilliant work *The Dream of Scipio*. And *Consolation* can certainly take its place in the general history of prison literature as well.[34]

But to cite the exception to this rule is to understand it: John Kennedy Toole's *A Confederacy of Dunces*. Its hero, Ignatius J. Reilly, is a scholar gone mad, compiling endless notebooks of rant against the world, quoting from *Consolation*, appealing to Fortuna and her wheel, clinging to Boethius, and so becoming utterly estranged from the corrupt world of New Orleans. His own text of *Consolation* becomes, through a series of misadventures, a prop in a widely distributed pornographic picture with a schoolhouse theme: a book, a globe, and a female teacher in a provocative pose. *Consolation* has here become a symbol of wisdom out of place.

In *A Confederacy of Dunces*, Philosophy appears in the person of one Myra Minkoff, a friend from college with whom Ignatius used to assail the modern academic and intellectual orthodoxies; she now wants to liberate him from his mother and New Orleans with promises of sex and New York and wants him to abandon his notebooks and run away. He resists her strenuously and will not take her path until the very end when he is still trying to grab armfuls of his notebooks to stuff into her car, trying for salvation on his own terms. One description of Myra is certainly drawn from the beginning of *Consolation*, in the Philosophy who has been attacked (cf. 1.1.5; 1.3.7):

I have seen that liberated doxy a few times since then, for, from time to time she embarks on an "inspection tour" of the South, stopping eventually in New Orleans to harangue me and to attempt to seduce me with the grim prison and chain-gang songs she strums on her guitar. Myrna is very sincere; unfortunately, she is also offensive. When I saw her after her last "inspection tour" she was rather bedraggled. She had stopped throughout the rural South to teach Negroes folk songs she had learned at the Library of Congress. . . . Although the Negroes had tried to ignore her, the whites had shown great interest in her. Bands of crackers and rednecks had chased her from the villages, slashed her tires, whipped her a bit about the arms. She had been hunted by bloodhounds, shocked by cattle prods, chewed by police dogs, peppered lightly with shotgun pellets. She had loved every minute of it, showing me quite proudly (and, I might add,

suggestively) a fang mark on her upper thigh. My stunned and disbe-
lieving eyes had noticed that on that occasion she was wearing dark
stockings and not leotards. My blood, however, failed to rise.[35]

We see the new Muses and the promise of true music, prison music; the descent from the true homeland, the delight in persecution, the promise of
union and return. And what of the revealing of her thigh? After all, Philosophy's robes are torn; and it is Alan of Lille who depicts a similar appa-
rition (Natura, like Lydia the Tattooed Lady, with an encyclopedia of the
natural world on her cloak) to a narrator who finds himself wondering just
what is to be found above the tops of her boots.[36]

Every student of *Consolation* should read *A Confederacy of Dunces*, but
clearly it *proves* nothing about the essential nature of *Consolation*. *A Confederacy of Dunces* could be just a parody of a serious *Consolation*. The counter-
argument that the novel, by a comic use of *Consolation*, points to a comic
potential in *Consolation* is not necessarily convincing. And I should not like
to undertake a proof that Toole had a knowledge of Alan of Lille. But the
novel is part of *Consolation*'s modern reception, and this creative use of
the text is at the very least a useful antidote to interpretations that presume
the text to be a serious, inspirational, but ultimately unusable, demonstration
of a particular set of philosophical worldviews that can no longer find a truly
sympathetic audience in the twentieth century.[37]

My interest in the reception of *Consolation* is not to attempt to speak of
its forward and outspreading influence. This is a vast topic.[38] Rather, I am
interested in working backward, to see what elements in the reception of
Consolation may bear some probative weight as concerns the reading that I
have presented. There is no difficulty in documenting that the first Latin
texts to use *Consolation* suggest a battle between a Muse and an author in
which the author is overpowered; or that the lack of self-definition was a defect that needed to be made up; or that the presence of Job was felt. And the
twelfth century and what used to be called the School of Chartres saw in
Consolation a work that emphasized the difficulty of transcendence through
Philosophy and accordingly offered a view of the world in which Theology
explains what Philosophy cannot and thus can make a universe that human
beings fit in.[39]

In what follows I attempt a close reading of the text, pointing to details
of dramatization and argument, and to parallel texts in antecedent philo-

sophic, comic, and consolatory traditions, that will make, I hope, the point
that *Consolation* is to be seen as a work that does not accomplish what it sets
out to do, that it does so intentionally, and that its larger goal is to demonstrate the limits of philosophy as understood, or misunderstood, by an author who refuses to accept its transcendent nature. In other words, I will
present as fully as possible that interpretation of *Consolation* which enabled
me in the first place to see what the nature of classical Menippean satire is,
and then suggest classical models, contemporary analogs, and later adapta-
tions that show similar themes and structures at work. Because I see the
text's goals and methods very differently, the parallels that I will bring to
bear are frequently not those of more standard analyses. I try to keep these
discussions brief, being content more to suggest and point the way to future
study than to pretend to exhaustive proofs of dependence or influence. I will
consider the consolatory tradition; some classical texts whose plots parallel
that of *Consolation* (Plato's *Crito,* in which the philosopher cannot escape
his prison *because* he is a philosopher; various dialogues of Lucian, especially
Jupiter Confutatus, in which the impudent questioner exposes the absurdity
of the lofty figure of authority); sixth- and seventh-century analogues and
reactions (a poem of Agathias Scholasticus on the irreconcilability of Plato
and Aristotle; the reading of *Consolation* implied by Maximian's *Third
Elegy;* Isidore of Seville's *Synonyma,* which tries to make up some of the perceived deficiencies of *Consolation*); and late medieval vernacular literature
(see William Heise's chapter on personification allegories in Dante, Alan,
The Romance of the Rose, and Langland). I will also address in passing parallels within Christian literature (*Consolation* as a Christianization of Job;
as apocalypse; and as autobiography after the manner of Augustine).

    Consolation is a book of stunning depth and complexity. To speak of it as
play does not label it as trivial: it is an experiment on an ambitious scale, an
intellectual autobiography, an attempt to identify the author's self in the
context of his thoughts and of his political world. This self is quite particular, that of a Roman proud to be Rome's last patriot, last poet, last scholar,
and last philosopher; and a Roman who makes humble discoveries about
himself and learns to make modest claims. *Consolation,* accordingly, can be
seen not just as Menippean satire, but as satire in its more original sense, an
exploratory attempt at self-definition through confrontation with other-
ness.[40] To those who have taken the patience to dwell on its details and its
poetic resonances, there is revealed a world of bitter emotion, vast longing,

and unexpected beauty. My contentions do not demean, nor can they exhaust, the dazzling potentialities of this text; I do hope to offer a new and cogent way of looking at it. In speaking of irony and parody I do not intend to claim that there is no serious philosophical content in *Consolation*, or that the author is not interested in advancing serious arguments. Nor will I just claim that it is context that makes us realize the relative worth of, and thus devalue, philosophical abstractions. We ought not argue from the fact that there is no escape from the prison that the abstractions of Philosophy are valueless, as if she should have brought the prisoner a cake with a file in it instead. Plato shows us the value of irony as a tool for stating philosophical truths; are we really to be satisfied with understanding *Consolation* as having a happy ending? I think that *Consolation* dramatizes what happens to a man who limits himself to words when questions of the soul and its true home are paramount. The philosopher who returns to the world of Aristotelian commentary to score a point against Philosophy herself, and then finds that it is prayer and not logic that is the way home, makes a painful but hopeful and helpful discovery. The prisoner's silence is the end of the book, the silence of prayer and the silence of Job, beyond the realm of discursive thought. And the marvel is that the author has constructed, quite strictly within the limits of his professional competence, a tale about those limits.

Chapter Two

Two Digressions and a Pointed Conclusion

Consolation of Philosophy presents a dialogue between an unnamed exile (we gradually learn that this character is to represent the historical Boethius and infer that he is in prison) and the heavenly Muse Philosophy, who has come to assert her irredentist claims over him and take him home with her. They are much alike and belong together; he had once been hers; her program of reeducation is designed to make him worthy to follow her yet again. She does not accomplish what she sets out to do. The discussion never explicitly reaches the promised question of who the exile truly is;[1] the promised harsher remedies are never administered; the promised homeland is never seen. These omissions are not signs of incompleteness, for the work is too tightly patterned for that; nor would I argue that the dialogue merely intends to lead the exile up to the point at which he is ready to have all of these promises fulfilled. *Consolation* is complete in itself; a dialogue that reaches the surprising conclusion that Chance is an agent of Providence can be allowed to assert the divine nature of what seem at first to be its accidents. My claim is that Philosophy does not achieve the ends that she sets out for herself because she loses control of the work and is never allowed to console *in the way that she had planned*. The prisoner gains confidence as Philosophy revives him, and he changes the course of the discussion as he raises questions and pursues topics that Philosophy does not want to address. She wanted a martyr, one ready to die to prove himself the last true philosopher, and she would be vindicated if she could so persuade him;[2] but she has reawakened someone who really wants her to talk about Aristotle, buried treasure, and future contingents. To borrow the language of book 5: in the confluence of their two very different causal streams is found the unexpected discovery that is the conclusion of *Consolation*.

The Progress of the Argument

Consolation ends far from its beginning. Philosophy is said almost to be starting over when, in 4.6, she discusses the nature of divine Providence. The Fortune that was largely dismissed as irrelevant to true happiness in books 2 and 3 is here redefined as Fate, the tool of divine Providence unfolding itself in time. The "Problem of Providence" dealt with in 4.5–5.2 reaches the conclusion that individual volitions are indeed free, even if their effects are not; events are bound up in the causal chain of events which is the divine Providence. The concluding sections (5.3–6) of *Consolation* address the "Problem of Prescience," ultimately reaching the finely articulated conclusion that God's eternal knowledge of the outcome of events is analogous to a human's knowledge of events occurring in the present, a knowledge that imparts no necessity to contingent events.[3]

Divine Providence and divine knowledge are separate truths, and the freedom of the human will is asserted and satisfactorily defended. But then comes the collapse when these two problems are conflated. The prisoner had objected at 5.3.15–16 that the claim that God knows how things are going to happen is no more than an assertion that events are the cause of divine Providence, and that something outside of God is a cause of God's knowledge (Marenbon 2003, 144). Philosophy accepts the force of this objection when she speaks to it near the end of her arguments, near the end of *Consolation* itself, when she says that God derives knowledge not from things but from "his own proper simplicity" (5.6.41: *ex propria . . . simplicitate*). God has now passed from the noninterventionist final cause of book 3—that which all things naturally desire because they desire true happiness which is the good which is God—to the God who causally determines all things by being the cause of all that he knows. Marenbon, whom I follow generally in this and the following account of the argument of *Consolation,* adds: "Philosophy's long and impressive defence of human freedom is ruined—but she seems not to have noticed" (Marenbon 2003, 145). Her concluding exhortation to moral virtue, addressed to the readers as well as to the prisoner, begins with a stunning negation of what she just said, a claim that humans do have freedom of the will (5.6.44): "And since this is the way things are, this remains unchanged for mortals: an inviolate freedom of independent judgment. Laws are not unjust, and they assign rewards and punishments to wills that are free of every necessity." It is inconceivable that Boethius, philosopher and author, is unaware of the contradictions that he has just placed in Philosophy's mouth. Nor is the reference to the justice of punishments assigned by law a consoling, or even a neutral, way to speak to the prisoner. How did we get here?

We must begin at the beginning. In the course of book 1 we learn the prisoner's view of his own condition and what Philosophy thinks about that condition and about the prisoner's reaction to it. Not only has he suffered loss, he thinks, but it seems that this is the way of the world, that the evil hold sway over the virtuous. Philosophy has to convince the prisoner that, as a philosopher, he has suffered no loss at all; this constitutes an approach to consolation, one that defines the nature of true happiness, which is primarily personal. But when the prisoner complains that God seems not to bring human actions under his governance (articulated eloquently in 1.m.5, the third of the prisoner's mere four poems in *Consolation,* the last being 5.m.3), Philosophy realizes that she has to teach (or reeducate) the prisoner *how* it is that God governs all things; *that* God governs them is emphatically not doubted. This avenue to consolation is more universal, a demonstration of how God is the final cause of all creation. A third and ultimate problem arises: when Philosophy discovers by interrogation that the prisoner no longer knows what he is, no longer knows that his nature is more than that of a rational, mortal animal, she labels this ignorance the greatest cause of his sickness. Just what sort of consolation such a definition would have provided had it been specifically offered is uncertain. The question of the relative claims of universality and particularity in the presentation of the person of the prisoner in *Consolation* is treated here in chapter 3; for now it is enough to note that that this self-knowledge is supposed to cure the prisoner, which is not necessarily the same thing as consoling him.[4]

Marenbon's analysis of the subsequent arguments makes a number of interesting points that I offer here as an overview of *Consolation*. While a complex view of true happiness is developed from the beginning of book 2 through 3.8, the final sections of book 3 offer a different, radically more simple approach to the nature of true happiness, which relates it to the nature of God as final cause; Marenbon believes as well that an answer is given in passing to the third question, about the nature of human beings. The issues raised in book 1 are satisfied, but the change of direction in the final sections of book 3 is telling—there are further complications to come. *Consolation* could have ended plausibly after book 3, but it does not. Books 4 and 5 are a problem, in that they make increasingly problematic a solution to the prisoner's problems that had just seemed to be sufficient. Book 4, a development of the thesis that the good are never really assaulted and that the evil are never truly happy (4.1–4), is opposed by the prisoner (4.5), and the revised solution proposed in the second half is inconsistent with the first half of book 4 as well as with the end of book 3. "Book V increases rather than resolves the tensions. And, just as the second half of Book IV and Book V do not fit neatly and unproblematically with the core arguments of the *Consolation* proposed from Book III.9 to Book IV.4, so too the approach of the section from the beginning of Book II to III.8 turns out to be at odds with them" (Marenbon 2003, 102).

To return to details, book 2 discusses happiness and true happiness: *felicitas* and *beatitudo*. The goods of Fortune are of two sorts, ornamental and nonornamental; the former—riches, status, power, and the like—contribute only to felicity but are not valueless if appreciated for the transitory things that they are; the other gifts of Fortune, the prisoner's family, rank higher and are real goods, which are more valuable than life and remain to him still. But these gifts do not confer true happiness; in the second half of book 2, Philosophy argues that they are not only transitory but that they have other essential defects, not the least of which is that evil people can possess them. Internal good qualities are far more important than external gifts of Fortune.

The material of the latter half of book 2 (2.5–8) is gone over in the beginning of book 3 with a crucial difference: the gifts of Fortune that people seem to desire are really false goods (riches, positions of honor, kingdoms, glory, physical pleasures) desired by people who mistake them for true goods (self-sufficiency, preeminence, power, acclamation, and delight). Such people confuse means and ends, and false goods are not means to attain true goods. Again, Marenbon points out that ornamental goods, properly valued, can be conducive toward this true happiness. "On such a view of happiness, Philosophy could not claim that Boethius had lost nothing through his misfortune, but she would be left with plenty of material for consoling him. His downfall has stripped him of most of his ornamental goods of fortune but not of much that contributes to his true happiness" (Marenbon 2003, 106). But he also points out that Philosophy does not draw all of this together or use it to provide consolation. Instead, she changes direction at 3.9 to argue that the problem with most people is not that they pursue false instead of true goods, but rather that they pursue multiple goods instead of a unitary good. Philosophy, in other words, shifts from a "complex" view of happiness to a "monolithic" presentation of the good (Marenbon 2003, 107–12). True happiness, *beatitudo,* is the good; the good is God; every truly happy person is a God. By the end of 3.10, Philosophy has demonstrated the nature of true happiness, without defining the relationship between the particular prisoner and the God who is true happiness. The remaining sections of book 3 address the second problem of book 1: God rules the world by means of the good, by being the One that all things desire. The good, the rudder by which God guides the world, is the One is *beatitudo* is God himself. "Since everything naturally desires the good . . . , God's rule is not in the least oppressive: everything wants it, and there is nothing that either wishes to resist it or could resist it, supposing it wished to do so" (Marenbon 2003, 114).

This argument for what Marenbon describes as a "benignly self-ruling universe" is neither clichéd nor routine. "God is seen as completely non-interventionist: merely by being the highest good, which everything desires as its end, he regulates the universe." God the final cause would seem to answer every question: the nature of true happiness, the governance of the world, and the nature of humans (every truly happy person is a God). Philosophy begins book 4 seemingly confident that all has been answered. Though interrupted just as she is about to talk about something else, she takes the next step and makes a promise to take the exile back to his true fatherland, even though the prisoner has retreated, returning to the question of the apparent power wielded by the evil in this world. Philosophy argues strenuously and from many angles in 4.1–4 that good people always have power and that evil people do not, because the latter cannot attain their goals and are therefore unhappy, and the former, even if unjustly punished, remain good and therefore happy.

But this is not enough. In 4.5 the prisoner returns to the thoughts he had in book 1, talks of the real goods and real evils to be found in Fortune as people commonly understand it, and speaks of the incompatibility of the ascendancy of the evil with the rule of the world by God through the good. Philosophy has already answered these objections and could repeat what she said before; instead, as if beginning from a new starting point (4.6.7: *velut ab alio orsa principio*), she speaks in 4.6 of the intelligence of God and of the rule of the world through his Providence. This is a profound shift in argument, from God as noninterventionist final cause to God the engineer of the world, its planner and artisan, and it makes the prisoner's situation that much more difficult to understand. Now Philosophy speaks of all Fortune as good for those who are good, instead of generally dismissing its value as in book 2; all Fortune is bad for the bad; the loss of good fortune is in any event no longer a matter of indifference. God may be testing or improving the good by allowing them to be oppressed by the evil and the wicked; the prominence of the evil may be an example to the good.

Through the course of *Consolation*, the concept of goodness moves from an abstract and cosmic principle to a personal and ethical imperative. Marenbon points out that Philosophy is not entirely consistent in her use of the term good, and it is in any event true that the category of moral action is problematic for a prisoner alone in a cell, removed from the world of action.[5] The problem of free will, the essence of book 5, is specifically concerned with the moral quality of human actions if divine Providence is the source of all things. Philosophy's answer is consistent enough, if not obviously satisfactory to a reader; there is an all-encompassing web of interrelated actions, and Fate is the name for this working out in time of the substance of eternal Providence. Individual volitions are said to be free and not bound up in this chain of events only because it is the volitions themselves that are free, and not the effects of the volitions, which remain bound. And the volitions themselves are only truly free when truly rational, which is to say, closest to agreement with the divine mind and free from the influence of the passions.

But it is clear that this Problem of Providence, as Marenbon calls it, raises questions and creates responses far from the ground covered in the first three books. The conclusion of book 5 (5.3–6) has to deal with the nature of divine intelligence and the question of whether God's knowledge that an event will occur removes all freedom of the will. This Problem of Prescience is different from the Problem of Providence because now the question is not one of causality perceived as a chain or sequence of events, but whether, pure and simple, God's knowledge that an event will occur makes that event necessary and therefore not contingent. Philosophy's conclusion is that God's way of knowing all things is like the way in which humans know the present; his knowledge imparts no more necessity to individual events, contingent in their own nature, than our knowledge of present contingent events imparts necessity to them.[6]

The combination of the problems of Providence and Prescience results in the undermining of Philosophy's argument for the freedom of the human will, as has already been noted. This, then, is the basis of the arguments of the following chapters, that to a large extent books 4 and 5 are digressions, inspired by the prisoner's own interests, that keep Philosophy from her homeward journey and that, while forcing her into more and more sophisticated and intricate arguments and demonstrations, ultimately trip her up and force a reevaluation of what this particular consolation and this particular dialogue are all about. Therefore, at the outset I would draw attention to the introductions of these two last books, in which we see the narrator deflecting Philosophy from her program, and to the concluding paragraph, in which Philosophy takes an almost angry leave of the book. The following translations are supplied with context and brief commentary. For the Latin texts see appendix 1.

Book 4

After the climactic central poem of *Consolation* (3.m.9, *O qui perpetua*),[7] book 3 ends with a rapid series of brief and seemingly unobjectionable presentations on God and goodness and their unity. Her switch in this final section from discussing the pursuit of false over true goods to the pursuit of multiple goods over the unitary good has already been noted. What Philosophy thinks is the last point to be achieved before the exile can return home in safety, that evil is nothing (3.12.29), finally makes the prisoner object: her arguments have been a labyrinth (3.12.30), and he accuses Philosophy of using an entirely self-contained and self-referential set of arguments.[8] She cheerfully admits to the charge of circular reasoning: God is like a sphere, and, as Plato says, arguments should resemble the things that they discuss (3.12.37–8). She concludes the book with the well-known poem on the descent of Orpheus (3.m.12) and gives it an explicit moral, which is that those who try to lead their minds up to the light lose the objects of their search if they look back down to the land of the dead.[9] The exile, she hopes, will take her advice. Book 4 then begins as follows:

4.1.1. Philosophy had sung these words softly and sweetly, never losing the dignity of her appearance or the impressiveness of her speech, but I had not yet forgotten the sorrow that was planted within me, and so I interrupted her train of thought then, just as she was getting ready to say something else. I said, 2. "Yes, you are the one who leads on towards the true light, and the words that flowed from your pleading were not only obviously divine, examined in themselves, but also irrefragable, according to your arguments; still, though I had recently forgotten them in my depression because of the wrongs done to me, you have spoken things that were not completely unknown to me before. 3. But here is what is perhaps the greatest cause of my sorrow: the fact that evil things can exist at all, or that they can pass unpunished, when the helmsman of all things is good. Make no mistake: Only you can ponder this with the amazement that it deserves. 4. No, there is another, an even greater thing connected to it: I mean, when gross wickedness thrives and has dominion, that not only does virtue go without its true rewards, but it is even forced to grovel at the feet of lawless men and to be ground beneath their heels, subjected to punishments as if for crimes committed. 5. That such things happen in the kingdom of a God who knows all things, who is capable of all things, but who desires good things and the good alone—no one can be amazed at it, and no one can complain about it, as it deserves." 6. And then she said: "True, it would be everlastingly incomprehensible, a thing more monstrous than all other monstrosities if, as you reckon it, the cheap earthenware pots were prized, and the expensive ones defiled, in what I may call so great a master's perfectly appointed house.[10] 7. But that is not the way it is. If the conclusions we reached a little while ago have not been torn to pieces but still hold, then, by the agency of that same creator of whose kingdom we now speak, you will come to see that good people are always powerful, while evil people are always disreputable and unable to sustain themselves; that vices are never without punishment, and virtues never without reward; that things worthy of rejoicing always happen to good people, and disasters always happen to the evil. There are many other conclusions of this sort, and they can brace you with an unshakable steadfastness, when first your complaints have been laid to rest. 8. And since you have seen the essence of true happiness through my previous demonstrations, and have even come to recognize where it is to be found, I will show to you the way that can carry you back home, after we've run through all the things that I think I must first set before it. 9. In fact, I will equip your mind with wings, so it can raise itself on high, so that you can cast your confusion into exile and return recuperated to your fatherland, following my lead, along my path, by my conveyances."

Philosophy's intent is fairly clear. She wants the prisoner to stop worrying about his own particular situation, that of the wounded innocent, the victim of corrupt government. She wants the exile to remember heavenly things, but the prisoner refuses to forget his earthly sorrow. She had thought that the exile was already prepared for travel, but the prisoner thinks otherwise; she now has to satisfy his philosophical program. She still intends to have him fly home (and her language at the end of this passage, expanded on in her following poem, mirrors that of the end of book 3),[11] but his question has required a number of preliminaries that she had not thought necessary according to her own scheme. We may applaud the exile's interest in taking a hand in his own education, but the objectives of the two partners in the dialogue are not the same at this point. Philosophy had misunderstood the prisoner and his need to worry about the earthly order; she did not realize how difficult it would be for him to leave the world behind, and when we hear Philosophy reassert the value of her own scheme of redemption in her proud closing words, she appropriates the language that she had earlier reserved for talking about God: the exile shall return home, but "following *my* lead, along *my* path, by *my* conveyances" (italics mine).[12]

Book 5

In the course of book 4 Philosophy passes from the first half—through the fourth poem, consisting of arguments that establish that the good are always powerful and happy, while the evil are always powerless and un-happy—to the second half—a discussion of the difference between Fate and Providence—as if she were starting from a new point altogether.[13] Again, we note that Philosophy deals first with questions that touch on the unfortunate details of her interlocutor's life: rewards for the good and punishments for the wicked is a paradox that the unjustly punished prisoner has a hard time accepting. Or so I would infer, because he initiates the question and answer of the second half by continuing to wonder about the seeming confusion of the fortunes of good and wicked people (4.5.4). The prisoner continues to try to restrict Philosophy to matters of more personal interest, while she labors to bring the exile from such sticky matters to a more lofty vision of things. Her discussion of Fate and Providence in this last half of book 4 is more in this ethereal vein, but it concludes with a piece of pointed moral advice addressed to the world at large and the exile in particular: "For the fortune that you prefer to fashion for yourselves has been placed in your own hands; indeed, every fortune that seems calamitous *does* punish you, unless it trains you or corrects you."[14] Her concluding poem gives mythical examples of successes that followed years of toil (Agamemnon's victory at Troy, Odysseus's return home, Hercules's labors and ultimate divine honors); this book ends as did book 3, with Philosophy assigning to her poem a moral that directs the plural listeners to look up: the act of renouncing the earth opens up the heavens.[15] Book 5 then begins:

5.5.1. So she concluded, and she was starting to turn the direction of her pleading toward the treatment and explanation of some other things. 2. But then I said: A proper encouragement to be sure, completely and absolutely worthy of your authority! But as to what you said previously about Providence, that it is a question bound up with many other questions—I know that by personal experience. 3. That is to say, I'm asking you whether you think there is such a thing as chance at all and, tell me, what sort of thing do you think it is? 4. Then she said: I'm hurrying to make good the debt of my promise, and to open up for you the path by which you may be carried back to your fatherland. 5. But these questions—even though they are quite useful to know, they are all the same a little off to one side of the path of what I had proposed. And it's reasonable for me to be afraid that you'll be exhausted on the sidetracks and won't be able to bear up for traveling the straight path through to its end. 6. I said: You must have absolutely no fear of that. For it will be like tranquil quiet for me to bring to mind the things in which I take the greatest delight. 7. And at the same time, when every side of your argument stands fixed, its trustworthiness undoubted, I want there to be no doubt at all about what follows. 8. Then she said: I'll humor you; and as she did so she began as follows.

This passage parallels closely the beginning of book 4. The word *oratio*, which I have translated "pleading," is used to describe speech only in these two passages in *Consolation* and when Philosophy refers to the prisoner's lengthy political apology of 1.4: ". . . but I would have had no idea just how far away your place of exile was, had your *set speech* not given it away."[16] It means more than speech; it is appropriate for an attempt at moral persuasion. The prisoner does not want to follow Philosophy's moral exhortation, and she, who was almost enthusiastic in the previous book when she started to deal with the prisoner's requests, is much more hesitant now. Why this withdrawal of enthusiasm? It is clear from 5.1.3 that the prisoner is motivated now by his inveterate intellectual curiosity; yet evidently Philosophy is not much impressed by this desire, even though it represents the longed-for forgetting of personal sorrow. "I'll humor you" is rather mordant; Philosophy must think that the prisoner's questions indeed run counter to the goals that she envisions. And the prisoner's solicitude for the status of Philosophy's argument is rather playful: the stability of her position is presented as the byproduct of his opportunity to return to the world of his beloved Aristotle. It is well known that this final book is substantially inspired by Boethius's commentaries on Aristotle's *De interpretatione*; but it should be pointed out that Boethius the author has the prisoner acknowledge the fact. What he knows from personal experience about the involved nature of arguments about Providence he knows from his work on Aristotle; the great delight that he will take in seeing familiar things is the delight that will come from returning to Aristotelian texts and issues. Philosophy knows this, and Aristotle will appear by name in what follows out of deference to the prisoner:[17]

5.1.8 [*continued*] She said: If someone were to define chance as a result that is a product of random motion, without any interweaving of causes, I would state that chance is nothing at all; my judgment is that it is a word absolutely devoid of meaning, in the absence of any signification of any underlying reality. I mean, what place can be left for randomness, when there is a God who keeps all things in bounds, binding them into order? 9. For that axiom is true, which none of the old philosophers ever spoke against: Nothing comes from nothing.[18] (Granted, they laid this down as a sort of foundation for all of their theories about the natural world only in consideration of the subject material, not the active first principle.) 10. But should something arise from no causes, it will seem to have arisen from nothing; but if this can't happen, then it is impossible that there be chance of the sort that we have just now defined. 11. Well then! I said. Is there really nothing that can rightly be called chance or accident? Or is there something that these words are appropriate for, even if it is hidden from the common herd? 12. She said: It is in his *Physics* that my good Aristotle has defined it, in a brief demonstration that is very near to the truth. I said: Tell me, in what way? 13. She said: Whenever something is done for some one particular purpose, and something other than what was intended occurs, from whatever causes—this is called chance. For example: if someone plows the earth in order to cultivate a field, and finds a mass of buried gold. 14. And so it is that this is actually believed to have happened accidentally, but it is not from nothing, because it has its own causes, and it is the unforeseen and unexpected confluence of these causes that seems to have engineered a chance occurrence. 15. For if the cultivator of the field were not plowing the earth, and if the one who hid the money had not hidden it in that very place, the gold would not have been found.

Philosophy clearly enjoys this sort of luxuriation in Aristotelian detail.[19] She will make her point a few more times in what follows, the concluding portion of this prose section; but I think that there is a special point to be made in this talk of buried gold:

> 5.1.16. And so these are the causes of the accidental profit, which arose not from the intention of the doer but from intersecting and confluent causes. 17. For neither the one who buried the gold nor the one who worked the field intended that this money be found but, as I've said, that the one dug where the other had buried—this is a coincidence and a confluence. 18. We may therefore define chance as follows: In the realm of things done for some particular reason, it is an unexpected outcome, deriving from confluent causes. 19. Further, the order that makes these causes coincident and confluent proceeds in an unescapable interweaving of causes; it descends from the source of Providence and arranges all things in their proper places and in their proper times.

This is not just a step in an argument, but a statement of programmatic intent very carefully placed by Boethius the author. Philosophy, who has stated that she will now have to lead the exile along the byways and fears that she will not be able to take him home by the main path, talks at length about discovery of gold in an unexpected place, about the providential nature of the unforeseen. It is not inevitable that Philosophy realizes the implications of her words. This could be irony in its proper sense: Philosophy may not hear what we can hear, that in the story of the man who finds what he was not supposed to find is the core story of *Consolation* itself. Or she may be well aware of the possibility that the prisoner will find what Philosophy had not intended, for the reader is reminded of book 2, at the end of its central poem on the glories of the Golden Age, when she calls down curses on those corrupted by wealth, and on the one who dug up gold and "the jewels that longed to lie hidden."[20]

Consolation has an unexpected outcome, as I shall make clear below; and the prisoner is responsible for this because of the digressions by which he interrupts Philosophy's plans. We can identify the particular point in the dialogue that inspired him to act so, and can see the motivation as well: he saw a possibility of extracting a Christian truth from this pagan source of wisdom, and it is this Christian truth that Philosophy is generally unwilling to provide. I return to the end of book 3, to the passages first discussed above. In 3.12, Philosophy establishes that God is the highest good and controls all things, and there can be no opposition to this highest good. Her conclusion of this line of argument is simple and positive (3.12.22): "It is therefore the highest Good, she said, that governs all things forcefully and arranges all things sweetly."[21] These are words from Scripture (Wisdom 8.1: "She [sc. Wisdom] reacheth therefore from end to end mightily and ordereth all things sweetly").[22] The prisoner's reaction is one of pleasure and surprise: "It is not only the summary of your arguments, which you have just completed, that delights me; what delight me much more are the words themselves that you have used! Now at long last they make the stupidity that rips apart great things ashamed of itself."[23] As Chadwick puts it: "Fancy you, of all people, knowing the Bible."[24] That which has been ripped apart is Philosophy herself, and we think of her torn robe in book 1; but if it is a biblical text that makes the prisoner himself repent of such actions, we must infer that he begins to see the possibility of the seamless integration of philosophy and revelation.

But *Consolation* is not a text which operates on the principle that the truths of pagan philosophy and Christian revelation are compatible; what we have here would seem at first to be only a particular example of a widely acknowledged overlap. But after the prisoner commends her for her biblical allusion, Philosophy hardly follows up on it, but goes on to talk about the Giants and their war on heaven. She then asks if the prisoner would like to have her set her arguments against each other (3.12.25);[25] when she does so and proves that evil is nothing, he objects to her circular reasoning; his dissatisfaction leads him to interrupt her at the beginning of book 4, as we have already seen. She is teasing him, leading him to interrupt her, not satisfying the expectations that the prisoner now has after hearing the scriptural words that made him repent his foolishness. The pursuit of philosophical niceties is presented as the opponent of the prisoner's newfound religious perceptions and sensibilities. This Philosophy, who is philosophy as Boethius had practiced it, an intellectual system that primarily functions apart from faith, does not want the prisoner to make the vital connection between the two. The reader could not say at this point whether Philosophy's refusal is arrogant or an admission of the limits of her inquiries.

But I do not think that Philosophy herself is aware at its beginning of the religious turn that the prisoner's interests are about to take in the course of book 5. The exile asks about free will in the second prose section and has his last real speech in the third, in which he complains that divine foreknowledge imposes a necessity on human actions and threatens the value of prayer, the one and only bond between the human and divine (5.3.33–36). How could you pray to avoid anything, if foreknowledge binds human actions in an inflexible series? (In appendix 2 will be found a parallel to this, a translation of a section of Boethius's *Second Commentary on Aristotle's De Interpretatione*, dealing with divination, rewards and punishments, the limitations of God's knowledge, and the impiety of anyone who would strip God of his free will or his foreknowledge.) Prayer is a surprise in *Consolation*, and consequently it cannot be said that the text presents an increasingly rational presentation of the abstractions of theory, nor is the prisoner stripped of his emotions. The exile's last poem (5.m.3) is an agonized series of staccato questions, full of Augustinian worries about how a knower who longs to know what he does not know can know what to long for:

Sed cur tanto flagrat amore
ueri tectas reperire notas?
Scitne quod appetit anxia nosse?
Sed quis nota scire laborat?
At si nescit, quid caeca petit?
Quis enim quicquam nescius optet?
Aut quis ualeat nescita sequi
quoue inueniat? Quisue reppertam
queat ignarus noscere formam?
(5.m.3.11–19)[26]

Bút whý does it (the mind, *mens*) búrn wíth súch a great lóve
To discóver the trúth, trúth's hidden sígn-posts?
Does it knów ít knóws what it frétfully seéks?
Whó strúggles to knów thát which he doés know?
Bút íf he knows nót, whý look for blínd things?
Whát ígnorant mán coúld máke any choíce?
Whó hás the stréngth tó chàse the unknówn?
Whére would he fínd it? Whó then could seé it,
Its fórm thus discóvered, íf unenlíghtened?

Philosophy will end the book by saying that it is proper to pray: free will exists; humble entreaties to heaven will have their effect (5.6.44–46; see below). In effect: "If you want to pray, then pray!" But in this same closing passage she will refer uncomfortably to the prisoner's particular condition when she says that laws appropriately dispense rewards and punishments, and that God in his foreknowledge does the same.[27] Here Philosophy will return to the physical world of the prisoner even as he seems finally to have left it behind. I submit that this a sort of game of cat and mouse, and what is at stake here is what path to God is to be chosen, and by whose authority.

But the reader is not at the conclusion yet. In the first half of book 5, we may say that the prisoner is thinking in Aristotelian terms, quoting himself, and looking for Aristotelian answers; Philosophy answers him as he wants. In Philosophy's half of this book (from 5.4 on) there is a change in the philosophical timbre of the argument, a change from an Aristotelian to an Augustinian perspective, inspired by the prisoner's questions and concerns.[28] Philosophy defines God's foreknowledge as timeless, as of an eternal now; knowledge is dependent upon the knower, not upon the thing known. Philosophy brings Boethius's earlier thoughts on causality and Providence onto a new plane by claiming that all coincidence flows from divine Providence, thus making possible the allegorization of Fortune as the agent of Providence that the Middle Ages are so fond of, even as the text argues against its independent reality.[29] Boethius's formulations and solutions are obviously incisive and deservedly influential; we would expect them to be climactic in the context of this dialogue. But Philosophy will not let go of the prisoner's argument about the imposition of necessity, and she even grants his point that there is a sort of necessity imposed on human actions that only a theologian can deal with.[30] She ends her discourse by saying that a person's free change of intentions cannot change the nature of God's knowledge, and that it is impossible to avoid the eye of God (5.6.38). Her concluding words, in fact, the concluding words of *Consolation*, can hardly satisfy the intentions that she had at the beginning of this dialogue; they appeal to the prisoner and to us all to direct our prayers upward and in this way return to the true homeland, not in the language of journey or vision, as we had been led to expect (5.6.44–48):

5.6.44. And since this is the way things are, this remains unchanged for mortals: an inviolate freedom of independent judgment. Laws are not unjust, and they assign rewards and punishments to wills that are free of every necessity. 45. God also remains unchanged, looking down from on high with foreknowledge of all things; the ever-present eternity of his vision keeps pace with the future quality of our actions, dispensing rewards to good people and punishments to the bad. 46. Nor are hopes and prayers placed in God in vain; they cannot help but be effective, provided that they are blameless. 47. Therefore, all of you: Avoid vices; cherish virtues; raise up your minds to blameless hopes; extend your humble prayers into the lofty heights. 48. Unless you want to hide the truth, there *is* a great necessity imposed upon you—the necessity of righteousness, since you act before the eyes of a judge who beholds all things.

It is hard to avoid the conclusion that Philosophy's last use of the word "necessity" is a pointed one; even if we are now in the moral sphere, in which the sentence "You must do right" has a rather different feel, the comment is made in direct response to the exile's question. It is also important to notice that the language of flight home has been replaced by the language of prayer; specifically, access to God through humble prayer, which is undoubtedly a Christian sentiment, and one introduced into the discussion by the exile himself at the end of his speech at 5.3.[31] Philosophy provides the exile a conclusion that is not what she had intended; she is not the path to this God, as she had hoped to be; there is no flight here on the wings of the mind, no philosophical conveyances; this is an ascent that the exile can make on his own.

If the conclusion is genuine, and I believe that it is, as it is so closely tied in theme and in language to the matter that has gone before, then we may say that Philosophy resignedly allows the exile to be satisfied with something other than what she had hoped to offer. She may be motivated by two different impulses: first, the author may have so constructed her that she is reluctant to claim that there is a path that leads from philosophy to Christian piety, and she would operate on the principle that a line of demarcation is to be drawn between the two. But a second motive is closer to the action of the dialogue: humble prayer is the act of one who chooses to live, and Philosophy's talk of return home is the language of death. The prisoner chooses not to die but to live; and Philosophy is deprived of a last martyr and companion. The conclusion does hark back to the beginning: Gruber rightly points out that the word *manet* in 5.6.44 and 45, "stands firm" ("remains unchanged" in my translation), draws us back to the end of the first poem: "Qui cecidit, stabili non erat ille gradu" [He who has fallen was never on a stable rung].[32] The prisoner chooses to abide, having forced out of Philosophy a justification for access to God without a flight to heaven. But we have also learned of the justice of the laws, a very awkward point to raise, given the injustice of the prisoner's incarceration. It was the prisoner who raised the objection at 5.3.31–32 that the fixed order of events required by divine Providence would cancel out the notions of virtuous and evil behavior and would make a mockery of temporal law, which rewards the one and punishes the other.[33] Philosophy does not doubt the truth of her counter-arguments; but to the one to whom she had hoped to give a transcendent vision she can give only the command to pray, couched in philosophical terms (necessity, foreknowledge) that make it problematic. She had always hoped that the exile would leave behind his worries about his own situation and break free of the bonds of earth. By bringing him back to the question of just punishments she rubs his nose in his own intransigence; the last point made is, in effect, that the prisoner's punishment is providential. He could have avoided these difficulties if he had acquiesced and escaped with her to the world above.

Our narrator reproduces a dialogue in which he can be seen rejecting Philosophy's lead and refusing to take the easy way out. This is surprising: a book that first speaks of rising above Fortune ultimately rejects transcendence and accepts a Fortune redefined as divine Providence. It does not insult the status that *Consolation* enjoys as an inspirational text to state that it is about forgetting the vision of the divine realm in order to do something harder, to accept physical reality as divine reality. But readers need to observe that this change has been made, and that, along the way, shifting values have been assigned to the injustices done to the prisoner, and the definition of what is the land of the living and what the land of the dead has altered. By the end of *Consolation*, the prisoner, who had finally given up his obsession with justice in the Aristotelian part of book 5, rediscovers prayer as a hopeful way to avoid coming misfortune; Philosophy, who had fought to make the prisoner leave the earthly world behind to see the realm of God above, ends by speaking of the workings of the justice of God in this world. What is at issue is a matter of perspective, constantly appearing in these terms: Is it wrong for the prisoner to look down? Is it right for the exile to look up? These are points to which we shall return many times.

The questions that I think we ought to raise in the light of these considerations, if I have presented the argument fairly in summary, are in four clusters: (1) Has the exile been resisting Philosophy, and has he manipulated the conversation consciously in order to achieve the conclusion that *Consolation* offers? (2) Is it good that the exile is so concerned with his own life throughout the course of *Consolation*? In other words, has the exile gotten less or more than Philosophy wanted to give him because of his insistence? (3) Has Philosophy consoled the exile? If so, did he take from her the consolation that she wanted to give? (4) Why would a text that tries so hard to present the author's mature philosophical thought on crucial issues do so in a context in which these truths are shown to be of lesser value than the path of humble prayer? These questions admit of coherent answers when *Consolation of Philosophy* takes its place in the history and traditions of Menippean satire.

Chapter Three

Universality and Particularity

Lerer makes the excellent point that Roman philosophical dialogue consciously presents itself as the process of making new books out of old books.[1] Boethius has done so in *Consolation,* and we can, as we pay attention to his sources, see where his prior commentaries on Aristotle and where other Neoplatonic commentaries have been blended together. But the author tries very hard not to present his book as a book in this sense at all. At the beginning of his apology he complains bitterly to Philosophy that he is not now in the proper environment for the writing of philosophical texts (1.4.3): "Is this the library which you yourself had chosen in my house to be your ever-fixèd dwelling place, in which you often stayed with me and would discourse upon knowledge of things both human and divine?"[2] How strange that he should meet Philosophy here, outside of the world of books; she will in fact want to take him in flight to where his books cannot go and has him drop his pen. While we realize the labor of memory that went into creating *Consolation,* Boethius wants us to see both the process and the result as other than those of just another book.

To the extent that *Consolation* is about how *Consolation* came to be written, it is in the traditions of Menippean satire, in which a narrator's debate with his Muse and their struggle for control of the text are quite common.[3]

Further, even as we try to avoid the biographical fallacy, *Consolation* calls out to be read in the context of the life of Boethius, its author. We are asked to recognize him in his apology at 1.4 as more than an abstraction, and we watch as that particular person chooses to dramatize his own approach to death. In this approach, he becomes ever more his true self, changing from elegiac poet to politician to disappointed man of the world to Aristotelian commentator. The prisoner of the beginning of book 5 is finally the Boethius that we know; the Boethius of the end of book 5, chastened by Philosophy, is a new Boethius, living in a new world. Such a dramatization is also at home in Menippean satire: in *Apocolocyntosis,* Seneca imagines Claudius's death and his arrival at the Hades from which he will never return; but Menippus spoke of his own journey to the land of the dead and his path back; so too does Lucian animate him in *Icaromenippus* and *Necyomantia;* a similar fantasy motivates Julian's *Caesars.* To approach the other world and then come back alive, having learned there the value of life here, is very much in the Menippean tradition. *Consolation* is one man's fiction, Boethius's fiction, his personal attempt to keep apocalypse at bay, to choose to stay alive and live the simple, pious life.

To read *Consolation* we must move away from simple attempts to deduce its intentions or its meanings from the fact of its composition or from the events surrounding its composition. Circumstances did not dictate it. *Consolation* is at every turn an unexpected book. It is worth remembering that Boethius was under no compulsion to write at all; or, having chosen to write, that he locate his book in a prison; or, setting it in a prison, that he should present himself as one embarrassed by Philosophy when he tries to complain of the wrongs done him, and that he should dramatize a struggle within himself.[4] Certainly, by its very form, it tries to dissociate itself from other philosophical, religious, and consolatory texts. Menippean satire, a mold in which to pour the shape and substance of a dozen other works and genres, provides a paradoxical framework for the presentation of intellectual truths. The conflicts between the prisoner's life and eternal life, his thoughts and eternal thought, are reflected and worked out in many ways, both stylistic and structural (the dialogue form, the mixture of prose and verse) and thematic and doctrinal (the concurrence of human temporal life and divine atemporal knowledge, the paradoxical necessity of free will). The spirit of Augustine broods over these Menippean waters. In *Consolation* we sense the desire to encompass the whole world within the limits of a book, but what kind of book could do so?[5] Perhaps Boethius the author, unlike Augustine, was not able to climb the ladder from the world of pagan knowledge to the world of Christian truth, [6] but rather insisted on their fundamental disparity; and the prisoner does not make that particular Augustinian ascent either. I do not believe that *Consolation* represents such a reconciliation of opposites. The complexities of *Consolation* will allow ascent only by a path that is not in evidence at its beginning.

If we speak of a reconciliation of poetry and philosophy achieved within its confines, we tend to describe an impersonal *Consolation* that addresses grand abstractions: the human and the divine, the temporal and the eternal, the world as viewed by the individual and the world as viewed through the eye of God, the return of the soul to its source. One of the great accomplishments of this dialogue is on this account a carefully patterned integration of the human and the cosmic perspectives.[7] Menippean satire can be invoked here in Bakhtinian terms as a medium that allows the different voices of poetry and philosophy to contribute to a polyphonic whole: the world in all its multiplicities is contained within the covers of a single book. But *Consolation* does not provide the expected Menippean view of the universe as a whole, of heaven and of earth, that we see in Seneca's *Apocolocyntosis* or in Martianus Capella's *Marriage*. We do have in *Consolation* one expected Menippean element, the *catascopia*, the Olympian view of life on earth, but without a corresponding vision of the other world. The point at which the genre of Menippean satire and the genre of consolation overlap is precisely where Boethius's Menippean consolation frustrates us, in denying us a vision of worlds beyond this one; so too is the return of the soul, so frequently addressed, never achieved. *Consolation* stops short, implying worlds that it does not see and imagining journeys that it does not take. Therefore, in the absence of these expected universal structures and themes, we should be cautious and not speak so freely of the prisoner's point of view as representative of humanity at large. And it is certainly difficult to make universal an interlocutor who is pleased to engage Philosophy in the material of his laborious Aristotelian commentaries. It is reasonable to raise the question of whether the narrator's perspective may be that of a specific individual, determined by particular historical and personal circumstances; in short, of the extraordinary philosopher-statesman Boethius.

The reader's strong desire to take the text of *Consolation* as something more than, or at least something other than, a record of its author's inner life is certainly justifiable. There is a point at which the topic is not the prisoner, but Everyman; Philosophy tries to console not only the prisoner, but the reader as well, addressing a plural audience at a number of key points; the prisoner's Platonic struggle to remember what he once knew and to locate himself in the eternal pattern of the world is our struggle. Similar forces operate on the reader of Augustine's *Confessions*. And it is not mere naïveté or wishful thinking or ahistorical habits of reading that make us try for a universal reading. Boethius the author has put into the text a running disagreement on whether the quotidian details of the prisoner's life should be removed from consideration. The lengthy apology in the first book (1.4), an account of the virtue of the prisoner's political actions in this world, is of no concern to Philosophy, except that it reveals how great his exile truly is;[8] it shows that the prisoner had placed his hopes in transient things; and when he resumes his narrator's function at 1.5, he labels this episode dog speech, which he had bayed until he could bay no more.[9] It is a bad apology, and in the context of a tale of a philosopher in prison, the dog reference makes us compare its speaker unflatteringly to Socrates. It is also functionally a mock encomium, praise of that which ought to be treated with contempt. The prisoner has been called to remember himself (1.2.6), but Philosophy is being paradoxical:[10] to do this the prisoner must forget himself, as the physical world is the obstacle to eternity and eternal thought.

Philosophy's propaedeutic is the lengthy assault on Fortune (the substance of book 2 and first half of book 3). What remains after this dismissal of the pagan Muses and the phenomenal world is a very abstract notion of human life; accordingly, the argument of the last two books tries to be thoroughly theoretical. The discussion of the coexistence of God and evil in book 4 is not intended as an occasion for reconsidering the prisoner's unjust condemnation, but for pondering the nature of God; similarly, the debate in book 5 on the relation of divine foreknowledge to human free will does not raise the question of how human beings are to act in this world until Philosophy speaks her enigmatic final words. Philosophy is trying all along not to give practical advice to the prisoner.[11] All of this was foreshadowed by the ladder on Philosophy's dress (1.1.4); we have been climbing the ladder from Practice to Theory; the intelligible realm is what truly exists, and the prisoner's recovered memories, if I may use the term, are to constitute a Socratic/Platonic ascent.

The prisoner's solitude, ruthlessly constructed, also contributes to this theoretical stance; it is like that of the monk in his cell or the body in its tomb. Philosophy even implies that a cell is desirable, as it is a place of retreat that separates the true believer from the rest of the mad world.[12] The reader awaits not the prisoner's release from prison so much as the recalling of the exile, but it is the exchange of one lonely place for another: Philosophy intends that the exile not be returned to the world but that he find himself in his true homeland.[13] Here is another paradox, though one common to Stoic contemplative literature: our narrator is closer to the real world because he is so withdrawn from the physical world, and isolation should itself prove liberating. And so we watch as this exile is stripped of everything extrinsic. Not only is there no possibility of moral action in this prison, as he is shut out from any communion with any other human being, not even having the company of a jailer, as Socrates had;[14] he even finally loses the power of speech (which he so laboriously gained at the beginning of book 1) when Philosophy puts an end to the dialogue halfway through book 5, delivers a lengthy monologue, and imagines the exile's questions and answers in her own voice.[15] And the little that he has, his life within his cell, he is supposed to leave behind.

His place of exile is an image both of the world and of his physical self. The flight home that Philosophy promises the exile at the beginning of book 4, and which she says she fears he will not achieve at the beginning of book 5, certainly puts us in mind of death, and the escape from the prison would be the escape from the body. Much of *Consolation* can be shown to turn on a painful working out of the maxim that philosophy is the practice of death.[16] But Philosophy first speaks of the flight home soon after the prisoner accuses her of circular reasoning and labyrinthine logic at the end of book 3 (3.12.30); the reader hears in this a hope for liberation from the bonds of discursive thought, for the mystic's impersonal transcendence of this world and ecstatic union with the divine, Plotinus's "flight of the Alone to the Alone."[17] And, of course, release from the prison; but, as we have seen, the prisoner objects to Philosophy's logic, and as we never hear what she had in mind for the subsequent stages of her argument, we imagine that the prisoner may make his own attempt at escape. But if flight from the labyrinth puts the reader in mind of Daedalus and Icarus, the possibility of disaster makes the reader pause—would a failure to achieve Philosophy's homeland be laid at the narrator's door or at humanity's?[18]

Now the self as microcosm may mirror the macrocosm; but if we are to have a universal text, then this self should be as generic as possible. If the prisoner and Philosophy represent two halves of the author's personality, the temporal and the eternal, and if *Consolation* dramatizes an attempt at reintegration of what had been split, then the more we see of the historical Boethius, the less universal the text becomes. This would be one of the reasons why it is so crucial to Philosophy and her goals that the narrator disappear at the end of the work, that she herself take over all of the burden of speech—for her to represent the union of the halves of the self, she would be that self without history, without context, without attachment to the world of particulars and individuals.

This stance, were it a fair representation of Boethius's authorial intentions, would frustrate us. We would miss the psychological insight of Augustine, who discerns the eternal patterns of God and the individual soul in an analysis of his own particular sins. Augustine sees in this personal way that he has two selves, and that they may not coincide;[19] Boethius's two selves would seem to be split on purely theoretical grounds. But we may doubt that Boethius the author could actually succeed in such a rigorous denial, in such a delimitation of human nature; similarly, the integration of such separate halves would be hard to achieve. For Philosophy continually asks the prisoner to follow her and take *her* way out, but they do not travel together, and she is forced to point the way rather than to lead. And the fact of the composition of text that is before the reader shows that the prisoner ultimately chose a different path and did something other than follow Philosophy, for he chose to live and write a book. Philosophy's ultimate goal, that the exile achieve a definition of what a human being is and therefore of what he himself is, is never reached; or, at least, never explicitly reached. If the prisoner is seen resisting Philosophy's abstractions, then he may not wish to allow her to define him, and I would conclude that *Consolation* does not want the reader to contemplate the prisoner's humanity in Philosophy's universal terms.[20] Of course, these positions and oppositions develop over time in *Consolation*. After all, it is the prisoner himself who, in his impassioned poem at 1.m.5, wishes that the love of heaven could rule the hearts of all people; and it is Philosophy, in a poem at the conclusion of book 2 that speaks of this same love in much the same terms, who raises the possibility that it is in Boethius himself that we find the only one whose love was true on this earth, and who kept holy the bonds that bind people and society together.[21]

Consolation has other, built-in obstacles to a universalist reading. These are a group of narrative gambits and authorial stances that define it as a very personal and introspective text. There is no addressee, and only at the ends of the three final books does Philosophy speak to a plurality, who may be imagined as the readers of the book.[22] The author has taken great pains to disguise his presence as an author; that is, to avoid the trappings of authorship and its implications of *auctoritas: Consolation* begins with the prisoner laying down his pen (at 1.1.1 he only says that he wrote down the first poem; at 1.1.7, that he was then taking dictation from his Muses), and Philosophy never tells him to pick it up again. *Consolation* is not presented as a teacher-student dialogue, and there is no command, typical in that genre, to write down the lessons learned;[23] when it finally dawns on the reader that the narrator has written down the dialogue as it were in retrospect and in peace, it is hard to escape the conclusion that he did so for his own benefit, and as an expression of a personal benefit gained.[24] Like *Confessions, Consolation* affects to be a work without an external audience, a meditation, but it cannot be viewed as a work without an author.[25]

A further obstacle to a universalist reading is another strong desire; namely, to read *Consolation* as a martyr's last will and testament.[26] The resolution of the wounded innocent, who refuses to speak of Death even in the presence of Death, who seeks not the comfort of visions of heavenly bliss but the intellectual satisfaction of hard questions well answered, who without fear rejects the things of this world and follows his mind where it will take him, makes of the author and the text inspiring exempla. The particular circumstances of its composition and the very fact of its composition are at least as important to this view of *Consolation* as the content: the virtuous Roman Republican spits in the eye of Theoderic and Empire.[27] That Boethius may in fact be guilty of treason as charged, inviting intervention in Roman affairs from Byzantium, is not particularly relevant to this reading, though it does cast the exculpatory arguments of his apology in a new and more Socratic light.[28]

Still, the author seems not to want us to dwell on such a thing as heroic resolve in the face of death. Death is more of a latent reality; it is made explicit only in the apology that Philosophy dismisses as proof of the prisoner's sickness (1.4.36; quoted in chapter 3, n. 13). And rather like his brother

Job, who proverbially has a reputation for patience that is wholly undeserved once he opens his mouth, Boethius's prisoner is not all that calm.[29] Philosophy would lead him, but he is not always willing to be led; both of the final books begin with Philosophy about to take the prisoner onward, upward, homeward, but she is frustrated by the prisoner, who forces her to answer questions that she thinks are irrelevant to her main task. The prisoner will achieve a sort of Pyrrhic victory when Philosophy feels compelled to admit to his debater's point, that in divine foreknowledge there is a sort of necessity imposed on human actions (5.6.25).

In brief, if I have read the tone of her closing remarks correctly, Philosophy's offer to escort him home along her own path has been rejected by the prisoner, who chooses not the path of transcendence but the path of humble approach—prayer is valued over Philosophy's abstractions. Ultimately, all that Philosophy has provided is an assertion of the value of prayer (although one would not call it a logical argument for belief in the efficacy of prayer): the necessity of God's knowledge of the future does not violate it. But the important point to make here is that it is Christian prayer that is in evidence; not just the abstract prayer of praise, but the particular prayer by which one hopes to avoid anticipated misfortunes: not *precari,* but *deprecari.* Other specific terms of this language of prayer are easily paralled in Christian liturgy.[30] The whole of book 5 can be shown to be quite different from the other four in its language and rhetorical structures, leading us to suspect a general change of direction.[31]

But from the beginning there has been a Christian presence: the use of the Greek letters Π and Θ to create, with the ladder, a unified symbol of Philosophy to adorn her robe, owes its inspiration more to Christian monograms, or gammadia, than to pagan sources.[32] Even for Philosophy's torn robes, emblematic of the division of her unity at the hands of vicious sectarians, there is a powerful Christian parallel: the clothing of Jesus, divided into four parts, for which the soldiers cast lots, and the seamless and indivisible tunic (Matthew 27.35, John 19.23; cf. Psalms 21.19) are taken by Augustine as anticipations of the heresies that would divide the church and of the divine love that cannot be divided.[33] It is not unreasonable to view Augustine's *Soliloquies,* with its dialogue between Augustine and his Reason, as one of the most important models for *Consolation.* And it has been argued that, throughout *Consolation,* in its poems, Boethius writes according to principles of numerical composition that are biblical, and that *Consolation* is one of the crucial texts for transmitting these principles to the Latin West.[34]

The Christian presence in *Consolation* has therefore been gaining emphasis in various recent studies; we are in a position to extend these still further, but with this twist: what is Christian in *Consolation* is not necessarily universal, but has to bear on a very specific prisoner. Consider again Philosophy's final words in book 5, which put this question of particular and universal interpretations of *Consolation* into sharp relief:

5.6.47. Therefore, all of you: Avoid vices, cherish virtues; raise up your minds to blameless hopes; extend your humble prayers into the lofty heights. 48. Unless you want to hide the truth, there *is* a great necessity imposed upon you—the necessity of righteousness, since you act before the eyes of a judge who beholds all things.

Philosophy has her last dig at the prisoner when she speaks of the necessity imposed on his actions, but she is actually speaking in his defense. The last words ("ante oculos agitis iudicis cuncta cernentis") are widely admitted to appeal to Scripture, Esther 16.4: "sed Dei quoque cuncta cernentis arbitrantur se posse fugere sententiam." But the context of the passage in Esther seems not to have been pursued by other critics of *Consolation*.[35] In this apocryphal chapter, Artaxerxes in a decree speaks of those ministers of his who had abused their powers and so attacked his subjects; not only do they hatch plots against their benefactors, but they even think that they can avoid the eye of God; Artaxerxes will see to it that unworthy holders of office and power are punished.[36] He speaks on behalf of the innocent Jews and against the evil Haman. The decree begins:

The great king Artaxerxes, from India to Ethiopia, to the governors and princes of a hundred and twenty-seven provinces, which obey our command, sendeth greeting. 2. Many have abused unto pride the goodness of princes and the honour that hath been bestowed upon them: 3. And not only endeavor to oppress the king's subjects; but not bearing the glory that is given them, take in hand to practise also against them that gave it. 4. Neither are they content not to return thanks for benefits received, and to violate in themselves the laws of humanity: but they think they can also escape the justice of God who seeth all things. 5. And they break out into so great madness, as to endeavour to undermine by lies such as observe diligently the offices committed to them, and do all things in such manner as to be worthy of all men's praise: 6. While with crafty fraud they deceive the ears of princes that are well meaning, and judge of others by their own nature. 7. Now this is proved both from ancient histories, and by the things which are done daily, how the good designs of kings are depraved by the evil suggestions of certain men. 8. Wherefore we must provide for the peace of the provinces.[37]

What is to prevent the reader from applying this context to the circumstances of Boethius before the court of Theoderic?[38] Why should we not read this as Boethius the author, not the prisoner, hoping for vengeance against those who accused and imprisoned him, still longing for the overthrow of a corrupt government? The fact of the composition of *Consolation* itself is, perhaps, some sort of indication that Boethius the author had a reason to expect that he might be released.[39] We could label this conclusion another instance of false modesty, as when, in book 1, Philosophy stopped the prisoner's mouth when he spoke of the injustices done to him. The author would only pretend to hide his life behind the prisoner's acquiescence to Philosophy's demands for self-forgetfulness. The "universal appeal" of Philosophy's little homily could be much more particular, that of a figure of absolute authority attacking temporal authority. Philosophy on this account could effectively silence the prisoner, telling him to attend to his prayers;[40] she will deal with the outside world.

Even to a particularist reading, this seems uncomfortably specific. A literary consolation could imagine in a vision the rewards of the virtuous and the punishments of sinners, but in this conclusion the prisoner does not seem truly to have found his peace. The lessons in Philosophy's diatribes against Fortune and worldly honor now seem to have been forgotten by Philosophy herself. Philosophy, who betrayed her own lack of sang-froid when she complained of the injustices done to her by unworthy philosophers who dragged her away as she kicked and screamed (1.3.4–14), has perhaps lacked all along the tranquillity that she tries to instill in the prisoner. This is not the end product of the dramatization of the process of thought, as Curley describes the action of *Consolation,* or a reconciliation of temporal and eternal perspectives. And in any event, this particular appeal to virtuous behavior should not include the prisoner who, alone in his cell, is beyond the realm of such actions.[41] He may pray humbly now, but Philosophy's finger-wagging "Don't think you can escape; God sees all; you must do right" is directed toward those who wish to hide the truth. The universalist reading suffers most because of the Esther passage: it would speak not to all of us, but to those who betrayed Boethius the author.

These may seem to be conclusions too great for the words *cuncta cernentis* to bear, but Boethius is a highly literate and highly allusive author; and were this a matter of Vergil alluding to Homer, we would go this far in analysis and still further. There is a simple expedient, one often taken: we can claim that the work is unfinished, and that either Boethius's hastily written final paragraph or a pious addition by a redactor has violated the tone and the truth of the text.[42] The end is certainly a problem, but not one that can be wished away. There are promises made in *Consolation* that are never fulfilled; these broken promises are consistent with its surprising redirections of thought and argument. There is a Christian sentiment in the text that becomes more intense toward the end, and the conclusion speaks to issues that were raised before in Christian terms. If do we not end up where we thought we would at the beginning of *Consolation,* it is because the text has been carefully crafted to surprise us. The author has not allowed Philosophy to provide the consolation that she had hoped to give; and the prisoner has taken from her a consolation that she had not expected to offer.

AT THE BEGINNING of this chapter, I noted the prisoner's complaint "Is this my library?" The author is, perhaps, frustrated not to be able to die as Augustine did, with time and preparation, able to make out of a life's worth of writing a coherent and revised library.[43] Boethius, who had hoped to write so much more than he did, found himself with his grand goals unachieved, and deprived of the opportunity to write his own *Retractions.* At the point of his own death, Augustine had copies of the penitential psalms put on the walls of his room so that he could spend his last days in tears and in reading, pondering the authority of the written word;[44] Boethius, who could not depict this end for himself, tries to come out from the shadow of Augustine by showing himself tearfully pondering the act of writing, rather than reading. Augustine's *Retractions* is a new kind of book, being a new sort of *Confessions*; so is *Consolation,* a kind of mixture of *Soliloquies* and *Retractions.* Boethius the author tries to do so much in *Consolation* to suggest a lifetime's writing, much of which must remain unwritten: it is exhortation and protreptic, Stoic moral essay and Platonic dialogue and Aristotelian commentary; it is autobiography and confession, prose and poetry.[45] Reading is for Augustine the fundamental act of self-awareness and self-definition, but our prisoner is now beyond reading, and we can see *Consolation* profitably as a work that tries to separate itself, both in structure and in theme, from the examples of Augustine.[46] It is good to note that the experience of the reader of *Consolation* is not that of the prisoner, who does not read; *Consolation* is a tale of a writer who finds a reason to continue to write. What he writes is autobiographical and confessional; it is unfortunate that *Consolation* is so frequently ignored in modern studies of autobiography.[47] To read it purely as an inspirational philosophical essay is to miss the sophistication of the author's self-presentation. For even as it is a particular and personal text, the personality of the author is hidden within it; *Consolation* is Boethius's attempt at self-discovery, and the reader is invited to search for this hidden author as well.[48]

It is to the implications of these positions that the following chapters are dedicated, to saving the phenomena of a book that is frustrated with its bookish form. One may say the same about Platonic dialogues, in which dialogue is in fact denied to the reader who cannot cross-examine them. The written word is not an apt medium for transcendent truths; Boethius the author is trying to keep himself within the bounds of a propriety that Plato defines but cannot adhere to. In rejecting apocalypse and transcendent vision he keeps language focused on where it may be most meaningful.[49] The fact that Boethius is a philosopher who knows his Plato, and who draws so clearly on Plato here, should make us wary of seeing his written words as an expression of unbounded confidence in the powers of human language and human thought.

The world of particulars is resistant to the tyranny of theory, and I have argued that Menippean satire takes the theorist's belief that the world may be comprehended and bounded by theory and shows it for its inadequacies, for its inability to define what is truly human. In other ancient Menippean satires, humans are incomprehensible because they are mad or corrupt; in *Consolation* humans are comprehensible in the gaze of God alone, but not to themselves. Kaplan argues that this very refusal to subordinate particulars to theory is at the heart of modern Menippean satire, a rejection of causal *nexus,* as he puts it; we do not have to accept his categorizations of modern literature to see that his fundamental argument illuminates *Consolation* (Kaplan 2000, 24):

> Wittengenstein wanted to eradicate this superstition of causal rela-
> tionships from the philosopher's mind. By seeing things this way, by
> seeing facts as they really are, as particular, the philosopher will per-
> ceive the world in a highly unusual way. The philosopher will see
> facts, so to speak, in a frozen frame—essentially unconnected with
> respect to time, to what comes before and to what comes after. The
> philosopher will see facts "*sub specie aeternitatis*" or from the "view-
> point of eternity." Wittgenstein says, "viewing the world *sub specie ae-
> ternitatis* is the good life." Facts perceived in this manner lose the ex-
> plainability which they have when they can be related to other facts.

Consolation is an attempt by Boethius the author to understand himself from this Olympian, eternal viewpoint; he does not wish to have himself understood, just as Job does not, within the web of causality that Philosophy would weave around him.

Chapter Four

Consolation and the Genre of Consolation

Edward Gibbon has some appreciative words about *Consolation,* a book valued more for its relative than its absolute merits. They are frequently cited, yet are worth a closer look:

> While Boethius, oppressed with fetters, expected each moment the sentence or the stroke of death, he composed in the tower of Pavia the *Consolation of Philosophy;* a golden volume not unworthy of the leisure of Plato or Tully, but which claims incomparable merit from the barbarism of the times and the situation of the author. The celestial guide whom he had so long invoked at Rome and Athens now condescended to illumine his dungeon, to revive his courage, and to pour into his wounds her salutary balm. . . . From the earth Boethius ascended to heaven in search of the SUPREME GOOD; explored the metaphysical labyrinth of chance and destiny; and generously attempted to reconcile the perfect attributes of the Deity with the apparent disorders of his moral and physical government. Such topics of consolation, so obvious, so vague, or so abstruse, are ineffectual to subdue the feelings of human nature. Yet the sense of misfortune may be diverted by the labour of thought; and the sage who could artfully combine in the

same work the various riches of philosophy, poetry, and eloquence, must already have possessed the intrepid calmness which he affected to seek.[1]

There are three acute observations here. First, *Consolation* is a debate recalled and written down by one who has already learned its lessons. We may say that one of the more curious aspects of *Consolation* is the dramatization and problematization of its own composition (after the narrator dictates the first poem, evidently in his sleep, just how does the rest get down on paper?);[2] but Gibbon is certainly right to recommend it to us as a dialogue composed in tranquillity. Second, it is a consolation. It is to this, and not to any belief in its truth, that Gibbon refers with the words "golden book,"[3] for so does Cicero describe the περὶ πένθους, "On Grief," of Crantor, the direct inspiration for his own *Consolation* on the death of his daughter Tullia.[4] Third, as consolations go, it is not very effective. This last point is a particularly welcome comment, for modern studies of consolatory literature in general, and studies of Boethius in particular, avoid the objection by not discussing *Consolation* as a consolation at all. The standard commentary on the *Consolatio ad Apollonium* ascribed to Plutarch (Kassel 1958), a great mine of information on the topoi of consolation, does not mention Boethius, despite the fact that a good deal of Boethius's book I has parallels in the *Ad Apollonium*.[5] Favez does not include Boethius in his book *La consolation latine chrétienne* (1937).[6] In von Moos's four-volume work on the consolatory genre in the Middle Ages, we read that Boethius's *Consolation*, insofar as it is a consolation, had only a limited influence in the Middle Ages, for the simple reason that *Consolation* has very little to do with death.[7] The most recent study of consolation in late antiquity, a commentary on a consolation by St. Jerome, considers Boethius "not a typical representative of the genre," but does not discuss the text as an atypical consolation.[8]

The word consolation cannot help but bring to a reader's mind solace in the face of death; and this solace embraces such things as assertions of the immortality of the soul, descriptions of the rewards of the blessed, and visions of eternity. None of these is to be found in the text, despite the example of *Phaedo*, a dialogue we would otherwise expect to lurk behind *Consolation*, and one is tempted to side with those who deny its affiliation to consolatory literature. Further, *Consolation* offers no reasons why death is not to be feared and spends most of its time taking the narrator's impending death for granted, in order to talk of other things, none of which involves a beatific vision.[9] Certainly, the word "consolation" does not by itself a consolation make,[10] yet there remains the interesting question: Why label a work with what seems to be a false promise? This is an authorial question; there is no reason to doubt that this is the title that Boethius gave his dialogue. One avenue is to say that we have here the playful title of a Menippean satire, with an oxymoron in the tradition of Varro's *Cynic Satires* or Petronius's *Satyricon*: Philosophy's consolation is a paradoxical consolation.[11] But this is not enough. The title is a tease: it invokes generic expectations that the work will not fulfill. Rather than deny the connection between *Consolation* and consolatory literature, we should look at *Consolation* as not-a-consolation; in short, as a parody.[12] In fact, Boethius's *Consolation* does align itself in a number of thematic and structural ways with the traditions of consolation, but what Gibbon sees as defects I will argue are pointed refusals and meaningful frustrations of expectations.

While death is its primary focus, a classical consolation may be triggered by other things: exile, loss of property (runaway slaves), or disappointment in friendship.[13] Accordingly, we may say that we have in Boethius's text a consolation for the fickleness of Fortune, the topic of the first half of the work, including the second and the beginning of the third books. *Consolation* therefore falls into two halves, separated by the central poem *O qui perpetua* (3.m.9), which is the essential statement of belief in the Providence that guides the world.[14] We may speak of these two halves and their center of gravity in a number of ways. The structure mirrors the narrator's search for truth, and Courcelle rightly notes the Neoplatonic succession of πρόοδος, ἐπιστροφή, and ἄνοδος (descent; turning around, or conversion; and ascent) in the presentation of his instruction at the hands of Philosophy.[15] The narrator's "conversion" is an ἀνάμνησις (remembering), and as he turns from self-forgetfulness to the recognition of the divine order, the tone changes from that of the Cynic diatribe to that of Platonic discourse.[16] But most important is the observation of Alfonsi that in the *opposition* of the first half of *Consolation* (which is consolatory, practical, and negative, weaning the narrator away from false goods) and the second half (which is hortatory, theoretical, and positive, leading the narrator on to eternal truths) is found the tension that is the essence of the work.[17] This bipartition shows up in other ways as well: Klingner has demonstrated that the individual books are neatly divided into halves of preamble and instruction.[18]

However, the fact that consolatory material is found in the first half of *Consolation* does not mean that *Consolation* begins in one genre and ends in another, or that consolation is dropped as a generic model or influence in favor of philosophical dialogue. This point should be made: all consolations are essentially bipartite and include a movement away from the physical and practical toward the ethereal and abstract. The practical consolatory matter tends to be followed by some authoritative statement of why death is not to be feared, and those who are to be consoled are turned from their present predicaments toward a contemplation of eternal truths. The situation is rather as in the middle dialogues of Plato: there is a strong tendency to transcend dialogue and achieve an absolute monologic revealed wisdom.[19] The pseudo-Platonic *Axiochus*, which has much in common with *Consolation*, offers a striking parallel. It deals with a man who once praised virtue and led a philosophic life but who now, at the point of death, finds himself afraid. Socrates is called in by Axiochus's son to aid in the case and to reconcile the man to death; he finds him pacing in front of his bed. Socrates has some of the imperiousness of Philosophy in *Consolation*, and the parallels in scene are hardly fortuitous; but after a dialogue on the nature of life and death Socrates concludes the work with a ἕτερος λόγος or "second discourse," a myth in the Platonic mold said to be related to him by one Gobryes, a Persian sage (371a).[20]

Dio Chrysostom preserves an interesting work called the *Charidemus* in which the bereaved gather on the occasion of Charidemus's death and read the letter that the deceased has surprisingly left behind for the consolation of his mourners. We read first of a gloomy account of the prison which is this life and of the punishments of the afterlife, attributed to a certain "morose man"; and then Charidemus gives two positive and hopeful accounts, both attributed to an unnamed rustic.[21] Here too, on a more modest scale, we ascend to a vision of the divine order of the world. But the most important parallel between *Consolation* and consolatory literature is afforded by Cicero's *Tusculan Disputations*. The very fact that there are five books in *Consolation* shows the influence of the *Tusculans*. Further, the *Tusculans* are similarly divided in two: there is a consolatory portion, in which philosophy is extolled as the medicine for fear of death and all other disorders of the soul (books 1–4); and there is a concluding protreptic in which virtue is extolled as the sole requisite for the happy life (book 5).

Now we may say that *Consolation* attempts to be a true consolation, not using high-handed methods to shut off the narrator's concerns (as do the myths of Axiochus and Charidemus, precluding any discussion) but inviting a dialogue throughout the work. As is said of Antiphon, Philosophy may be trying to heal through discourse alone.[22] And the fact that *Consolation* presents itself to us as an idiosyncratic consolation is not in itself a reason to deny it the label of consolation, for the genre, in so far as one can label it so, is quite an experimental one, and there are many variations. The chief defect of studies of the genre has been an emphasis on the various topoi of consolation, without serious consideration of the structures in which these topoi are found. For example, there are the monologic letters on the order of Seneca's *Consolationes* and Plutarch's *ad Apollonium*; there are dialogues, such as *Axiochus*; Cicero claims to have been the first to write a work of self-consolation, the work occasioned by the death of his daughter;[23] Dio Chrysostom's *Charidemus*, in which the dead console the living, has already been mentioned.[24]

Boethius's *Consolation* can therefore be seen as yet another experiment in consolation: a dialogue in which the there is an attempt to continue dialogue and thus avoid the anticipated monologic pronouncement of truth. But whose idea is it to avoid this monologue? Our prisoner has to find his voice in the opening book, when Philosophy has to rouse him from his lethargy; she would then seem to want to silence that voice in the concluding books in order to be revelatory and thus consolatory, in satisfaction of expectations. From the beginning, the expectation that dialogue should be superseded by a vision or an appeal to some outside, irrefragable source of truth has been turned on its head, because the vision in this consolation precedes the dialogue in the very epiphany of Philosophy.[25] The prisoner's desire to continue to speak has the effect of forestalling Philosophy's intended consolation, which is the promised vision of the true home frustrated by the digressions of books 4 and 5; yet the work does end with the pointed silence of the narrator, so we must infer at some point the prisoner's acquiescence, and therefore interpret Philosophy's final words as a *surprising* sort of monologic consolatory speech, created by the dialogue with the prisoner. Because the work calls itself a consolation, the reader looks for an account of transcendent reality, which never comes. The prisoner must be seen as resisting consolation by the fact of his struggle to prevent Philosophy from taking him to his homeland; but Philosophy's absolute and final pronouncement must come as a surprise both to him and to the reader.

Title, Topoi, and Action

It is worth detailing the ways in which *Consolation,* from the very begin-ning, toys with the expectations created by its title. First, it is not addressed to anyone. Consolations always have an addressee (*Consolatio ad Liviam, Ad Helvetiam matrem,* παραμυθητικὸς πρὸς Ἀπολλώνιον); it is further remark-able that any prose work in the sixth century would lack a dedicatee, or that a prisoner would not attempt to address the emperor who had imprisoned him.[26] Second, once the author's name is included in the title, as *The Con-solation of Philosophy of Boethius,* not only is an addressee not specified, but a confusion is invited on the question of just who is consoling whom.[27] The familiarity of the title and the work should not make us blind to just how unusual and open-ended a title this is. "Philosophy's Act of Consoling Boe-thius" is one possible translation; so too is "Boethius, on Philosophy's Act of Consolation"; and why not "Boethius's Act of Consoling Philosophy"?[28] Further, there is no other consolation written in a mixture of prose and verse; and while a consolation could be entirely in verse (*Consolatio ad Liviam*), it stuns the reader of a consolation to hear a narrator complaining in an opening poem about himself and his physical ailments. There is no clear delineation of who the speaker is, or what the problem is, or for what there must be consolation. Other consolations set the stage much more clearly and unambiguously. By dramatizing a process of consolation and setting us down *in medias res,* the text elegantly confuses us.

A literary consolation is more than a collection of consolatory topoi—it is also an expectation of a meeting of equals,[29] of sympathetic address, of as-cent to an absolute statement of the true nature of the world, of a transcen-dence of the inevitability of death. But one particular complex of topoi has a special relevance to Boethius's *Consolation,* the relation of *consolator* and *consolandus* as doctor and patient.[30] Consider the following, to be found at the very beginning of pseudo-Plutarch, *Ad Apollonium.*[31] The best doctors do not heal too quickly but give humors in flux a chance to settle and then apply external medications to bring things to a head; a waiting period is ap-propriate before approaching the bereaved (102ab). Sorrow is viewed as a most grievous thing, leading some to madness, some to suicide. Apathy is not good; there must be some grieving (102cd). Fortune is a treacherous goddess, and her wheel should keep us from believing that our happiness is permanent; reason is the remedy against sorrow (103f).

These topoi, appropriate to the beginning of a consolation, view the bereaved as ill, in a dangerous state, apt to be corrupted by solitude, needing a
healer who adapts what needs to be said to the individual's ability to listen
and accept. To this extent the action of book 1 is fitting for a consolation:
Philosophy comes as the doctor, who diagnoses the patient's illness as lethargy, or a sort of stupor; part of healing is to make the lethargic prisoner see
the light.[32] Philosophy is a doctor, whose medicine is reason; this view of
wisdom is common in consolatory works, especially so in Cicero's *Tusculans*.
The title's appeal to the consolatory topoi prepares us for viewing a sick patient; the surprising details are the debate about what the true nature of the
illness is and this doctor's need to expel the quack doctors (the histrionic
Muses) from the room.

Yet once we think of patient and doctor, we may consider the proverbial
relations between them. There is such a thing in late antiquity as the "house
philosopher," who is summoned when members of a great family have need
of him. Plutarch, *De superstitione* 7 (168b–c), has a wonderful account of different types of despair: there is the man who blames fortune when things go
bad; the one who blames god; and the one who will not listen to the house
philosopher who comes to console him, but falls into melancholy.[33] Compare this to *De profectu in uirtute* (81f–82a) on the three types of sick people,
the worst being the melancholiac who will not let the doctor in. I think that
we can say that the use of the word "consolation" in the title prepares us for
this presentation of a melancholic narrator whose doctor must force her way
into his locked room. The physical reality of the prison is not nearly as important as the prison of the narrator's own device: he has shut her out.

It is now possible to see the significance of the fact that this doctor is a
woman. It does not surprise us to see a female embodiment of wisdom; but
a female doctor we would expect to be a midwife. This Socratic, maieutic
function is thoroughly appropriate in context, even if it is not made explicit
verbally: the prisoner has forgotten who he is, and Philosophy's plan is to
bring out of him what he already knows so that he may come to realize who
he truly is. A further point to be made is one common to the paradoxology
of consolation (and will be pursued further in the next chapter): Philosophy
the doctor wants to save the exile's soul, not heal his body, and her call for
him to follow her home is in fact a call for the separation of his soul from his
body. What she wants to bring forth from the prisoner, the redeemable true
self, can come out only at the price of death.

It is melancholy, not a physical ailment, that is at issue in this consolation, for whatever Philosophy may be, she is not the antidote to death but the promise of death. The prisoner's opening poem completely misrepresents his real condition with its description of the pains of premature old age. When Philosophy offers the diagnosis of lethargy (1.2.5), which she explains as a sort of self-forgetfulness, we are not just to applaud her diagnosis but also to realize that it is a reinterpretation of events that allows her to be useful. The study of philosophy and the aims of consolation have this in common: they intend to take their audience away from the obsession with the physical world to contemplation of the divine. And melancholy is a disease thematically appropriate for consolations in general and particularly apt for one of Boethius's nature; the medical authors of late antiquity, whether or not they accept the explanation of melancholy as a function of an excess of black bile, often relate the depressive aspects of the disease to intellectual activity.[34] Soranus's description of melancholy puts us in mind of Boethius: the melancholiac exhibits "mental anguish and distress, dejection, silence, animosity toward members of the household, sometimes a desire to live and at other times a longing for death, suspicion . . . that a plot is being hatched against him, weeping without reason, meaningless muttering and . . . occasional joviality."[35]

To return to the question of just what we find as we begin to read *Consolation*: there is no addressee, and the action is not clear. At this point we know neither of the prisoner nor the exile and cannot separate author and narrator; let us refer to the poet. Given the title and the maudlin and self-referential content of the opening poem, we can only conclude that the poet is trying to console himself and doing a bad job of it. Philosophy in pursuit of her own brand of consolation will have to banish the poet's Muses; by the end of the first prose section we infer that there are at least two consolations involved here, and that the work began with a false consolation:

Carmina qui quondam studio florente peregi,
    flebilis, heu, maestos cogor inire modos.

Í who was ónce at the heíght of my pówers a máster of vérsecraft—
    Woé is me!—weéping, coérced, énter the gríef-ridden móde.[36]

Boethius is said to have written a bucolic poem in his youth, but he was hardly a poet; the poet regrets having to write elegy now, but the compulsion that makes him do so is hard to see. He will go on to speak of his Muses, still his companions in prison, as his one eternal possession, proof against the ravages of Fortune. The poet indulges his grief; he tells us that he is old, abandoned, his skin slack, his white hair falling out. Clearly, this effusion is to strike the reader as a terrible piece of poetry, flawed in conception as well as execution. This is not unreasonable; the poem serves to show that its speaker, whover he is, is in great need of help. Philosophy appears in order to put an end to nonsense; in this, she is playing the part of the straight man of Menippean satire, interrupting out of impatience an absurd and self-absorbed speaker.[37] Also true to conventions of that genre, she changes the genre of *Consolation*: after her appearance the work is no longer a poem, but a mixture of prose and verse, and, as I have argued elsewhere, we see Philosophy first as the personification of a genre, philosophical discourse.[38]

Philosophy therefore appears in the prisoner's cell in order to put an end to one sort of self-consolation. But the work as a whole is still to be understood as the author Boethius's self-consolation. It is not merely the precedent of Cicero's self-consolation that makes us believe this. First of all, as becomes clear when reading an essay such as Plutarch's consolatory letter to his wife, *Ad uxorem,* the act of writing a consolation inevitably consoles its author.[39] More specifically, the lack of addressee in *Consolation* speaks to a purely internally realized sort of work. Further, the prisoner and Philosophy are very much alike: each has a battery of Muses, and Philosophy will replace the prisoner's Muses with her own (1.1.11).[40] The prisoner will remember who he is if he remembers who *she* is (1.2.6).[41] Crucial too is the fact that, after we learn that the opening poem has been dictated to the silent prisoner by his Muses, we hear no more of how the present text comes to be written down. Writing has ended, to be replaced by a debate without an addressee. Boethius is speaking to himself. And if he has chosen to divide himself in two and to represent opposing components of his own self, he does so in accordance with Stoic meditative literature (in particular *De remediis fortuitorum;* see here chapter 5).[42]

But if Philosophy comes to put an end to a false consolation, she should replace it with a true one. Consolation by music is admitted, even in Boethius's *De musica,* to be an unworthy thing.[43] The fact that the work is written in a mixture of prose and verse shows that Philosophy is adapting her methods to the prisoner's nature, and that her opening gambit is not the way that she would prefer to speak, because she must take her patient's health into account. The lack of verse at the end of book 5 then signals two things: first, that Philosophy is dissociating herself from the prisoner's preferred form of argument; second, that she is finally achieving the mode of address that the genre of consolation would have us expect. When Philosophy first comes to the narrator, she dismisses the Muses who were dictating poetry to him (cf. Plutarch's complaint about the "malignant women" who come to prolong grief),[44] challenges our first perceptions of him, and diagnoses his illness as a mental problem, not premature old age; she also changes the genre of his work and creates a prose/verse hybrid that must ultimately be transcended in the name of true consolation. Philosophy is unmoved by the prisoner's recitation of his public benefactions and of his betrayal by court politicians at 1.4; his real problem is that he has forgotten what a human being is and so laments his lost fortune. In general terms, Philosophy seeks to deny the physical realities of the narrator's plight and blames him directly for his affliction; we may sympathize with the prisoner against the harshness of Philosophy, who does not seem as mild as she ought to be for a consolatory healer. It is in her preservation of the prisoner's verse, and in her willingness to yield to the prisoner and defer the remedy that is death, that Philosophy shows her mildness.

Philosophy the psychiatrist therefore has two distinct functions to perform in the service of true consolation: (1) re-education, to restore her patient's intellectual abilities, his ability to see the light; and (2) revelation, to lead him from that stage to a higher level, in which his true nature shall be defined. Dialogue would seem to be important to Philosophy's aims only in the first of these. Philosophy must by careful steps lead the narrator back to where he started: she is not in the business of teaching him anything new in the first half of the work (books 1–3) but in reminding him of certain truths evident to him at an earlier time, some of which are still present in him in book 1.[45] After the habit of consolations, as argued above, our *Consolation* should fall into two halves; the narrator's illness necessitates this particular bifurcation, reminiscence before revelation, instead of *praecepta* before *solacia* and *exempla*.

But this promised second level is never really achieved. The actual bipartition of *Consolation* is along other lines. In books 4 and 5, increasingly difficult philosophical problems are subjected to scrutiny, with increasingly problematic results. Dialogue is largely preserved; we learn much of philosophy but little of transcendence; self-definition and revelation never come explicitly, though it is possible that they are implicit, both for the reader and for the prisoner, in the contemplation of the peculiar silence of the ending. The point that I wish to make here is that *Consolation* promises a consolation and structures itself as one, without satisfying that promise in any obvious way. Yet the title leads us to believe that Philosophy's consolation is different from traditional consolations. And what starts as a poor self-consolation—and cannot be understood as a proper consolation of a mourner by someone external—can and will return to the category of self-consolation when our prisoner refuses to go home with Philosophy. It is our idea of who the *consolandus* is that changes in a reading of *Consolation*: there is an evolution from poet and prisoner through exile and narrator to Boethius the living author.

But what of death? Not only does the the consolatory tradition lead us to expect some treatment of death; so too does the narrator's predicament. Death, dismissed within the text by Philosophy, has its reality outside of the text, in the narrator's anticipation of his own fate and the reader's expectation, created as much by literary parallels (*Phaedo, Crito*) as any historical consideration, that *Consolation* is the author's final work. The absence of death within the text is a telling one, and failure to treat it is significant. Philosophy wanted to speak of something else, perhaps of death, in each of the last two books; the question may be suppressed because the narrator does not want to die and chooses not to. In some sense, the prisoner does not want Philosophy's consolation, the consolation that is the acceptance of death itself, and avoids her conclusion, the upward vision of the true home. And while at the beginning of *Consolation* Philosophy tried to steer the prisoner away from his thoughts about his impending execution, by its end it is the prisoner who similarly is redirecting Philosophy. And in the absence of dialogue and the absence of poetry at the very end we see that Philosophy does have the last word.

Given the expectations of consolation, and of an unusual consolation, that the text has given us through its title, its presentation of the illness of the narrator, and its promise of revelation, and given the surprising variations on the consolatory traditions (the debate on the nature of the illness, the absence of death, the lack of vision of the supernal realms), we reach the following conclusion about the ending of *Consolation:* its discussion of the world from the perspective of God is part of the inversion of consolatory expectations—instead of seeing the world of the divine, we see the physical world from the perspective of the divine. This is not only philosophically but also literarily satisfying, for this Olympian vision, with its suppressed Olympian laughter, is in the Menippean tradition of the Cynic *catascopia:* a view of the world from a height would lead one to devalue the human world, but here its value is asserted, because all is Providential, even if the status of human free will remains inexplicable.[46] This latter surprising philosophical conclusion has a thematic value as well as a narrative one. Philosophy once promised the exile that she would show him a citadel from which he could look down and laugh at the world (1.3.13–14) or see that the tyrants are the true exiles (4.m.1.27–30); but ultimately the view that she offers takes the world very seriously, even justifying the prisoner's punishment in the name of Providence. Philosophy hoped to demonstrate to the exile that he was superior to the world, but the prisoner's relentless interest in the world creates a sort of vision of the totality of things in which he is both observer and integral part. It is a vision that owes much to the conclusion of Job and that in its turn offers much to later ages; it would seem to anticipate the end of Spenser's *Faerie Queene*.[47] This is the vision that is substituted for what consolation would have us expect. Since the text presents a struggle for control of the text, in which Philosophy at first overrules the poet's designs, and in which later the prisoner overrides Philosophy's plans; and since we are given the spectacle of warring approaches to consolation, this particular conclusion is neither what the poet nor Philosophy had in mind at the beginning of *Consolation*. Whether it is some sort of Hegelian synthesis of two opposing approaches, the spark struck by the collision of the prisoner's and Philosophy's worldviews,[48] or whether it really represents the prisoner's victory, asserting the terrible value of the phenomenal world, remains to be seen.

Chapter Five

Death and Meditation

All the same, he's gone to join the majority. It was the doctors
that got him; no, make that bad luck. After all, a doctor's nothing
but consolation for the soul.

Petronius

Considerations of the particularity of the prisoner—the discoverer of Philosophy's hidden gold—and of the consolatory genre argue that *Consolation*
presents a tale of death deferred. The imminence of death seems clear
enough in the text, in the prisoner's apology in book 1 and his account of
the author's downfall and condemnation, yet the rejection of Philosophy's
journey home is the rejection of Death itself. The author presents after the
fact what the narrator experienced. Let us forget impending execution and
notions of composition interrupted by the fatal knock on the door; *Consolation* is written in a reflective moment, viewing the encounter with Philosophy as a thing of the past. The act of writing *Consolation* is the act of one
who has survived his dialogue with Philosophy and Death. The question,
then, that needs to be asked next is why the author has summoned Death to
converse with his imprisoned self.

Some literary and historical parallels between Petronius and his *Satyricon* and Boethius and his *Consolation,* beyond the epigraph to this chapter,[1] are worth pursuing as a starting point. Theirs are the two most prosimetric texts of antiquity (Martianus Capella's *Marriage* would come in third), with the most extensive integration of verse into narration and the greatest variety and experimentation in metrical forms. The narrators of both works are scholars; both are distressed by the fact that their own theories about the world are contradicted by their experience. Encolpius the moralist and literary critic leads an immoral life and is trapped within the pages of an improper book;[2] Boethius's prisoner is forced to confront the fact that his prior ideas about justice and about good and evil are insufficient to explain the world of which his evidently just punishment is a part. One work presents a parody of the officious moralist, the other the embarrassment of the ambitious philosopher; in both, the unorthodox form and the multifarious content of the narrative suggest a vision of the world as a whole. Most important is that their respective worlds are death-centered. This fact is notorious in *Satyricon,* more latent in *Consolation;* but the title *Consolation* sets the tone and prepares for the entrance of Philosophy as a death figure.

Another intriguing parallel between the two authors lies in a biographical consideration. Petronius the author, condemned by Nero, refuses to ask for mercy and dramatizes his own death, slitting his wrists and sitting in a hot bath, now opening, now closing his wounds, disdaining to read serious works, dispensing rewards and punishments to his slaves, and writing a full account of Nero's immoralities.[3] It is a parody of a philosopher's death; both Socrates and Cato of Utica seem to be looking quizzically over Petronius's shoulder as he bravely makes his way to death while refusing to take his situation too seriously. And what of Boethius? Condemned by Theoderic, he too refuses to ask for mercy and goes out defiantly; with a censor's outrage and a satirist's anger he dares, like Lucilius, to name names; we read at 1.4.25 that Boethius wrote a separate account of his political involvements.[4] Philosophy's own history of philosophers as martyrs for philosophy in the face of corrupt authority clearly suggests that the prisoner, and Boethius the author, ought to take their place among them (1.3.4–10, 1.5.8–12). Yet for all of this Boethius presents himself in *Consolation* not in the realm of answers but of questions, as a man who refuses revelation and the apocalypse. Petronius's death was not to be found in his own dying testament, and neither is Boethius's: for both authors, composing a text is part of the larger process of dying, one by no means finished at the end of *Consolation;* to be implacably opposed to the emperor does not mean that either author is prepared to give a purely heroic accounting of himself. Boethius's narrator is not willing to be the martyr that Philosophy is looking for.

It is difficult to separate a reading of *Consolation* from an analysis of Boethius's own life; and while we still need to be wary of introducing biographical considerations into literary criticism, it is good to note that the irresistible attempts to locate *Consolation* in the context of Boethius's life view the book as a paradox. A difficulty is always imported: Where is Boethius's Christianity? The work's insistence upon pagan philosophical discourse in the face of death seems a sort of apostasy, yet one generally approved of by classicists and philosophers, as if the author had chosen the better path. On the other hand, it is clear that only those Neoplatonic doctrines that are compatible with Christian thought are to be found within it;[5] and Christian language and thought have long been detected within it, even when Christianity is admitted to have only a minor thematic presence.[6] As a non-Christian work that can be read in a Christian way, it could be uncharitably viewed as yet another instance of fence-sitting in the career of a man who is not known for taking sides in intellectual disputes but for being modestly orthodox in theological debates, for believing conventionally that all things can be reconciled.

Of course, it was not foreordained that Boethius had to abandon his religious beliefs in order to discuss his philosophical avocations; but the most common critical view of *Consolation* is that it seeks to reconcile reason and emotion, logical discourse and poetry, outside of the realm of the Christian religion. And even if my claim is true that this is a Christian work—and if we go further and adopt the language of theologians to say that in *Consolation* theology is what Boethius speaks *about,* while philosophy is what he speaks *through*—we are still entitled to wonder whether the reluctance to treat Christianity explicitly is a failure of nerve, or whether some subtler and profounder effect is sought. I would suggest that *Consolation,* designed as the author's less-than-perfect accounting of himself, points to that which is missing. It is a perplexing finale, though ultimately a satisfying finale, to the philosopher's abruptly curtailed lifetime of writing and study.[7]

This confusion of autobiography and literary interpretation is encouraged by the author, who makes it plain that the prisoner of the text is the

Boethius of the superscription. I have already argued that *Consolation* presents us with a prisoner-narrator who does not want to be Everyman; now we can look more closely at how Boethius the author contemplates the particularities of his own personality. Though the name Boethius nowhere appears in the text proper, when the prisoner in his apology names the names of those who conspired against him, he makes his identity clear to his contemporaries (1.4.10–17). The references that Philosophy makes to the prisoner's two sons who were coconsuls (2.4.5) and to his father-in-law, Symmachus (2.4.7), further pin down the author precisely. But this identification is made by the reader only slowly. The fact that it is a first-person narrative does not make us think immediately that the author speaks in his own person. Just as it takes the prisoner some time to realize that it is Philosophy who stands before him (1.3.2), and just as it takes Philosophy a while to come to know what she will understand to be the true causes of the prisoner's sorrow (1.6.17–21), so too with our realization that the prisoner is Boethius. If nothing else, the opening elegiac lament is most un-Boethian. The revelations that the narrator is a prisoner, and that the prisoner is the author, are unexpected parts of the unfolding of this story. Trying to define who the author is is both the reader's goal and the author's.

Now Philosophy wants to move the prisoner away from concerns with these details of his life and pass him on into a more abstract realm, in which the only self-awareness that matters is that which is divorced from the everyday world. The autobiographical concerns of his apology are ultimately separable, and, as we have seen, are said to have been written down separately. This account interests us for another reason as well: in the company of the first poem, it refers to an act of writing that is distinct from the dialogue which the prisoner is nowhere told to record. We know that we are not in the realm of revelatory literature or of that sort of instructional literature in which a master teaches a pupil mysteries that are to be written down. While the prisoner is interested in writing, Philosophy is not; part of her job seems to be to keep him from putting his trust in books. This is a surprise. Philosophy appears with a scepter in her left hand and books in her right (1.1.6); she is not herself a writer but the Muse of writers, yet she is not asking him to write, just as she never asked Socrates to write. There is an equivalence of the prisoner and Philosophy that would make such a division of labor inappropriate; this is to put us in mind of a theoretically pure Socratic dialogue, with partners on the same level; such equality is at the heart of the consolatory genre as well. *Consolation* is not composed as a transcript of the teachings of the wise Philosophy but, written down afterward and without Philosophy's expressed command, as Boethius's personal attempt at consoling himself and therefore of understanding himself.

Split Personalities

The equivalence of prisoner and Philosophy is made clear in a number of other ways as well, as has already been stated. Philosophy says that if the lethargic prisoner comes to recognize who she is, he will recognize who he is; that self-understanding and understanding of Philosophy are one and the same (1.2.6).[8] They both detail their unjust treatment, and Philosophy takes her own as seriously, and describes it as proudly, as the prisoner does his. When under attack, she retreats to the citadel that her general makes available to her and from whose Olympian height she looks down on the world; she invites the prisoner to see his prison cell as the philosopher's true home (1.3.4–14). The doctor-patient relationship will prove to be a Socratic, maieutic one; she must bring back to the prisoner's mind what he already knows, and these recovered memories will unite the two. But it is also implied in the conventions of consolatory literature—as the consoler and the consoled are on an equal footing—that the consoler, by consoling, achieves a measure of self-consolation as well.

I think it is clear that, because of the equality of the prisoner and Philosophy, we are to take this dialogue ultimately as an interior dialogue, between dramatizations of two different aspects of the author's own self. My point is not that an author inevitably concocts literature out of inner voices; or, because Philosophy didn't really appear to him, that Boethius made it all up and could not help but write the two halves of the dialogue. Rather, it is possible to see Philosophy "as an internal aspect of the consolee-narrator himself"; and that, given her claim that he will know himself once he recognizes her, there is very little difference between viewing her as a part of the narrator and viewing her as an external agent who has been internalized.[9] We say the same about Augustine's early *Soliloquies* and their presentation of Augustine and Reason.

There is a good deal of Platonic influence in the dialogue, but much of its thematic inspiration is Stoic. Stoicism is not just a function of the beginning books of *Consolation*; Lerer has argued that the Stoic dramas of Seneca provide a constant backdrop against which to measure the narrator's progress in assimilating Philosophy's teachings.[10] The setting and the action of this dialogue can also be related to those Stoic maxims, well represented in Senecan epistles and in the *Meditations* of Marcus Aurelius, that the Stoic should retreat within and find true life within rather than without. I submit that we have here in literary form the sort of self-examination recommended in Stoic literature.[11] But before considering the mechanisms of self-analysis, we need to look more closely at the presentation of the characters in the dialogue and the ways in which each one represents some aspect of the author's person.

One of the intriguing conclusions to be drawn from the assertion of the equivalence of prisoner and Philosophy is that we can then picture Philosophy not as a divine being, living in heaven, complete and self-sufficient, but as the human possession that Socrates is said to have transferred from heaven to earth. The Philosophy that lives on earth will be Philosophy as the prisoner had practiced her; further, to the extent that she represents a desire to escape to the other world, she is the author's mortal, not his immortal, part. The dialogue between the prisoner and Philosophy can be reasonably defined as a dialogue between emotion and reason, between experience and theory, between forgetfulness of purpose and knowledge of the right, between life and death within the specific individual who is Boethius; but reason, theory, and knowledge are represented by the death figure Philosophy. It is good to remember, considering the various Muses and musics of *Consolation,* that Boethius himself, in another musical context, thought that "the goal of a harmonic scholar should be to bring these two faculties, sense and reason, into concord."[12] But it is not at all clear that the action of *Consolation* with its rejection of apocalypse does dramatize any kind of reconciliation. The self-examination, the retreat within, that is effected by the dialogue between the prisoner and Philosophy results in the life of the author, and what Philosophy wants of the prisoner is not life but death—a martyr's death, but death all the same.

If the dialogue presents parts of the author's self, then the prisoner, who is a part, is distinct from the integrated whole, which is the author of *Consolation*. If we disengage the prisoner and the author, on the basis of the discrepancies between the two, we may allow that the dialogue that takes place within Boethius the author is aimed at reintegrating the author as a person, and that the author in his ideal wholeness does not need to be portrayed accurately in, or associated exclusively with, any one of the sides represented in this confrontation.[13] We see that the historical Boethius as author has in fact remade himself in a number of ways in the prisoner. Philosophy is portrayed as less than her ideal (in torn and smoke-covered clothes, lamenting her treatment by unworthy philosophers), and so is the prisoner. The whole that is aimed at should be greater than the sum of the parts.

The extent to which the introduction of *Consolation* surprises the reader by its frustration of expectations has already been discussed; let us consider further here the personality of the prisoner as revealed in the first book. To be specific, the prisoner's opening elegy is dictated to him by his Muses, and their goal as "malignant women" is to prolong grief; there is no reason why the poem should state any truth at all. Did Boethius ever compose poems in his youth? Cassiodorus tells us that he wrote a bucolic poem, but surely the point is that the Muses are exaggerating.[14] Boethius was primarily a translator and commentator of Aristotle and a writer of technical handbooks. He was little more than forty when he died; does this let him speak realistically of his white-haired old age and sagging skin, and can he be said to be anything other than a translator and commentator when he was in his prime (*studio florente;* 1.m.1.1)? The opening poem is a parody of an elegy and an index of his diseased mind.[15]

Nor does Boethius the author choose to misrepresent himself only here. Philosophy's first poem mocks the prisoner as a natural philosopher who can no longer see celestial realities but only the ground at his feet. He once knew the risings and settings of sun, moon, and stars, she says, and the cycle of the seasons (1.m.2.20–27):

Whó was the reáson that Fáll ín the year's fúllness,
Fértile and rích, overflóws, grápes full to búrsting—
Ít was his hábit to próbe áll of these quéstions,
Náture's root caúses to sólve, áll of them hídden.
Nów here he líes, and his mínd's bríghtness is bárren;
Weíghed down, draped óver his néck pónderous sháckles,
Weáring a fáce that looks dówn, bént by the deád weight—
Woé is him! trúly coérced he stáres at the hárd earth.[16]

Now Boethius is of course not a natural philosopher. He did write on astronomy, though this work has not survived; but such efforts were not central to his life's work.[17] When at 1.4.4 the prisoner speaks of Philosophy's instructing him on the order of the heavens in private, in his library, she is said to have directed this knowledge toward his moral education.[18] How different the poem would be if Philosophy had said, "Here's the man who wrote two commentaries on Aristotle's *De interpretatione,* and who needed to defend himself against charges of longwindedness and pride!"[19] The poem wants to stake out some ground for Boethius that he never really held; it certainly overlooks all of his work in rhetoric, logic, and music. Philosophy resumes in prose by saying that it is time for medicine, not complaint (1.2.1: "Sed medicinae, inquit, tempus est quam querelae"). We deduce that she has been teasing him: "Some universal philosopher you are!"

Why should the author choose to have Philosophy label the prisoner's intellectual efforts in this way, and why doesn't the prisoner correct her? Not merely because he is speechless at this point. Rather, Philosophy chides the narrator as one who has not had, but who should have had, some all-encompassing cosmic vision. Boethius as we know him was a prodigiously learned man who exhausted himself, if we may use the literary metaphor, in scaling only the lower slopes of Parnassus. He should have looked up, her poem concludes; but now he is forced to stare at the ground.[20] His whole career has been weighed in the balance and found wanting by that portion of the author's self that longs for universal vision. By the end of *Consolation,* however, the author will finally have achieved in his own way the sort of vision whose lack Philosophy here decries in the prisoner, and he will at that point disappear from the text, his new vision presented, in effect, as the scholar's hard-won crowning achievement.

I suspect that there is a latent criticism of Boethius as an Aristotelian in Philosophy's poem here, as one who examines the phenomena of the earth instead of attempting a Platonic experience of the unchanging realms above. When Philosophy tells proudly of her history at 1.3.4–10, Aristotle does not appear. It is a quick step from Socrates and Plato to the vicious schismatics, the Stoics and Epicureans, who carried her off, each taking only a fragment of her dress. Socrates is the philosopher of the unified Philosophy; Philosophy longs for her own earlier integral self and hopes to find it in Boethius, the Platonist and Socratic martyr. There is a terrific pride in an author who seeks to portray himself as the last real philosopher. Boethius was the scholastic wonder of his age, but let's be honest: Boethius is a translator, a master of other people's words and thoughts, never taking sides. Even in the *Tractates* he claims for himself no very large ground but only offers to submit his philological skills to the clarification of a number of terms and concepts for the benefit of others. And the significant doctrinal achievements of *Consolation*, particularly in the attempt of reconciling divine foreknowledge and human free will, are accomplished modestly, as the prisoner forces Philosophy to admit that necessity is still involved. The Philosophy that the prisoner debates is the Philosophy that Boethius has personally known, that has been limited by his own practice and experience of her; he is not wrestling with an angel, but he is trying to force his own beliefs toward some other goal and purpose. And so, at the end of book 5, Philosophy addresses the prisoner within Boethius's own Aristotelian terms; when she speaks of the providential value of the world below when seen through the eye of God, we can appreciate the author's depiction of a victory snatched from the jaws of defeat. It is a sort of triumph of Aristotle over Plato: looking down, not looking up, provides what will pass for consolation here.

Let us also say that there is no reason for Boethius to feel, at the end of his life, that he had accomplished his life's work. The fact that his version of the Organon formed a very influential body of texts says more about the Middle Ages than about his own desires. If he wanted to translate, comment on, and reconcile all of Aristotle and Plato he could only think that his life's work had just begun. If he were to compare himself to Plato, Aristotle, Porphyry, Iamblichus, or Augustine, he would be compelled to admit that he never achieved a coherent body of work; there are no great personal visions, no cosmic synthesis, no creative literature, no myths, no transcendence. When he turns to the writing of *Consolation* he finally allows himself to write something personal, something mythic, something creative. He clearly wants the reader to feel that he is trying to accomplish all that he had left undone before. Lerer and O'Daly document that a large part of *Consolation* is, within itself, the prisoner's search for a voice; I would say that this is true of Boethius outside of the text as well, in that Boethius's search for a personal voice in the corpus of his philosophical writings is also at issue. For *Consolation* is not just Boethius's final work but is also his first and only attempt at the Platonic corpus: not a translation or a commentary but a recreation of *Crito*, a prison dialogue on what it means to be loyal to the principles by which you have lived your life and on what it would mean to escape. But these have been very limited principles: Philosophy chides him for it and wishes to raise him to the grand vision he never had; what is remarkable is just how true to his principles our prisoner will prove to be when he refuses the grandeur that Philosophy offers and stays very much within the confines of what he has already had experience of.

The supernatural visitor is not Socrates' Spirit of the Laws of Athens, but the author's Muse, and to wrangle with a Muse is by classical convention to wrangle with memory, not in a personal but a historical sense.[21] Literary traditions do have an objective reality outside of the author, and one of the issues of this interior dialogue is the question of what genre the prisoner-author should align himself with. If the prisoner is to be proved to be the true philosopher, then the tattered and torn Philosophy herself gains a certain measure of reality; her desire to insert him into her tradition is a desire to validate herself. Philosophy in book 1 seems to upbraid the narrator for not writing philosophy (elegy here represents the antithesis of philosophy) and immediately invokes the memory of the philosophers of the past who had no trouble writing and living as philosophers despite their troubles. Philosophy wants to add the prisoner to her chain of philosophical martyrs, of whom Socrates is the type (1.3.6);[22] but what surprises us is that she does not want a book from him, but his life. The existence of the book before the reader's eyes proves to be an assertion of the prisoner's independence; so too is the genre in which the author has chosen to write. And so Philosophy will prove to be more than the prisoner's Muse, because she has goals quite different from those of the composition of the present text; and the prisoner will write his book in defiance of this Muse.

The characters have different goals in this dialogue because each is trying to become a different whole, to claim a different missing half, like the lovers in Aristophanes' tale in Plato's *Symposium*. The key to all of this is to insist that Philosophy is a death figure. This is seen in many ways. The theta on her robe marks the top of the ladder that reaches from *praxis* to *theoria;* but a theta on a robe of a prisoner is a sign of one marked for death.[23] The smoke that covers her robes at 1.1.3 reminds the prisoner (or rather the reader, as the prisoner is supposed to be too lethargic at this point to catch too many details) of the smoke on death masks in the halls of aristocratic families. She said she was carried away kicking and screaming by the schismatic Epicureans and Stoics, who had torn her clothes; she has been neglected for a long time; she gives every impression of coming back from where they had taken her. She speaks of the bitter remedies that she will give the prisoner to drink, and in this Socratic prison world she can only allude to the cup of hemlock. I have argued elsewhere that the opening scene is closely related to a motif of Old Comedy, in which a personified genre comes on stage to complain of her shabby treatment at the hands of moderns and to find a champion who will restore her to her former glory.[24] Philosophy wants the exile to walk off hand-in-hand with her into the sunset and is convinced that they need each other. But Philosophy is the practice of death; a good death will prove the philosopher, and Philosophy is eager for the prisoner to die well and thus to vindicate her.[25] I think that she comes from the Land of the Dead and intends to take the prisoner back down with her.

It may be naive to object to Philosophy's teachings on the grounds that they do not literally remove the prisoner from his cell; but it is not naive to point out that the prisoner doesn't die. Socrates' death is described at the end of *Phaedo*, and Philosophy refers to it lovingly here; and while it would be extraordinary for a living author of a first-person narrative to describe his own death (or to carry on like a Trimalchio or a Eumolpus and imagine it), the prisoner's being alive at the end of *Consolation* is to some extent a frustration of the design of Philosophy.[26] The prisoner is not Socrates. The prisoner has so acted in the course of the dialogue as to keep himself alive, not to be a martyr to her cause. As Philosophy is both death and half of the author's person, we may conclude that the author does not desire that these halves of himself be reconciled and united. And this conclusion has important ramifications in the vexing question of the text's ability to provide a definition of who the prisoner (or exile, or narrator, or author) really is. At first the prisoner admits only that he is a rational, mortal animal (1.6.15); now he is not so willing to accept his mortality.

Stoic Exercises

The author (possibly Seneca) of *De remediis fortuitorum* ("Cures for the Vicissitudes of Fortune") encourages people to engage in an internal dialogue as the best means of revealing their superiority to the slings and arrows of outrageous Fortune.[27] The resemblance of such a Stoic scheme to books 2 and 3 of *Consolation* is obvious. Let us say that Boethius the author has split himself in two in order to analyse the reality of Fortune, and that he has been successful in this attempt. Denial of Fortune has entailed a redefinition of person: the prisoner is neither the aging ex-poet nor the natural philosopher, and the physical realities of his life need to be put to one side. Abstraction accompanies correction; he is to make himself more a philosopher in his dialogue with Philosophy, but a sort of philosopher that he never was before, a mystic and a metaphysician. What I have already described as an attempt to forestall consolation, to continue dialogue and thus to avoid the monologic and transcendent vision, can now be seen as a diverting of cosmic Philosophy to the realms of discursive thought, realms familiar to the prisoner from long ago. The author has so structured the debate that the Philosophy who had hoped to lose her Boethian particularity ends up, in effect, quoting from Boethius's Aristotelian commentaries.[28] The prisoner, who had been urged to rise, keeps Philosophy from making her own ascent. This has a great survival value: as long as the prisoner can keep Philosophy talking, he can stay alive. In the presence of such large questions of life and death, the prisoner has wisely kept himself within himself; he has been unwilling to go to the extremes that Philosophy believes necessary to find the truth. In doing so, he has been true to the Stoic models of self-examination.

The choice between life and death is not that between escape and execution. Philosophy has quickly directed the narrator's concerns away from external realties to inner ones: he is responsible for his own life and death, and he is subject to temporal powers only by his assent. This is the language of Stoicism; one need go no farther than Marcus Aurelius's *Meditations* to read that a new choice of words or perceptions results in freedom from earthly distress and anxiety.[29] The debate must center around the narrator's ability to understand that his situation is entirely within his own control; and to this extent we can see that Stoic notions of dialogue are at work in *Consolation* as well, in the call to self-examination. Marcus Aurelius assures us that imagining oneself in the presence of Death is an appropriate starting place for such a dialogue (2.2.4):

Throw away your books, be no longer anxious: that was not your given role. Rather reflect thus as if death were now before you (ὡς ἤδη ἀπο-θνήσκων): "You are an old man, let this third part (sc. the directing mind, τὸ ἡγεμονικόν) be enslaved no longer, nor be a mere puppet on the strings of selfish desire; no longer let it be vexed by your past or present lot, or peer suspiciously into the future."[30]

Marcus Aurelius is also of the opinion that the proper philosopher does not make journeys to the underworld, and that the value of a flight to heaven is small.[31] Boethius the author keeps his prisoner within these life-giving boundaries; the prisoner will neither travel down nor up, but will keep the matter of his own soul within himself. I have also argued that a parallel to *Consolation* is to be found in a comic piece of the fifth-century Greek poet Agathias Scholasticus (translated in appendix 4), in which the student asks a teacher who has mastered all of philosophy (that is, all of Plato and Aristotle) whether the soul is mortal or immortal; the teacher is absolutely agnostic, saying that only death will answer the question, and that it is not good to try to find out too soon. The proper way to resolve such questions is to accept that there are things that only death will reveal, and that it is proper to keep oneself on this side of that great divide.

There are a number of reasons for us to view *Meditations* as a text parallel to *Consolation*. Like *Confessions*, *Meditations* is written in the presence of death by a scholar forced against his inclinations to act in the world of politics, trying to maintain his allegiance to the precepts of philosophy and writing in the solitude of his tent, for himself, in the moments of quiet afforded him by lulls in battle.[32] Resemblances between the two pass beyond the commonplaces of Stoic thought. For example, Marcus refers contemptuously to the sort of philosopher and the sort of situation that we find at the beginning of *Consolation* (10.28):

> Picture to yourself every man who is pained or dissatisfied with anything as being like a pig kicking and squealing when sacrificed; and so is the man who laments silently, alone in his bed, that we are bound by fate. Realize too that it is granted only to the rational creature to submit willingly to the course of events; merely to submit is inevitable for all creatures.[33]

Marcus too imagines Philosophy as a doctor to whom someone with bad vision must return, with the crucial addition that Philosophy is to be not merely a tutor of lessons (5.9.1–3):

Love that to which you are returning; do not return to philosophy as to a reproachful tutor, but as the victim of ophthalmia returns to his sponges and white of egg, or a sick man to his compresses and poultices. In this way you will show that obedience to Reason is no burden, but even a relief. Remember that philosophy only wants such things as your nature wants; it was you who wanted something else not in accord with nature.

This self-examination in the presence of the good doctor Philosophy is difficult to separate in *Consolation* from the self-examination in the presence of death. Philosophy herself is both the type of death (according to the prisoner) and its antitype (in her own estimation).

If we say that the narrator of *Consolation* is in his cell, a word that he does not use, let us not forget that a cell is home not only to the prisoner but to the monk, and that the monk's cell is a fortress of solitude (if I may borrow the phrase from Superman, though not out of place in the literature of the desert) that frees the mind to contemplate the truth.[34] It is a superior place, affording a vantage point from which to look down on the world (a *catascopia* in the Menippean tradition, at home among the Stoics as well).[35] Philosophy herself rejoices in the acquisition of such a citadel, from which she and her loyal troops can laugh at the enemy, which can only kill the body (1.3.13–14).[36] Philosophy constantly encourages the prisoner to enter her citadel, that is, to trade his current solitude for hers. This is another indication of their basic equality. The prisoner, by virtue of his solitude, friendlessness, lack of possessions, and the shock of retreat from society, is already able to contemplate his true self. This language of retreat (anachoresis, whence the monastic term anchorite) is Stoic, and again *Meditations* affords us a good parallel (4.3.1–3):

Men seek retreats for themselves in country places, on beaches and mountains, [and you yourself are wont to long for such retreats,] but that is altogether unenlightened when it is possible at any hour you please to find a retreat within yourself. For nowhere can a man withdraw to a more untroubled quietude than in his own soul, especially a man who has within him things of which the contemplation will at once put him perfectly at ease, and by ease I mean nothing other than orderly conduct. Grant yourself this withdrawal continually, and refresh yourself. Let these be brief and elemental doctrines which when present will suffice to overwhelm all sorrows and to send you back no longer resentful of the things to which you return.[37]

Will the meditative prisoner, who has achieved already the isolation necessary for the self-examination in the presence of death, trade one citadel for another? If so, it will be by an acceptance of death, a death not achieved in *Consolation*.

Yet is it possible to take Philosophy both as the death figure who comes for the narrator and as half of the narrator's own self? I think it is. For if Philosophy is abandoned and neglected, she has been abandoned and neglected by the narrator himself; his forgetfulness of her is a mortal blow; she must make him believe in her if she is to have any life, but she can offer no escape from death and will in fact make the point that, just as it is not politics but his mind that is his trouble, so it is his own belief and resolve, and not the actions of others, that will lead to his death. Just as he is said to be responsible for his true exile (which has nothing to do with politics and prisons) because of his forgetfulness of her (1.5.3), so too is his impending death in his own hands, and she is glad of this, provided it is a philosopher's death. His reintegration as she imagines it, a merging with the eternal, will bring about the good death that she desires, and this good death she views as true life. But to the extent that Philosophy represents the author's own nontranscendent studies, Aristotle and sea battles, reintegration is particular, a reassertion of the value of the prisoner's life. In a way, the author admits to the truth of Philosophy's charges by presenting his own philosophical interests and endeavors as schismatic and incomplete.

Boethius the author may depict the split between his life in the world and his intellectual pursuits, but he does so by depicting each portion of his unitary self as split: one half is the prisoner, confronted by the opposition of physical and intellectual life; the other half is Philosophy, who represents the particular practice of Boethius longing to become universal and absolute. Philosophy looks at the narrator in two ways: as the particular Boethius, last of the philosophers and victim of conspiracy, soon to be her martyr and thus her vindication; and as Everyman, the generalized, ahistorical victim of faulty reasoning. He looks at her as the embodiment of the wisdom he once mastered and as the promise of truth to come. He refuses to be Everyman and will not let her be his guide to the other world; he not only retreats within himself to find truth, but retreats from Philosophy herself. None of these restrictions of the possibilities of either philosopher or Philosophy is allowed to emerge as complete; no potential unification of these halves is achieved in effect.

Philosophy's double aspect is crucial to a reading of *Consolation*. This has been dramatized in the difference between her unitary self and her fragmented self; Philosophy needs to regain the prisoner in order to achieve her ideal status, and thus to become whole. The two Philosophies of the text will be discussed in chapter 7 as a device to be found in Lucian's *Piscator*, a dialogue that has more than a few resemblances to *Consolation*, but for now let us return to the difference between the earthly and the transcendent Philosophy as a plot device in *Consolation*. One of Philosophy's refrains is the exhortation to the prisoner to look up, to rise up, to fly up; she wants him to look down on the earth below and despise it from an Olympian height. She says that she wants to take the prisoner to his true homeland. The flight home out of the prison is also death, the separation of soul and body; and Philosophy offers death in two ways, physical death and spiritual transcendence. One Neoplatonic option that Philosophy does not offer is that of union with the One, or with God; but, whichever path the prisoner chooses, he cannot come back to earth again. It is the heavenly Philosophy who wants him to undertake a journey, and *Consolation* implies journeys of many sorts, but particularly that of descent and return. She needs the prisoner to abandon his earthbound philosophy and rise to heavenly heights. The challenge to the prisoner, who must keep himself within himself, is to resist this siren call, to contemplate the heavens but return to his earthly home. This is the myth of Homer's *Odyssey*, and it is to Odysseus that we now turn.

Chapter Six

The *Odyssey* of *Consolation*

Apuleius concludes his essay *On the God of Socrates* by speaking of how Socrates concerned himself only with those possessions that could be truly said to be his, the internal ones that were separate from fortune and family—the wise must not be praised for externals. Apuleius then quotes approvingly from the beginning of Accius's tragedy *Philoctetes,* in which Odysseus is addressed by many epithets but by his father's name, Laertes, last of all, because this is the least of all. Apuleius goes on to praise Odysseus himself, implying not only that Odysseus and Socrates are alike, but also that the quest of Odysseus is the philosopher's quest:

> And in the very person of Odysseus Homer teaches you no different, for he always wanted Odysseus to have Providence [*prudentia*] as his companion, whom he called Minerva [Athena], according to poetic license. And so, with this same woman as his companion, he underwent all frightful things, and overcame all the things that opposed him. To wit: with her help he entered the cave of the Cyclops, but came out again; he saw the cattle of the Sun, but did not eat them; he journeyed to the land of the dead and came back up. With this same wisdom as his companion he sailed past Scylla, but was not snatched up; he was enveloped by Charybdis but was not held fast; he drank

from Circe's cup and was not changed; he went to the land of the Lotos-Eaters and did not stay; he heard the Sirens and did not draw near.[1]

How appropriately this concludes a discussion of Socrates' demon, the voice in his ear that would say no but never yes. That philosophy consists of rejection more than of acceptance, and that it intersects with epic in that it is an escape from death and destruction, will prove to be a useful approach to *Consolation*, for the prisoner is both a Socrates and an Odysseus.

In her book *Job, Boethius, and Epic Truth*, Ann W. Astell makes the claim that there are secondary epics in the Middle Ages. Because *Consolation* is interpreted as an epic, and because Job is perceived as an epic hero, there is a wide range of literature—hagiographic, romantic, and chivalric—that deserves to be read in the light of a continuously developing tradition of classical epic. The medieval epic traditions need not detain us here, but this reading of *Consolation* is certainly right. The point is a simple one: in the Neoplatonic allegorization of Homer, Odysseus is frequently invoked as a model of the human soul, specifically, the soul that is not resigned to its fall into this world but is actively seeking to return home.[2] Since *Consolation* is obviously what *Odyssey* is covertly, a tale of the soul's wandering on this earth and its longing for heavenly return, it is an epic, because it is what epic is about. In other terms, we could call *Consolation* an epic myth without the epic integument.

The opening words of *Consolation*, the couplet that alludes to the false introduction to Vergil's *Aeneid*, would then put us immediately in mind of Aeneas;[3] but it is the wandering *Odyssey*, not the martial *Iliad* or *Aeneid*, that has the upper hand here. When Philosophy dismisses the prisoner's Muses as Sirens, "a sweetness unto death" (1.1.11), she makes us think of the prisoner as an Odysseus; accordingly, Philosophy does not just replace one set of Muses with another by this dismissal, but removes a seductive obstacle that would keep the exiled soul from returning to its proper home. Philosophy would be like Athena, and the robe that Philosophy is said to have made with her own hands would provide an association between the two from the very beginning of *Consolation* (*Consolation* 1.1.3; *Iliad* 5.733–37).[4] Athena and Philosophy are embodiments of wisdom and would lead the wise hero past pitfalls and dangers, the enticements of sleep, forgetfulness, and death to the home where he truly belongs.

Astell draws particular attention to the only three mythical poems of *Consolation*: 3.m.12, on Orpheus and Eurydice; 4.m.3, on Odysseus and Circe; 4.m.7, on Agamemnon, Odysseus, and Hercules. She claims that they speak respectively of mortality and passion, of reason, and of the soul's struggle to achieve heaven; the three poems taken together provide the definition of what a human being is (mortal, rational, and possessed of an immortal soul) that the prisoner cannot come up with at the beginning of *Consolation* and that Philosophy herself never explicitly reveals throughout its course. These poems, which frame book 4, would establish the prisoner's right to go on to the more theological topics and eternal visions of the concluding book.

But there is a problem in this argument, if I have interpreted correctly the prisoner's refusal to go away with Philosophy as his struggle to stay alive. Odysseus needs the help of Athena not only to fight the battle against death, which Apuleius so succinctly describes, but also to resist the lure of immortality, offered by Circe and Calypso, in order to return home. Boethius's prisoner must ultimately resist Philosophy and her offer of the immortality which would be conferred upon him by that homecoming, which is death. The prisoner is truer to the plot and the Neoplatonic interpretation of the *Odyssey* by refusing to follow Philosophy's lead to what Philosophy offers as his true home. The life of his soul, his spiritual Odyssey, requires that he stay on this earth and learn to reject Philosophy's lead as he follows another wisdom to his earthly home. Consequently, this chapter will be devoted to a further consideration of the Christian presence in the plot of *Consolation;* a restatement of the arguments made here and in the previous chapters will conclude this chapter, an outline of the action and the interpretation of this Menippean satire.

Resistance and Revelation

The metaphor of an "intellectual *Odyssey*" is surely faded beyond usefulness. But the text would have us think of *Odyssey* in a vital way.[5] It is not just homecoming that is at issue but the connection between homecoming and the refusal of immortality. The prisoner, who refuses to be led by Philosophy, may have achieved a homecoming in a different sense. If we look at the dialogue from the point of view of its author and its composition, we may say that Stoic introspection has been a successful exercise; the prisoner has kept himself within himself and thereby found himself anew. Only this self-realization will allow the prisoner to contemplate God; but rather than say that *Consolation* has only served to get the prisoner ready for a final leap, I think it better to say that it has been about the rediscovery of the self in relation to the world *as opposed to* locating it in the heavenly realms or the Isles of the Blessed. Because Philosophy is a death figure, she cannot offer directly to the prisoner knowledge of who he truly is, that revelation strikingly absent from her presentations.

The injunction "Know thyself" is frequently defined by pagan and Christian authors alike as living within oneself, so as to be ready for true revelation.[6] And if we keep in mind that *Consolation* presents us with a story, and that its philosophical arguments function as stages in a drama, then we can describe the changes in intention and outlook as part of a plot; interwoven in this plot is the complex character of Philosophy, genre, Muse, midwife, teacher, debater, and Death. The prisoner, and the reader, must come to realize who Philosophy is in all of her functions and aspects; in defining Philosophy, and in defining himself against Philosophy, the prisoner comes to the realization of what he is and where wisdom is to be found.

To approach the Land of the Dead and then return alive; to approach a source of otherworldly wisdom and to accept this wisdom as a reason to withdraw from it to the reality of the physical world—these are not only themes of epic, but central themes of Menippean satire, which draws on Odysseus and his quest as one of its formative influences.[7] Wisdom is found at one's feet, not in heaven or hell, as Teiresias says to Menippus in Lucian's *Necyomantia;* the life of the private citizen, not the philosopher, is best (*Necyomantia* 21). This Menippean truth is thoroughly exploited in Seneca's *Apocolocyntosis,* in which the afterlife is presented as a sham and a fraud; and it is present in different degrees in works as diverse as Varro's *Endymiones* and Martianus Capella's *Marriage.* Its most influential incarnation is in Lucian, who presents us tales of a Menippus who goes both to heaven and to hell, a Menippus who thus becomes a sort of Everyman. The fantastic voyage of Menippus's *Necyia* has been reworked in Lucian's *Necyomantia;* it was Lucian's innovation to make as a counterpart a heavenly voyage for Menippus, the *Icaromenippus.* The two together, a diptych, are very influential in later literature, especially in the Renaissance; they are equally parodies of the philosopher's quest.[8]

But even philosophers, or at least moral philosophers, will agree with this assessment of where truth is to be found. As his importance to an understanding of *Consolation* has already been established, it is worthwhile to examine Marcus Aurelius's objection to Plato on this score. For example, Plato has Socrates describe the "consummate philosopher" as follows (*Theaetetus* 173e): "The truth is that only his body has taken up residence in the city and can be found there, while his mind disdains all these matters, seeing them as petty and worthless, and wings its way everywhere, as Pindar says, 'from beneath the earth to above the heavens' [fr. 302 Bowra; fr. 292 Christ]—the plane surfaces of the earth being the province of geometry, the heavens of astronomy; his mind is constantly exploring the general nature of every entity as a whole, but no local object becomes its perch."[9] Both Galen (*Protrepticus* 1) and Porphyry (*De abstinentia* 1.36) refer to this Platonic passage with approval. Marcus Aurelius, however, does not, quoting the same Pindaric tag as he does so (2.13.1–2): "Nothing is more wretched than the man who runs around in circles busying himself with all kinds of things—investigating things below the earth, as the saying goes—always looking for signs of what his neighbors are feeling and thinking. He does not realize that it is enough to be concerned with the spirit within oneself and genuinely to serve it. This service consists in keeping it free from passions, aimlessness, and discontent with its fate at the hands of gods and men."[10] Marcus only speaks of searching below the earth here; the voyage to the heavens he mentions elsewhere, in a positive though limited way, in exactly the terms of the Cynic *catascopia*, the view that Philosophy herself urges the exile to achieve in the early stages of *Consolation* (*Meditations* 12.24.3–4): "If you were suddenly taken up into the sky and thence looked down on human affairs and noted the trickeries involved, you would despise it as you saw at the same time the crowd of beings around you who live in the air or the upper ether. And as often as you were thus lifted upwards you would see the same things below: monotony, and shortness of life; and these are the objects of your vanity."[11]

There is little physical action in *Consolation*; all ideas of movement have to do with the movement of ideas and the paths suggested by poetry and implied by conversion. The prisoner has not actually travelled to the other world to see Philosophy; she has come to him. His retreat from her offer of the journey home is his intellectual return to his own boundaries; and his view of the phenomenal world at the end of book 5, which inverts the traditional *catascopia* by asserting the divine value of that world, is yet another retreat, a flight from heaven back down to the earth below. To the extent that the prisoner is a voyager, *Consolation* is parallel to a number of Lucian's pieces, and these are parallels that will be treated in the following chapter. But let us examine the prisoner's rejection of Philosophy's lead from her point of view. Philosophy herself was ready to travel to the world above, and I have suggested that, in her guise as death, she has also come to take the prisoner with her on a journey below. When the prisoner stymies her and redirects her energies and her arguments, he keeps her from traveling as well. We can speak of the prisoner's act of self-preservation, but this is also an act of kindness toward Philosophy. He has kept her from unwanted flights of fancy to the ends of the earth and has kept her within herself. By the end of *Consolation,* she too is made susceptible of revelation by being so restricted and can come to a realization of who she truly is. Both prisoner and Philosophy are grounded, in both senses of the term, by the prisoner's questions and Philosophy's description of the world as seen by God. We are not told what Philosophy does after her final words. A simple ending, like that of Cicero's *Dream of Scipio,* might have been welcome: "She left, and I awoke from sleep."[12] But evidently both are left to puzzle over what has happened and what has been said.[13] One thinks of *Waiting for Godot*: They do not move.

We are now in a good position to answer what I consider to be the fundamental question of interpretation of *Consolation*: whether the prisoner, as he resists Philosophy, intends at any point to arrive at the conclusion that he wrests from her. I would say, simply, no. In structure, the conclusion of *Consolation* reveals a monologic consolation finally achieved; and the gist of it, the inversion of our expectations, the vision of earth and the providential nature of all its phenomena, is wholly unexpected. The prisoner is forced ultimately to confront not his beloved Aristotle but the essential rightness of the injustice of his punishment. Philosophy did not anticipate this either. It is clear that the prisoner consciously tried to divert Philosophy from her course, and that he did so after he realized the Christian sentiments of which Philosophy was capable. Philosophy wanted to administer the cup of hemlock and did not; she is surprised to find a philosopher who prefers to stay in this world, and while she makes it clear that acceptance of the world involves some bitter paradoxes that a mere acceptance of the life to come in the realms of the blessed does not, she reaches a vision of life through the eyes of God that contradicts her early, cynical assertions about the folly that would be seen by anyone who looked down from above. The necessity that the prisoner worries about, the logical objection to free will, is not so important as the necessity of moral action; the connection between him and God is provided by humble prayer. She would be surprised that the prisoner will now go on to write *Consolation*, which we must view as a moral act, in fact the only moral act of which the socially isolated prisoner is capable. Her teaching has converted the prisoner from her teachings; he accepts the transcendence of God, and from the conversion of the prisoner's point of view Boethius the author leaves behind a document for the rest of us.

The conclusion of *Consolation* is the theodicy of Job. I know of no classical work that ends with a mystical assertion of the value of the earth, beyond the comprehension of the human being who is invited to leave behind his threadbare notions of justice and try for himself the vision of God. The prisoner must admit to the inadequacy of his own categories of thought, surrender himself, and fall silent.[14] But Philosophy is not God; nor is she Eliphaz, Bildad, and Zophar. She forced the prisoner to contemplate the nature of God, and this is the substitute for the harsher remedies that she could not administer. The prisoner has unwittingly forced her to administer it, so that she can only express her amazement at his folly ("Well, if you must have it, here is your necessity") of taking this downward view of the world instead of the upward view of heaven. At any event, the end of *Consolation* provides a far more problematic vision of the nature of the prisoner than would something as simple, or as clichéd, as an assertion of the prisoner's beatific life to come in the eternal realm. At the end of *Consolation* the prisoner does not go off to die with a good hope, but is told to pray in spite of the providential nature of his punishment, and in spite of the imposition of necessity on his actions. Philosophy knows that it is Christian prayer that she is recommending; she could not provide a seamless exposition of pagan wisdom leading up to heaven, nor is she prepared to assert that pagan learning and Christian revelation are compatible. Her final teachings must surprise even herself. *Consolation* is hardly a martyr's text. Boethius, who would have us understand the prisoner's escape from death, modestly and usefully reveals the limits of the Philosophy that he had known and practiced, and his dissatisfaction with how he had limited her. But he knows who he is and as an author writes another philosophical book instead of merely flying away, a book that in its own way now attempts the moral dimensions and universal visions that Philosophy could not find in his work up to this point and for whose lack she insulted him in her second poem.

The gold that the prisoner is surprised to find and that Philosophy did not know lay buried in her field is this assertion of the value of the earth as seen through the eyes of God. And perhaps the sentence on which *Consolation* hinges is not so much the prisoner's delight in hearing the words of Scripture at 3.12.22, but Philosophy's subsequent question at 3.12.25:

> Sed uisne rationes ipsas inuicem collidamus? Forsitan ex huius modi conflictatione pulchra quaedam ueritatis scintilla dissiliat. — Tuo, inquam, arbitratu.

> But do you want us to smash the arguments themselves into each other? Perhaps from a striking of this sort some beautiful spark of truth may fly out. I said: As you think best.

I would argue that the *rationes* to be set against each other prove to be philosophy and revelation. If this is then an invitation by the Muse to the prisoner to engage in a game in which each tries to have the upper hand in the creation and interpretation of *Consolation,* it would be directly parallel to the passage in Martianus Capella (3.221–22) in which Satura (called Camena, or "The Muse") argues against the scribe-author that myth is necessary for the presentation of truth. The passage ends enigmatically: "Do you decline?" The scribe answers, "I shall join the game together."[15] But as in *Marriage of Philology and Mercury,* in which neither participant is satisfied with the resultant attempt at a synthesis of myth and learning, so too here: neither the prisoner nor Philosophy knows where the dialogue will end up. And so we can explain that lack of explicit reference to Christianity in this Christian work: because *Consolation* is an epic, a philosophical Odyssey, it spends its time en route to the goal, traveling past that which must be rejected, and not so much at the goal itself. Odysseus's actual time spent as lord of the manor to which he returns is quite small; similarly, Lucius spends only a little time as a priest of Isis in the expanse of the *Golden Ass.* Still, Christianity is the religion that dares not speak its name in *Consolation*; but this epic shows what our hero can achieve under his own power. It is the philosopher's discovery, by philosophical means, of the limits of philosophy and what lies just beyond its grasp.

Recapitulation: The Action of *Consolation*

With this much said, I think that we can proceed to a description of the twists and turns of the plot and give an outline of a reading of *Consolation*. Not only the purposes of the speakers, and of the work, change in the course of the dialogue; the characters themselves change as they assume different functions. One thing leads to another: some initial concerns are forgotten along the way, some new issues force their way in. This is a plausible enough way to present a dialogue, even within the philosophical tradition. Boethius's *Consolation* does not present an ordered march from diagnosis to cure. If we search for the structure of *Consolation*, we will not find it by tabulating its philosophical sources, but by considering the the links that connect the various sections, and the feints and dodges of the text.

The very pace of the text is an important part of its structure, and a few remarks about it need to come first. The first three books are very slow, with a sudden acceleration at the end of book 3, when Philosophy passes rapidly through demonstrations that lead to the conclusion that evil does not exist. It is at this point that the prisoner becomes restive; he tries to slow her down. The implications are interesting. The author had in his youth designed to translate and comment upon all of Aristotle and Plato and in so doing demonstrate their fundamental unity and consistency. It is possible to attach too much significance to what must be considered a naive remark and an overly ambitious project. We certainly should not think that at the beginning of his academic life Boethius saw all of his predecessors steady and saw them whole, for current studies of his translations and commentaries on Aristotle's logical works demonstrate that he learned his logic as he went along.[16] In the world of Neoplatonism and its philosophical commentaries, Aristotle is the necessary groundwork for Platonic study, but Boethius, though a Platonist, spent all of his time on Aristotle and may be thought of as frustrated with his own methodical approach. Note how Philosophy only attempts to show the prisoner what he already knows, and how she always insists on slow and careful preparation, on many cautious first steps, before she can reach in book 3 what the prisoner knew in book 1, that the world is ruled by God. Note too that in keeping Philosophy from moving on to higher things, he forces her to remain slow and methodical and restricts her to the world of Aristotle. It is reasonable to see his *Consolation* as Boethius's first and last attempt on the Platonic corpus. But he does not set before himself the myth-making Plato, the Plato of the middle dialogues with the doctrines of transcendent forms; we rather applaud his method and his modesty, for his model is not *Phaedo* but *Crito,* an elenctic dialogue. The struggle between Philosophy's desire for transcendence and the prisoner's desire for theodicy could be seen as a confrontation of the metaphysical Socrates of the middle dialogues and the ethical Socrates of the early ones.

Consolation repeatedly shifts its focus, creating and destroying expectations. The first of these redirections has to do with the title and the reader's expectations of what a consolation is. To retranslate: "Boethius's Philosophy's Consolation's book 1: I who once when in my prime did compose fair poetry, am now compelled, alas, to take up depressive strains." The title signals an unusual consolation; the first line of the poem invokes epic expectations; the second line, which is elegiac, destroys one sort of epic expectation, inverting in the process the beginning of Ovid's *Metamorphoses*.[17] But can it be a consolation in verse if its opening words are those of one who requires consolation? We would not expect a consolatory dialogue in verse. The poem is soon recognized for the dreadful composition that it is, full of "alas!" and "alack!" and laments for the white hairs of old age, as if senility will be discovered to be the prisoner's real problem. But we do not know yet who the speaker is. We begin with a conundrum: this consolation is not a consolation.

The issue is temporarily resolved with the appearance of Philosophy and the famous banishment of the author's Muses. The prisoner is not allowed to continue as he had begun, the tearful amanuensis of histrionic whores. The appearance of Philosophy shows her to be a Muse, changing the narrator's work, both its direction and its genre; again, like the beginning of the *Metamorphoses*. What seemed to begin as verse consolation is now prosimetric philosophy, in the camp of Menippean satire. Yet the change of genre accompanies the laying down of the pen that wrote the first poem, and the prisoner does not pick it up again. The language in which he does so confuses our understanding of what we have just read (1.1.1): "As I was conning these words over within myself [*mecum*] in silence, and putting my seal on this tearful complaint with the aid of my pen, there appeared to me a woman who had taken her stand directly above my head." Visions regularly appear standing over the viewer's head in dreams; we learn that he is on his bed, and we wonder if he is asleep.

The poem and the beginning of the first prose section, which puts an end to the poem, serve to characterize the confused state of the author's mind. In this it is in the tradition of Menippean satire: consider the introductory poems of Martianus Capella's *De Nuptiis* and Fulgentius's *Mythologies*. But there is more at work. An abstraction appears in order to put an end to the poetic babblings of the self-absorbed speaker, again as in *Mythologies,* or in Lucian's *Jupiter Tragoedus, Necyomantia,* and *Icaromenippus.* Like the narrators in Martianus and Fulgentius, Boethius's prisoner must also have his genre changed by his Muse, and this is the second redirection.[18] Before Philosophy is a source of wisdom or an embodiment of a tradition, she is first a personification of a genre. This scene is to be understood in the light of the tradition of Old Comedy, no doubt mediated to Boethius by Varro's *Menippean Satires,* in which a personified genre appears on stage to complain about the unworthy treatment that she is subjected to by moderns.[19] The Philosophy who appears in *Consolation* in tattered robes that are marked with a theta (in the manner of condemned prisoners) and are covered with soot (like the death masks kept in an aristocratic atrium), the Philosophy who complains that she had been carried away kicking and screaming by partisans who destroyed the unity of philosophy (1.3.6–7) can come to the prisoner's cell only from the Land of the Dead. She needs a champion, she needs a true philosopher to vindicate her; part of her horror in finding a lethargic narrator in the company of the Muses is that he is of no use to her in this state. To justify herself, she must find a true philosopher who understands that philosophy is the practice of death, who knows that death proves the philosopher. Philosophy at first does not want to argue death away but make him accept it; she has come to take another philosopher with her back to the Land of the Dead. This is what her promise of "stronger remedies" entails. She rejoices in the death of Socrates, and she stood by him as he died; the language she uses here, speaking of the victory of his death, has clear Christian overtones (1.3.6): "Surely in the court of the ancients as well, even before the era of our beloved Plato, we often fought the great fight against the insolence of stupidity; and though he himself survived, his teacher Socrates won the victory of an unjust death while I stood at his side."[20]

So our second redirection, away from elegiac poetry to philosophical prose and dialogue, further frustrates our expectations of consolation by this exultation in death. We do not have consolation against death but the consolation that death itself brings. But to return to the crucial complication: the narrator and his Muse are now collaborators in a new venture, but just who is wielding the pen of *Consolation*?[21] Boethius draws attention to the fact that the prisoner wrote the first poem as a scribe, but we are not told who writes the rest, as Philosophy never tells the prisoner to write anything down. Nor is it irrelevant that her own Muses, to whom she would leave the prisoner, never appear. Consequently, *Consolation* presents itself not only as a dialogue in progress, but also as an interruption in the act of writing. The book is not being written by the prisoner or Philosophy as we listen in on them, but is the author's creation, recalled after the fact. It is cobbled together of pieces of very different origin: the written text of the poem and the memory of the dialogue.

Consolation wishes to be read as a true dialogue, not as the creation of a pat text. Its characters need to be defined for us; we learn in time that the prisoner is Boethius; he realizes in time that the woman who stands before him is Philosophy. But we are forced to notice the difference between a book and a dialogue: the author's desire to create a book out of a conversation with his Muse is very different from a presentation of himself as inspired by his Muse. The book that she would dictate, or that her Muses would inspire, is not what we have before us; we do have the dramatization of a confrontation, not a philosophical handbook. The dialogue is of a provisional nature, and the book is a celebration of that provisional nature. This is not Philosophy's book.

The prosimetric nature of the text participates in and is emblematic of this fact. Philosophy is a prosaic Muse, and Boethius had been in thrall to poetic Muses. The one wishes to celebrate reason; the other, emotion. Philosophy feels that she needs to speak in verse in order to get through to the narrator; as verse becomes less and less prominent in books 4 and 5, we see Philosophy becoming more her true self and less in tune with the nature and needs of the prisoner. It has long been noted that prose and verse in *Consolation* represent two different worldviews, two different agenda, two different desires; it has been noted as well that there is a longing to make a union out of the two, to make a philosophical truth become a heartfelt reality. If Philosophy had dictated the prosimetric text to the narrator, we could conclude that this union was made. But she does not, and the silence at the end of *Consolation,* the absence of the poem that seems structurally and emotionally so necessary, may point to the prisoner's prayer, but it also points to the lack of reconciliation.

The beginning of the second book is the third redirection. Philosophy here undertakes to demonstrate that the prisoner's real sorrow comes from a sense of loss of his former prosperity. Consolation against the instability of Fortune is a plausible enough topic, and it may correspond to Philosophy's notion of what is a good place to start the exile's reeducation, but it is hardly on the same level as her diagnosis of book 1, that the root cause of the prisoner's problem is that he has forgotten who he is. Not only does she thus trivialize the prisoner's stated reasons for his discontent, and her own as well, but by the end of the book she only achieves the conclusion that the prisoner himself had reached by the middle of book 1, a hope that heavenly peace may prove to be what guides the affairs of earth:

> Rapidos, rector, comprime fluctus
> et quo caelum regis immensum
> firma stabiles foedere terras.
> > (Prisoner, 1.m.5.46–48)

> Ó hélmsman, make cálm the swíft-running seá swell,
> Máke stáble the eárth in the sáme cóncórd
> Wíth which you pílot the límitless heávens.

> O felix hominum genus,
> si uestros animos amor
> quo caelum regitur regat!
> > (Philosophy, 2.m.8.28–30)

> Ó hów háppy the mórtal ráce,
> Wére Lóve kíng over áll your heárts,
> Lóve that heáven accépts as kíng!

Philosophy, who had responded to the narrator's poem by saying that she didn't realize until then just how sick the narrator was, practically repeats his words. Note that what is at issue is the theme of the Lord's prayer (*fiat uoluntas tua sicut in caelo et in terra*). In book 3, up to the central poem *O qui perpetua*, she proceeds to go over the substance of book 2; she shifts from discussing the transitory nature of the gifts of Fortune to labeling these goods as false goods. Philosophy is perhaps laying the groundwork for the larger shift, that what is good is really unitary, and that the problem with people is that they pursue multiple goods instead of the good. But at the end of book 2 she repeats the prisoner's thoughts, and in the middle of book 3 she is still discussing Fortune. Philosophy will not reach new and vital topics except at the prodding of the prisoner. Philosophy does not seek to engage the exile as a philosopher until she has dealt with him as poet, author, politician, prisoner, and man of the world.

The philosophical material just preceding 3.m.9 breaks new ground in its assertion that all good things that mortals desire are one in substance. After the poem, we move at a breathless pace, reading that true happiness, the good, and God are the same (3.10); that all things strive toward God because they desire unity and God is one (3.11); that God rules the world because of his goodness, answering the question about divine governance asked at 1.6.7 (3.12). But then Philosophy says that evil does not exist, because God is omnipotent, and now the prisoner is upset, accusing her of making an inescapable labyrinth of purely theoretical and circular reasoning (3.12.30), a charge she playfully admits to: God is spherical, arguments should conform to their subjects, so of course her reasoning is circular (3.12.36–38). The poem that she sings next tells of Orpheus and Eurydice, making the point that you cannot climb to heaven if you look back down to hell; her first poem in book 4 will speak of flying to heaven so as to look down on the earth and despise it. The poems clearly form a pair, but we think of Icarus in this flight to heaven out of the narrator's labyrinth. We wonder whether it will be successful.

The first prose section of book 4 is another redirection, coming between these two poems. Philosophy is about to go off on some other topic (we never learn what), but the prisoner, still in the grip of his old melancholy, interrupts her. Her arguments at the end of the third book have made him nervous; he wants an absolutely and internally consistent argument, just as Philosophy said was proper. Book 4, on the coexistence of an all-powerful

God and evil, is a topic raised by the prisoner when Philosophy wanted to talk about something else. The same matter that had been secure before, about the love of God controlling the earth as well as heaven, seems to have come unstuck. The prisoner assigns a new "greatest" cause of sorrow to himself, as if reeducation has only peeled away the layers of sorrow. The prisoner is pointed in his words; what he calls the greatest cause of his grief is not what Philosophy so labelled back in book 1; there it was self-forget-fulness, now it is a question of theodicy. Philosophy did not understand what was truly the prisoner's problem when she spoke of the exile's deficien-cies. Now the prisoner says that the existence, or the lack of punishment, of evil is the sole thing which is worthy of great amazement (4.1.3). This and the free-will debate in book 5 are matters that Philosophy would just as soon not talk about; as becomes clear, she cannot resolve all of his logical ques-tions cleanly, and there remain difficulties that only theologians can handle. The logical high road to heaven becomes impossible; all that remains is the devotional low road of prayer.

What Philosophy does in the brief sermon that ends *Consolation* is un-derline what she considers the lack of success that our prisoner has had: there has been no transcendence. God is at the height that the narrator has not scaled; the physical world is still present. But this disconcerting series of assertions does not make nonesense out of all that has gone before; rather, the prisoner has a bitter pill to swallow, if we may revive the medical imag-ery of book 1 and suggest that here ultimately are to be found the *ualidiora remedia* that Philosophy had spoken of. If Death had been a topic of *Conso-lation,* then we could have heard proper Plotinian lessons about the good of death;[22] nor is there room for a depiction of human life as a drama in which each player has a part to fill.[23] But ultimately we cannot look down and de-spise the world or even embrace death in *Consolation*. This is the lesson that Philosophy herself learns, and her exile learns it along with her. And it is at this point that I think we can speak of conversion in *Consolation*. The text is, with *Confessions,* at the head of the traditions of autobiography; and the text certainly has its influence in the Middle Ages in autobiographical works. A recent study of religion and autobiography makes the good point that it is typically impossible for autobiographers to assert what values they embraced without describing what values they have left behind.[24] But if the concluding paragraph leaves us with the truths that are to be embraced, then Boethius has spent most of *Consolation* describing the philosophical system that he had to leave behind, from which he was "deconverted." It would certainly come as a surprise to discover at the very end of the work that the rug has been pulled out from under us, but this is precisely a pattern of Menippean satire. For the change of perspective is obvious: our exile must no longer try to look up but to look down.

We now turn to hopes and prayers (5.6.46): "Nor are hopes and prayers placed in God in vain; they cannot help but be effective, provided that they are blameless."[25] Note that God is here a source of favors—God rewards those who pray sincerely. But what is effectiveness here?[26] The sentence answers the prisoner's objections at 5.3.33–36, which need to be given in full, for they, along with the impassioned poem that follows them, are in effect the last words that the prisoner speaks:

33. Therefore: There is no reason to hope for something or to pray for deliverance; for what would a person hope for or even pray to be delivered from if an unbendable sequence weaves together all the things that could be chosen? 34. Therefore: That one and only avenue of exchange[27] between human beings and God will be taken away, the avenue of hope and prayer for deliverance; provided, of course, that for the price of our rightful humility we deserve the return of divine grace,[28] which is beyond price. This is the only way by which human beings seem to be able to speak with God—by the act of supplication—and to be joined to that inapproachable light[29] even before they succeed in attaining it. 35. Once the necessity of future events is accepted, if these hopes and prayers are then believed to have no force,[30] what will there be by which we can be woven together with and cling to that most high ruler of all things?[31] 36. And so it is, just as you were singing a little while ago [at 4.m.6.40–43], that it will necessarily be the case that the human race, separated and "cut off from its source, will burst at the seams."[32]

The prisoner is agitated and wants results; when he asks, "What about prayer?" Philosophy will, in her own good time, answer, "Pray!" It is quite clear that in this section of book 5 our prisoner is using Christian language: devotional humility, divine grace, the inapproachable light of 1 Timothy 6.16, the achievement of life with God after death, binding oneself to God instead of becoming one with God. After the Aristotelian details, Philosophy reaches a Christian answer. All of the elaborate argumentation has served the sole purpose of making prayer a meaningful thing.

Much of the prisoner's material in 5.3 comes from his second commentary on Aristotle's *On Interpretation.* There too the question of divination travels along with the question of the relation of human free will to divine foreknowledge. But prayer is not to be found in the commentary, yet is to be found in *Consolation.* I think that we have to deal with Christianity as another in the changes of gears of *Consolation,* and one which corresponds to an insight of the author's that either he did not make before or did not put into print. But when Philosophy answers this way, she no longer addresses the prisoner. Now her address is universal (5.6.47): "Therefore, all of you: Avoid vices; cherish virtues; raise up your minds to blameless hopes; extend your humble prayers into the lofty heights." It is not that this briefest of Christian sermons is a sign of the incompleteness of the text; it was prepared for at the end of 5.3. What has not been prepared for is the disappearance of the prisoner. To C. S. Lewis, this is a masterstroke;[33] Lerer speaks of the prisoner, who was not a participant in Philosophy's recent monologue, as merging with the reader of the text, which "affirms the act of reading as the key to intellectual growth and self-awareness."[34] But can we not say that the prisoner is no longer present because, according to the only ways by which action and motion have been implied all along in *Consolation,* he has gone away to his homeland? The exhortation to Christian piety, which precludes the exile's return with Philosophy to the homeland that she had in mind, is shown to be the path out, the escape from Philosophy's labyrinth and from prison itself. The absent prisoner is the text from which Philosophy, now abandoned, takes her sermon. The prisoner has learned humility, and now that he has learned his lesson, we may learn ours. We are of course free to doubt the sincerity of this stance. Granted, Boethius the author is no longer thinking of himself as the last true philosopher after Plato, the man whose death would give new life to pagan Philosophy; granted too that the writing of *Consolation of Philosophy* is a covert act, neither enjoined upon him by his Muse nor boldly claimed by the prisoner; we are still left with a book that claims to find a way out, an unexpected path to heaven. But I would insist on Boethius's modesty: this is a personal text, about a personal attempt to work through a philosopher's limits to the truth that lies beyond them. The epic hero has survived his struggle; and we may be thankful that, having had no Homer or Vergil to do it for him, he decided to write it down for us himself.

WEINBROT IS RIGHT to object that studies of modern Menippean satire speak too much of ideas alone and seek to include too many works under an increasingly large and unmanageable umbrella. He prefers a more structural approach to satire: "Menippean satire, then, is a form that uses at least two other genres, languages, cultures, or changes of voice to oppose a dangerous, false, or specious and threatening orthodoxy. In different exemplars, the satire may use either of two tones: the severe, in which the threatened, angry satirist fails and becomes angrier still, or the muted, in which the threatened, angry satirist offers a partial antidote to the poison he knows remains."[35] But now that it is clear that *Consolation* is not about the exaltation of Philosophy's revealed truths but a philosopher's discovery of how he must oppose those truths in order the preserve his life and save his soul, of how he can in silence retreat from Philosophy to pursue the wisdom that Philosophy knows of but which is not really hers, it may be seen that *Consolation* does belong to the genre of Menippean satire as Weinbrot sees it. I have offered an analysis that demonstrates the similarities in intellectual stance and in conventions of character, plot, and rhetoric that align it with the antecedent traditions of classical Menippean satire, and I shall have more to say in the coming chapters about analogues to *Consolation* in classical and medieval literary traditions. We may be gratified to realize that, despite the extraordinariness of *Consolation*, it does belongs to traditions that have never ceased to make their presence felt.

Chapter Seven

Models and Rewritings

The conclusions reached in the previous chapters are sufficient, I think, to establish the plausibility of a Christian reading of *Consolation*, that is, that the professed methods and intended goals of Philosophy are resisted by a prisoner who chooses the path to God of Christian prayer rather than of pagan transcendence. But now it is time to tie this reading into the web of the history of Western literature, and to look for other works that operate along similar lines, have similar characters, or achieve similar ends. Again, I do not intend to repeat the methods or the conclusions of *Ancient Menippean Satire* here, but only to adduce parallels in earlier and later literature in a range of genres and thus support the interpretation thus far advanced. If I am brief in the following discussions and documentations, it is only because I follow this rather limited goal, allowing reception to suggest rather than to prove; all of the following texts are offered to curious readers of *Consolation* as companion pieces; each is worthy of further study as a model for, or as a sign of the influence of, the ironies of the text.

The wide range of literary and philosophical influences on *Consolation* and the presence of a great number of other genres within it (consolation, protreptic, dialogue, meditation, apocalyptic, and poetry in genres from lyric and elegiac to epic) can be assigned to the general voraciousness of the Menippean genre. And *Consolation* as the nexus of all these traditions, is an intertext for all of them and thus has influence in the Middle Ages over a dizzying variety of texts and genres. But the claim is too easily made that this is a work like no other; the label Menippean satire has frequently functioned as an excuse not to consider the possibility of parallels. True, *Consolation* does not have the heavenly fantasies of Lucian's pieces or of *Apocolocyntosis*, the linguistic play of Martianus's *Marriage of Philology and Mercury*, the social critique of Petronius's *Satyricon*, or, seemingly, any humor at all. Such similarities as do exist seem not as important as the fundamental seriousness of *Consolation*, and prose and verse gain a disproportionate share of critical interest because the presence of their mixture seems part and parcel of a Bakhtinian polyphony that suggests the voice of a new truth arising from the clash of theory and experience.[1]

My argument and procedure here are along other lines. First, at the time of its composition, I claim that *Consolation* was not unique in its myth; that is, in the basic structure of its action. I will adduce as parallels Plato's *Crito*, some dialogues of Lucian, and a poem of Agathias Scholasticus, none of which I consider Menippean satires by the definition achieved in *Ancient Menippean Satire*. Second, I argue that *Consolation*, soon after its publication, elicited literary responses that show an awareness of its particular ironies, again in works that are not all generically Menippean satires. For this early reception history I will consider Fulgentius's *Mythologies*, Maximian's *Elegies*, and Isidore of Seville's *Synonyma*.[2]

Plato

The claim has been made, reasonably, that *Phaedo* is one of the pervasive influences in *Consolation*. The basic contention is a historical one: Boethius, knowing that he is about to die, draws inspiration from the traditions concerning Socrates; the cure that Philosophy offers, the *ualidiora remedia* of 1.6.21, is Socrates' cup of hemlock. But *Phaedo* certainly presents no parallel for the material of *Consolation*, even if in it we read of Socrates composing hymns in prison (*Phaedo*, 60c–61b). *Phaedo* offers reasons why the soul must be immortal, and this is a question that never really arises in *Consolation*. But it is *Crito* that offers parallels in action and in content.

To summarize: Socrates in prison argues against his well-meaning friend Crito, who is encouraging him to escape; Socrates never yields to the temptation. In the concluding pages of the dialogue, Socrates imagines the laws and constitution of Athens appearing to him in his cell as he prepares to run away and convincing him that flight would be hypocritical and a rejection of the principles by which he had always lived. True to his habit, Socrates imagines an otherworldly voice that only dissuades him from a possible course of action; and realistically, Socrates the narrator was never in doubt. Thus there are significant differences between Boethius's *Consolation* and *Crito:* what is imagined in *Crito* becomes a true fantasy in *Consolation*,[3] and *Consolation* offers true dialogue between the abstraction and the interlocutor, who is not always willing to accept the truths that are being revealed to him. But the parallels are impressive: an abstraction appearing in jail to discuss matters of life-and-death importance, an abstraction that lays claim to the narrator's loyalty because the narrator was raised and educated under the abstraction's wings. And, what is most important, the question in *Crito* is framed this way: are you going to leave the prison or not? The true philosopher stays in prison, accepting the decision of his city, and will drink the hemlock and die. The true philosopher is proved by his unwillingness to escape the consequences of his actions.

But consider *Consolation*: Boethius's prisoner does not raise the possibility of physical escape. The debate takes place on a more metaphysical plane: questions of flight and perseverance are cast in terms of loyalty to beliefs.[4] The prisoner may escape Philosophy but not his cell, and as far as the action of *Consolation* goes, there is no possibility of a future outside of the prison walls. Socrates, on the other hand, knows very well that he can leave the prison and live in exile. But Philosophy does present the picture of life outside of the prison; or rather she hints at it, when, at the beginnings of books 4 and 5, she refers to the wings that she will attach to the narrator's mind that will enable him to rise up and see his true home. She wants the narrator to escape. Boethius's prisoner, like Socrates in *Crito*, will stay in his cell. Socrates does so in obedience to his revelation, in order to die; Boethius's narrator does so in spite of his guide's intentions, in order to live. But, like Socrates, Boethius's prisoner hears the word "no" and stays put.

Consolation is a parody, or, if you will, a travesty of *Crito*: the prisoner in effect refuses to drink the hemlock. The only gift that Philosophy can offer him is death, and *Consolation* is so structured as to make the reader see the limits of this pagan revelation. The prisoner proves himself a true philosopher in a remarkable way, by staying in prison despite Philosophy's efforts to lead him out. Boethius's prisoner reenacts, in physical terms, the action of *Crito*; yet he does find a spiritual escape by a different route, by keeping himself within himself. From the author's point of view, this is simply achieved in that Stoic contemplation of the presence of death; but from the prisoner's, this attempt to avoid the hemlock must come with the introduction to book 4—he is diverting her from her stronger medicines, though he does not know then where he will end up.

Not only does the structure of *Consolation* derive in large part from Plato, through *Crito*; *Consolation* 1.3 brings in the character of Socrates explicitly as well. Philosophy gladly tells of how she has always been at the prisoner's side; she boasts that death is ever the reward of the true philosopher; in her following poem (1.m.4) she describes the security of those who can, by absence of emotion, hope, and fear, disarm the tyrants and all the madness of the world. One property of Menippean satire is that it takes serious authors and works and ideas and travesties them; as such, Plato has tremendous influence in the history of the genre, being a towering figure of strange ideas. His myths and theories and literary forms are a major inspiration to Menippean satire, which deals freely in apocalypse, myth, dialogue, symposium, and criticism of ideas and intellectuals.[5] A travestied *Crito* is a structural source of *Consolation,* and a general desire to point out the difference between what is true and what words can say is a Platonic legacy that animates much of its intellectual content; but we may ask what conditions this travesty, and what other works have had an influence in turning *Crito* on its head. The need of the prisoner to prove himself a true philosopher and Philosophy's habit of formulating questions of allegiance to old beliefs in terms of exile, running away, and returning home are crucial here, and parallels in Lucian can be brought to bear.

Lucian

The dialogues of Lucian are important for an understanding of Boethius's *Consolation* in three ways, all as plot devices. First, for dramatizations of Philosophy herself, upset at the opinions of self-professed philosophers; second, for parallels to an imperious figure demanding an accounting from a narrator who is presumed to be at some remove from the truths of his profession; third, for parallels to a narrator quizzing his source of super-natural truth regarding certain eternal questions and naggingly insoluble problems.[6]

The first of these parallels is most important, as we need to take seriously the resemblances between *Consolation* and the only other ancient works in which Philosophy appears as a character in a debate. Consider Lucian's *Piscator (The Fisherman)*.[7] The protagonist (Parrhesiades, or Frank Talk) stands trial before Philosophy herself and a number of other abstractions on the grounds, brought by the various late dogmatic philosophers, that he insulted Philosophy through his disgraceful treatment of dead philosophers in the companion piece to this work, *Philosophers for Sale*.[8] He tells the philosophers that when he went looking for Philosophy, all he found was a strumpet pretender to the name; the true Philosophy, accompanied by Truth and others, appears from the Ceramicus in Athens to preside over the trial, at which Diogenes the Cynic is called upon to make the most of the speech for the prosecution. The narrator mounts a successful defense on the grounds that he attacked only false pretenders to the name of philosopher in *Philosophers for Sale*, hypocrites who were only interested in the power and prestige that they could gain while aping the dress and habits of true philosophers. The reader may object that the defense is wholly unsatisfactory, as, of course, the narrator did mean to insult all of philosophy and all philosophers, and his defense that he was attacking only those who brought her into disrepute rings very hollow.

There are two Philosophies in *Piscator*, a false and a true one, and a distinction is made between false and true philosophers on trial. Philosophy, Frank Talk, and the true philosophers end the dialogue by occupying a hill and fighting off the false philosophers, who try to storm it; some are snagged by a fishhook and removed, whence the dialogue's name.[9] Now there is no judge, jury, or trial in *Consolation*, but there is a curious parallel in this: the philosopher who is presumed not to be a true philosopher must reveal himself to be one. Boethius's Philosophy, like Lucian's, is not the judge of human beings, but the judge of philosophers. One of the questions raised in *Consolation* is whether our narrator is a real philosopher, and the parallels to *Crito* show that the prisoner is proved to be one in a paradoxical way. Philosophy in *Consolation* must of course apply much effort to make him shake off his lethargy and rise again to the heights of his earlier perceptions; but it is in the last two books that the prisoner, on his own and without the encouragement of Philosophy, who wants to go on to other matters, proves himself to be a true philosopher, but this time at his cost.

Another of Lucian's pieces in which Philosophy appears and is disgusted at the pretensions of those who claim to be philosophers is *The Fugitive Philosophers*.[10] Philosophy complains before Zeus of those who take her name in vain; specifically, three runaway slaves who have masqueraded as philosophers in order to accomplish various criminal acts. Philosophy, accompanied by Heracles and Hermes, goes down to earth and meets (among others) the runaways, a wronged woman, Orpheus, and some slave owners. In Greek philosophical language, to reject a particular philosophical school and its teachings after having lived according to its principles is to run away, to be a fugitive. Here too, antiphilosophical fantasy makes the metaphoric real; the dialogue creates the image of false philosophers as runaway slaves, and there must of course be some sort of contention for them to find their true owners.[11] The appearances of Philosophy in Lucian allow us to see the narrator's self-defense as a philosopher undergirding *Consolation*. The implicit question in the appearance of Philosophy is whether the narrator is a true philosopher; *Consolation* does not just chart the ways in which Philosophy reeducates the exile to remind him of who he truly is, but it also allows us to see just how the prisoner proves himself a philosopher.

There is another, more general sort of parallel between the dialogues of Lucian and *Consolation* that can be outlined here. *Zeus the Tragedian* and *Zeus Catechized* may stand in as two examples out of many.[12] The mocker of divine Providence always brings up two objections in Lucian: the existence of evil in a world run by divine Providence (specifically the fact that virtuous people suffer and the blasphemous escape divine vengeance) and the relation of Fate and free will among the gods. In *Zeus the Tragedian*, in two intertwined dialogues (one in heaven and one on earth), Momus among the gods and Damis the atheist among mortals have a field day assailing the notion of divine Providence on these grounds, and even Zeus is forced to agree. Now it is a running joke in Lucian that the true and enlightened argument has no effect: what does it mean to have Zeus admit that he doesn't exist, or that he cannot act as he would want to, but is constrained by Fate? The existence of the gods in these intellectual fantasies is proof that we cannot take too seriously the arguments that set out to deny them. The standard philosophical conundrums still prevail: why it is that good people suffer in this world, and why does the world seem to be in such disarray, if the gods have *pronoia* (Providence); and how it is that people can have free will in a universe in which *pronoia* or *ananke* (what Boethius the philosopher would call the "violence of necessity") rules? Logic has only a specious claim to their solution; this is much of the point of *Consolation*.

In her consideration of Lucian as a Menippean satirist, Payne argues that, in the dialogue *Zeus Catechized*, the true protagonist is Cyniscus, the Cynic philosopher, who travels to Olympus to ask Zeus embarrassing questions about Fate and free will; Zeus is the minor character.[13] It is the minor characters in Lucian who, according to Payne, worry about history, about the realities of human life, and about the contingencies of existence; the questioner is the man on a mission, a maniacal character who can understand the world only according to his one fixed opinion, usually that of a logical debunker of myth. In the dynamics of the dialogue, the concerns of the minor characters serve to balance the intellectual abstractions and so keep before the reader the terrible beauty of the phenomenal world. But I think that this analysis does not pay enough attention to plot. In the dialogue *Zeus Catechized*, I see Cyniscus as a student who seeks to deflate the great wise man; it is the inability of Zeus specifically to provide satisfactory answers about human free will and the relation of fate and divine foreknowledge that leads him, compromised as he is, to an embarrassing impasse. Zeus will not answer any more questions; it is not right for him to do so; Cyniscus is a bully and a sophist; Zeus will turn his back on him and leave. Cyniscus calls out a few final questions about the three Fates; he thanks Zeus for the answers he gave to the previous questions and figures that it probably is not fated for him to hear any further. The one who goes back to earth has the upper hand, being now in possession, through his skeptical inquiry, of a wisdom far greater than that of the Zeus who stays in heaven. As such, the plot of this dialogue is very close to that of *Consolation*.

Agathias

The confrontation of Philosophy and prisoner is not presented as that of teacher and student; Lucian suggests that judge and apostate may be a better parallel; so too the model of wisdom figure and questioner, or guru and seeker. This last is neatly exemplified in a poem of the fifth-century Greek poet Agathias, an editor of *The Greek Anthology*, who was careful to anthologize more of his own work than anyone else's. The text of this poem (*A.P.* 11.354) will be found here in appendix 4 with translation and notes. It is an account of a confrontation between an eager student, who wants to know the nature of the soul, and the philosopher Nicostratus, presented as a master of all of Aristotle and Plato, who, because of the contradictory nature of Plato's and Aristotle's teachings about the soul, can only say that if the soul has a nature, then it must be either mortal or immortal.

Nicostratus is clearly a comic figure; he gains more of our sympathy and respect when he modestly adds that the truth about such things can only be found after death. If the student wants to "know himself," he will wait until death reveals all and not hurry to find the answers to questions that are insoluble in this world. The poem plays with the wisdom figure while also making the sensible point that it is best for those that would pursue wisdom to keep themselves on this side of the line between life and death. Agathias's presentation of this particular resolution of this particular problem is itself of Christian inspiration, and here too, as in *Consolation*, the author's Christianity makes no overt appearance. I haved claimed that this poem is in fact a brief analogue to the whole of *Consolation* (Relihan 1990a); further discussion is not required here.

Fulgentius

I have discussed Fulgentius's *Mythologies* at length in *Ancient Menippean Satire*. Parallels between the epiphany of Philosophy in Boethius and that of Calliope in Fulgentius have long been noted.[14] Both works would begin with a scholar whose literary intentions must be turned by a Muse who bends the work to Menippean satire and takes the work out of the narrator's hands; the result is an encyclopedic and didactic work that does not quite do what its author or its Muse desired. There are also to be found in the presentation of Calliope and the narrator in *Mythologies* a great number of parallels with the presentation of Vergil and his interlocutor in Fulgentius's *Allegorical Content of Vergil*.[15] I have suggested that these two works are two sides of the same coin: despised pagan mythology reveals trivial moralizings, while the honored pagan Vergil yields Chistian truths. Despite the similarities in presentation, there is a great difference in the actual content of the pieces because of the need to protect the reputation of Vergil; and it is Menippean satire that is the chosen form only for the *Mythologies*.

But the argument has recently been made that *Consolation*, instead of being written after *Mythologies* as I had supposed,[16] may actually have been written before it, as the motifs that are to be found concentrated in the beginning of *Consolation* (1.1.1–6) are found scattered through the prologue of *Mythologies* and in *Allegorical Content of Vergil*: I am now convinced that Fulgentius's borrowing from Boethius is the easier conjecture.[17] This suggests that Fulgentius found in *Consolation* a model for two different comic pieces on the relation between Christian revelation and pagan learning. Even if one were to insist that this is just an example of the sort of anti-Boethian hostility evidenced in Ennodius and Maximian, these authors taken together at least make it clear that it was not hard to see in *Consolation* a model for a confrontation between learned source and feckless interlocutor in which the source of Wisdom is also held up to ridicule.

Maximian

The *Third Elegy* of the sixth-century Latin poet Maximian has always claimed the attention of students of *Consolation*, because Boethius appears in it in a rather unflattering way, and because the poet clearly alludes to *Consolation* within it.[18] It purports to be an autobiographical poem; the poet tells how he once, as a youth, went to Boethius for advice on how to conduct a love affair and received very peculiar advice. Boethius proposes a program of action whose ostensible goal is the exact opposite of what he hopes Maximian will achieve; in short, he encourages the poet to indulge his passion, knowing that familiarity will breed contempt, and that virtue will be taught by the blandishments of carnality. I suggest that the poet derived this picture of Boethius the ironic teacher from Philosophy in *Consolation*.

With the exception of the *Third Elegy*, Maximian's poetry, which consists entirely of bitter and self-deprecatory tales of lost love, is largely neglected.[19] The *Elegy* is typically assigned to a period after Boethius's death in which his memory is under attack.[20] But, as is usual in Maximian's poetry, the poet himself receives most of the abuse for his unseasonable emotional excess and his hypocrisy in disappointed love. The Latin text of the *Third Elegy*, with translation and notes, may be found here in appendix 3.

To summarize: The poet recounts a scene from his youth, hoping that the reader will abandon the contemplation of the dizzying world to view the poet's sorrow (1–4). He was once in love with one Aquilina, and his own naïveté drove him mad (5–8); she too did not know how to satisfy her longing (9–16). Their anxieties are compounded by his watchful pedagogue and her suspicious mother (17–20); they resort to secret meetings after trying unsuccessfully to hide their passion (21–28). Her mother finds out and beats the girl, fanning the flames of her desire; she tells the poet that she has now bought him at the price of her wounds and has given meaning to her love through pain (29–42). He is now caught between languor and ardor, beginning to lose interest in what he can achieve (43–46). At this point he appeals to Boethius, whom he calls *magnarum scrutator maxime rerum*, "loftiest investigator of all lofty things" (47–48).

Boethius here is modeled on Philosophy in *Consolation*. He perceives the poet's sadness but not its cause; he asks, in gentle words, that the poet open his heart (49–52). Like Philosophy, Boethius is a doctor who wants to cure his patient (53–56). The poet is too ashamed to confess, but Boethius tells him not to be afraid. The poet tells him everything, in tears (57–62). Boethius's advice is blunt and surprising: get the girl. The poet, though at first unwilling, follows it (63–70). Boethius then actually plays the pander and bribes the girl's parents; they come to approve of their daughter's liaison (71–74). They provide opportunities for the two to meet alone (75–76). Opportunity breeds contempt in him, and she abandons the boy who would not be her lover (77–80). The poet is now cured, and he bids the girl an ironic and contemptuous farewell, claiming that he is the cause of her sudden virtue (81–84). Boethius learns of this and congratulates the poet on his victory (85–90). The poet himself pronounces the concluding moral (91–94):

> The free opportunity, once it was granted to me, stole away my eagerness for error, and the very desire for such things bolted and ran. Unsatisfied and depressed alike we both departed—the cause of the divorce was a life of chastity.

This conclusion particularly draws our attention. I think that Shanzer is right to assign *ambo,* "we both," to Boethius and the poet, not to the poet and Aquilina, who was dismissed ten lines earlier.[21] We do not hear that the poet is thrilled to have been taught his lesson. While Boethius may have taught the lesson that he wanted to teach, there is no clear indication that the poet was pleased to have learned this lesson in this way. Here as elsewhere in his *Elegies*, Maximian uses his Christianity as a last-minute justification for despising the woman he cannot or will not have, and he asks us to see his own behavior as contemptible. Surely the Boethius of the poem could have reached the same conclusion.

There are numerous verbal reminiscences of *Consolation* in the *Third Elegy*, and Maximian's knowledge of Boethius's work is assured.[22] Maximian places himself before Boethius as Boethius depicted himself in the presence of Philosophy, as a man in great emotional distress before a doctor who demands a full accounting and gives unexpected advice. Philosophy tells Boethius that she will make him remember himself, Boethius tells Maximian that he will help him get the girl; both teachers allow their pupils to go to their natural extremes (philosophical inquiry, a love affair) to learn by the failure of such studies that their hearts lie elsewhere. Maximian tells us of a Boethius who teaches through irony, through an excess of the wrong advice. Maximian therefore imitates *Consolation,* albeit on a small scale, in the *Third Elegy*. But it is now possible to see the entire suite of six *Elegies* as a reworking of the themes of *Consolation,* according to the excellent arguments of Barnish 1990, who sees in them a work of "Swiftian despair" and lets us think that Maximian knew very much what *Consolation* was about.[23] Barnish insists on the essential seriousness and political relevance of the *Elegies*. He offers a quick reading of the first five *Elegies* as a commentary on *Consolation* (the sixth is a mere ten-line epilogue).[24] I would expand on his observations as follows.

The first *Elegy,* in 292 verses, is a lengthy complaint on old age. So is the first poem of *Consolation*. Maximian has it that only old age has reduced him from virtue to vice; in his youth, he was capable of Socratic virtue, including that of being incapable of getting drunk (1.41–48). In this lament, the poet touches on a number of themes found in *Consolation*: the poet is no longer capable of remembering who he is (1.123–24); his vision is such that he cannot see true light, but the clouds before his eyes are themselves bright (1.139–50); he cannot look up, but is forced to look down (1.217–18); he will not complain about the laws of nature (1.267–68); he loses his former friends and pupils (1.280–86); the worst punishment of old age is the memory of former joys (1.289–92).[25]

Barnish assigns all of *Elegy* 2 to the theme of the loss of former false friends, but it is possible to be much more specific. He speaks of Lycoris, who despises him now that he is old. But this Lycoris is like Philosophy, discovering a Boethius who is not what she had a reason to expect on the basis of their former associations. Boethius's Philosophy is disdainful and insults the prisoner before she condescends to help him; Maximian's Lycoris does not so condescend. She is still beautiful, with flame beneath the ash (2.29–30); the poet remembers how they used to be equal and hopes that his former satisfaction may still please her now (2.55–59); he offers her his poems as he did in his youth (2.63–64); he prays that reason may prevail (2.71–72).

Barnish devotes little space to *Elegy* 4, but it is in fact a very nice recasting of the opening of *Consolation*. Here the poet recalls his love for Candida, a musician; he is wounded by his love and enjoys his wounds in silence (4.15–16). He begins to talk to himself, to imagine her presence when she is not there; everyone thinks him mad, and ultimately his passions are betrayed when he talks of his love in his sleep, and the girl's father overhears (4.31–48). Rather as Philosophy finds Boethius embarrassingly in thrall to the Muses, so does Candida's father find the poet. The humiliation that the poet now professes is out of synch with the humor that we were led to expect in the introduction of the poem. The moral is poignant and worth quoting in full (4.49–60):

> Sic ego, qui cunctis sanctae grauitatis habebar,
>   proditus indicio sum miser ipse meo:
> et nunc infelix tota est in crimine uita,
>   et peccare senem non potuisse pudet.
> Deserimur uitiis, fugit indignata uoluptas;
>   nec quod non possum non uoluisse meum est.
> Hoc etiam meminisse licet, quod serior aetas
>   intulit, et gemitus, quos mihi lingua dedit,
> si quis has possit naturae adtingere partes,
>   gnarus cur sapiens noxia saepe uelit.
> Interdum rapimur uitiis trahimurque uidentes,
>   et quod non cupiunt pectora bruta uolunt.

And so it was that I, whom everyone thought to be a man of holy dignity, was myself miserably betrayed by my own confession. Now the whole of my wretched life is on trial [*in crimine*], and it is shameful that an old man was incapable of sin. We are abandoned by our vices, and contemptuous Desire takes to her heels, nor can I claim that I did not want what I cannot achieve. But this I can bring to mind, which too old age has brought upon me; and the groanings too, which are the gift of my tongue to me: in hopes that someone be able to comprehend these aspects of human nature, why it is that a wise man willingly often wishes for what will do him harm. But in the meantime we are tumbled along by our vices, dragged along with our eyes open, and our bestial hearts desire that which they do not want.

This is a fascinating conflation of most of the contents of the first book of *Consolation*. Boethius's political difficulties and the accusations against him appear here in an erotic context. Boethius's prisoner certainly feels that his whole life is on trial; he is unrepentant for having done the deed that led to the accusation; he regrets that he cannot achieve his ends, not that he does not desire them. Maximian's embarrassment and groaning he can offer as a problem and as a cautionary tale to others; but these things seem to arise from him passively (the groans are given him by his tongue, rather as the prisoner sets down words dictated by the Muses). The general problem however is that of *Consolation* as a whole: why is it that the wise man desires what does him no good? While it may go too far to say that the *Elegies* as a whole form a sort of moral, protreptic textbook, it is true that the particular erotic events are seen to have much wider implications. This is the bridge to the fifth *Elegy*.

Barnish considers this the elegy "most reminiscent of the *Consolation*."[26] In it, an anonymous Greek girl (the poet does not quite understand her singing, but is enthralled by it) seduces him while he is on a diplomatic mission to the Eastern Empire. Theirs is, to say the least, a checkered affair, fully detailed: a first sexual attempt results in a lost erection after she complains of his weight; he is successful during a first night together, but the strain is almost too much for an old man; he proves impotent on the next night, and she cannot arouse him by masturbation, though she tries twice. After the first attempt, she accuses him of infidelity and then exhorts him to forget his cares; he pleads that his condition is not the result of any lack of willpower, but when her second attempt to arouse him fails, she delivers two powerful speeches, each addressed to his penis.[27] The first laments the loss of a friend and confidant, who is now to be considered dead; the second moves from the particular to the universal. The poet had suggested that her reaction to his impotence showed that she suffered from a far greater affliction. She objects angrily: with this loss, the whole fabric of the universe comes undone (109–52). She begins:

> Illa furens: "nescis, ut cerno, perfide, nescis:
>   non fleo priuatum, sed generale chaos.
> Haec genus humanum, pecudum uolucrumque, ferarum
>   et quicquid toto spirat in orbe, creat.
> Hac sine diuersi nulla est concordia sexus,
>   hac sine coniugii gratia summa perit.
> Haec geminas tanto constringit foedere mentes,
>   unius ut faciat corporis esse duo.

In a rage, she said: "I see it now: you don't get it, you traitor, you just don't get it. I do not weep for a personal but for a universal chaos. This thing creates the race of human beings, of flocks and birds and wild animals—whatever draws breath throughout the world. Without this there is no coming together of the opposite sexes; without this the un-surpassable delight of marriage is lost. This joins together twin minds in such a bond that it makes one body out of two."

He shows that the universe has fallen apart. At the end of her tirade she leaves him for dead, her speech in effect a parody of a eulogy (5.153–54): "Finally she fell silent, having had her fill of mourning; she left me, as if my funeral were now over."[28] As in all of the *Elegies*, the end mocks the poet; the ironic praise of the *mentula* is rather like the praise of the poet's virtue at the end of the *Third Elegy:* "Brief is your anger, long is your loyalty, and Desire rises up again; and when the ability is lost, the intention remains nevertheless the same."[29] This reproduction of confrontations of puzzled poets and imperious mentors is an intelligent interpretation of things crucial to *Consolation*.

To be sure, the Greek girl who tries to stimulate the languid poet owes something to Ovid's *Amores*, but it is also reminiscent of the Philosophy who strokes the prisoner's breast in *Consolation*.[30] And the leap from physical love to universal metapysics is well established in philosophical and mystical traditions; Martianus's *Marriage* celebrates this explicitly, the opening poem corresponding in some details to the Greek girl's second address. Maximian comprehends not only the beginning of *Consolation*, its lament for old age, its concern with political missions, its regret for things left undone, its opposition of desire and capability, but also its end, with its collapse of dialogue and its doubtful departures.

Isidore of Seville

The seventh-century Latin bishop, author of the *Etymologies* and the two books *On Distinctions between Words*, combines his linguistic and moral interests in a strange work called *Synonyma*, subtitled "The Lament of the Sinful Soul." Braulio, who aided the publication of some of Isidore's works and catalogued them after his death, provides the first reader's reaction recorded: "He wrote two books called *Synonyma*, by which he raised the soul up to consolation and to the hope of the winning of pardon, through the intercession of the exhortations of reason."[31] Fontaine, in a lengthy and perceptive article, notes that Braulio's opinion would make us think of *Consolation*, but he insists that Isidore knew only of Boethius the logician and rhetorician, and that there is no connection between *Consolation* and *Synonyma*.[32] The conjunction of reason and hope is characteristic of the spirituality of late antiquity and there, Fontaine argues, the overlap ends.

I would suggest that *Synonyma* is in fact a response to *Consolation*. It falls into two books, the first a conversation between *homo* and *ratio*, the second between *homo* and *anima*. The first is an encouragement to *homo* to rise above misfortune, to find instruction in chastisement, to look inside; *homo* complains of the wrongs done to him and hopes that there is reward for prayer. The second is largely moral, encompassing such things as the golden rule, a condemnation of fornication, rules for judges, and the fall of princes. The dialogue is explicitly Christian, and at first sight it is not particularly profound, seeming to be more in a distant line of descent from Augustine's *Soliloquies* than related to *Consolation*. But the book's fascination comes from its language: it is essentially a preacher's handbook, giving endless variations of stock phrases by which one might encourage the sinful to seek salvation. It has a power and an insistence that comes from a relation to the formulaic repetitions of Hebrew verse. But to my eye it is a text that organizes these thoughts around the complaints of a man who finds that the world has turned against him, and who must be encouraged to know himself, and so know his relation to God. *Synonyma* may be taken as making up what it perceives to be the deficiencies of *Consolation,* and in doing so merges the unfortunate victim of political intrigue and Job, so that allusions to Job abound.[33] Observe this movement from a Boethian to a Joban lament near the beginning of the work. *Homo* speaks (1.11–12):

> I am judged by the false and vicious judgment of witnesses and judges; innocent, I am led to death by the false judgment of witnesses; from the same assembly come the witnesses and the judges, and from the same throng come the accusers; they put against me false judges, they cast at me false witnesses, in whose testimony they have confidence. No one disagrees with them; no one objects, no one rejects their plan. To whom may I speak? In whom may I trust? Whom may I address? Whom may I approach? From whom may I receive advice? To whom may I entrust my spirit? Whom should I seek out first of all?
>
> 12. I am hateful to all, I am deserted by everyone's love, all cast me from themselves, with loathing they all loath me, all shudder to see me, all reject me, they threaten to disown me. I want to take refuge with them, but they frighten me; I desire to entreat their footsteps, but they run away; they oppose me and hate me; by supplication I want to make them gracious to me, but they become even more offensive. At times they attach themselves to me in pretended love, not for consolation, but for temptation; they speak rehearsed, and if they are silent their silence is not simple; they search for accusations to make; they search for rumors to hear; they search for betrayals to make, they look for ways to deceive me.[34]

We learn that *homo,* like Boethius's prisoner, is an exile (1.15: "And so I am driven into exile; so I am condemned to exile; so I mourn the punishment of exile; so I groan for the condemnation of exile"); like Job he regrets that he was ever born (1.19: "Why was I born accursed? Why was I cast into this wretched life? For what purpose have I in my misery seen the light?"; cf. Job 3.3 ff.). *Ratio* appears and begs *homo* to resist depression (1.22: "O *homo,* why put so little trust in your spirit? Why are you so enervated in the mind? Why do you dismiss all hope and trust? Why are you so torn apart in spirit? . . . Dismiss sadness; cease to be sad; push sadness away from you; refuse to yield to depression; refuse to give yourself over so to depression"). The key to his recovery is *ratio* (1.27: "Place reason before you; be a participant in reason; let reason prevail in you; control your spirit with reason; let reason strengthen your soul; let reason check the violence of such grief"). *Ratio* assures *homo* that nothing bad could happen to him with divine approval (1.32); *homo* acknowledges his sinful nature, takes the blame for his misfortune, and admits that it is hard to reject sinful ways (1.43–45). *Ratio* encourages *homo* to think of punishments in the world to come (1.46–48). One could go on.

Clearly, the ethics and the theology of *Synonyma* are utterly different from those of *Consolation*. But sometimes we hear an almost Boethian voice, as when *homo* asks whether confession works (1.52; cf. the prisoner's concerns about the value of prayer at *Consolation* 5.m.3.):

> But this I ask; this I want to know, this I desire particularly to understand: is there hope in confession? Is there a keeping of promises? Is there forgiveness? Is there pardon? Is there indulgence? Is there through penance an opportunity to return to justice?

The second book shifts gears; *anima* takes the place of *ratio*, and the first item on the agenda is that *homo* come to know just who he is (2.2: "*Homo*, know thyself; know who you are; know why you came into being; know why you were born, for what purpose you were given birth, why you were made, on what terms you were brought into the world, or why you were engendered in this age"). Another curious detail with Boethian resonances is that *anima* encourages *homo* to learn the value of silence when in duress (2.32: "You be quiet, you be silent; hide what you feel; be disdainful; do not speak; practice silence"). *Anima* returns to the topic of silence later on (2.46). The book ends with what seems to be advice for confessors, using the language of medicinal wisdom familiar from the topoi of consolation (2.69: "The doctor's speech will be in accordance with the listener's perceptions; instruction is to be imparted according to an individual's habits. Remedies are to be applied in accordance with the wound; different wills desire different instruction; each one is to be taught in accordance with the particular station in life").

Synonyma is not so tightly organized that the reader is to see a progression from wailing sin to quiet endurance to useful teaching, as if the *homo* of book 1 were so well instructed by the end of book 2 as to be able to go out into the world and preach and hear confessions. But the division into two books is suggestive of the basic bipartite consolatory structure; the movement from *ratio* to *anima* can be taken as an elevation in source; in this light, *Synonyma* would not accept Philosophy's claim that she is able to deal both with the rational and the spiritual life. Admittedly, Boethius's *Consolation* is not a typical text of Christian spirituality, and any Christian book that covers any of Boethius's ground could be said to try to do correctly what Boethius attempted idiosyncratically. One does not need *Consolation* to read *Synonyma*. But I think that any readers of *Synonyma*, whether in the seventh or the twentieth century, who bring *Consolation* to it will find their understanding of Boethius's text enhanced. Not only does it show how much religious value *Consolation* assigns to the physical world, by making it quite clear that *Consolation*'s morality is not based on a fear of hell or a hope of heaven; it shows that the ability to know who one is, is strictly in the province of *anima*, not *ratio,* and so helps to explain why *Consolation* never reaches an explicit definition of what *homo* is.

OTHER PARALLELS raised in the previous chapters may be briefly mentioned here. The pseudo-Platonic consolation *Axiochus*, with Socrates as the wisdom figure who consoles the sick man on his bed who fears death; more controversially, the Book of Job, with its account of the innocent who must learn the wisdom that is to be found in accepting injustice as divine and seeing through it the transcendence of God; most controversially, the *Satyricon,* also an intensively prosimetric tale of a scholar who takes on the mantle of Homer's Odysseus to wander through a death-centered world. Some may prove to be more persuasive than others. But what must be acknowledged, I think, is that there are many texts which speak of a search for the truth in ways that suggest that truth is beyond the grasp of its rational seekers. This reading of Boethius's *Consolation* proves to be inspirational in the Middle Ages, in literature that is keenly concerned with the questions of the limits of human reason and the transcendence of faith. It is to these medieval uses that we now turn.

Chapter Eight

The Menippean Boethius in
the Personification Allegories of
the Middle Ages

WILLIAM E. HEISE

In the thousand years following the death of its author, *Consolation of Philosophy* exercised an enormous influence on literary culture. The work has generally been understood to have been written and received without the self-conscious Menippean ironies detailed in the previous chapters. The neglect of the Menippean elements of *Consolation* can be attributed to the modern scholastic approach to medieval literature. Medievalists tend to try to point to medieval sources that show that a particular reading or point of view was propounded in the period. At first glance, it would appear easy to defend the practice of neglecting the Menippean elements of *Consolation*, since knowledge of the genre was not widespread in the period. However, the Menippean ironies may be found by the traditional method of close reading, which questions the self-consistency of arguments. That a

Menippean reading has not emerged for *Consolation* is a testament to the historicist approach to literature that is characteristic among medievalists.[1]

The reliance on medieval source material to support readings was most strongly emphasized by Robertson's *Preface to Chaucer* (1962). Robertson insisted that medieval literature should be read in its cultural context, but tended to see medieval culture as as "otherworldly" and allegorical. Robertson and those who followed him believed that medieval literature contained an allegorical "inner" spiritual core that was available to the faithful. Believing that the practice of close reading allowed too much freedom from cultural material that should guide the reader, Robertson rejected the practice of close reading, arguing that "[s]cientific scholarship insists on confining itself to what a text 'actually says.'"[2] All religious skepticism or debate that one might find in a medieval work was likely to be the product of close readers who pressed their interpretations into the text, rather than accepting the guidance provided by medieval culture. The approach was controversial from its introduction, but the usefulness of looking at medieval source material for producing subtle readings of medieval literature made Robertson's approach popular, even among those who did not accept his strict interpretation of the limitations of the medieval mind.

Following a source-based approach to medieval literature, it would be easy to overlook Menippean elements in *Consolation*. Furthermore, the medieval commentary tradition on Boethius emphasizes the poem's reconciliation of Philosophy's teachings with Christianity. Thus, the study of Patch (1970) of the influence of Boethius on the Middle Ages points to no medieval concerns about the difficulties of interpreting Philosophy's argument in a Christian context.

We are left, then, with a view that the poem was an authority for medieval Christians seeking "otherworldly" guidance, and that it was perhaps written as such. Thus, Peter Dronke, for example, betrays no sense that Menippean ironies have helped shape *Consolation* when he maintains that Philosophy "is the ideal love of [Boethius's] mind, the embodiment of all he could hope to know of truth on earth" and that "Boethius believed passionately in the truth of what was revealed to him."[3] The extent to which the medievalists' approach to literature has colored his reading of the poem may be indicated by the fact that he supports his view of what Boethius intended by pointing to the thirteenth-century introduction to the work by Jean de Meun.

Despite the arguments presented in the previous chapters that the elements of the Menippean satire are central to our understanding of the work, it is possible that medievalists might respond that the Menippean tradition is not central to our understanding of its reception in the Middle Ages. First, the Menippean satire was not a major genre in the Middle Ages, and the Menippean works upon which Boethius draws were not widely known in the period. In the medieval literary tradition, *Consolation* is most often imitated in the genre of the personification allegory, which might or might not be cast in the prosimetric form that characterizes Menippean satire. Second, medievalists treating the influence of *Consolation* have tended to treat Boethius as another of the sanctioned *auctores* whose works are borrowed from and imitated because they contain a dogmatically sound and morally sensible point of view, not because *Consolation* offers ironies to be explored. Many medieval historicists argue that a work must be understood in terms of the generally religious orientation of the readers and writers of the time. The fate of the unjustly accused Boethius may be read in a framework provided by other, more characteristic medieval genres such as the legend of the martyred saint: as Boethius dies he is disabused of his love of the world and learns of a higher good. Finally, Boethius may be found in the tenth circle of Dante's *Paradiso*, a treatment that would hardly be warranted if the satiric elements that undermine the teaching of Philosophy were widely recognized in the Middle Ages. It would be easy to continue to argue that the Menippean ironies of the work were simply lost on the medieval readership.

Yet there are instances in medieval literature in which an author imitating the debate between Philosophy and the imprisoned Boethius entangles an allegorical personification in the same sorts of difficulties that trouble Philosophy as she argues with Boethius. The personification of Nature in the twelfth-century *Complaint of Nature* occasionally stumbles in her argument, just as Boethius's Philosophy does. The personification of Reason in Jean de Meun's section of the *Roman de la Rose*, also modeled on Boethius's Philosophy, displays a petulance and lack of self-understanding that exaggerate the Menippean elements of *Consolation*. Even the character of Holy Church in William Langland's *Piers Plowman* can be shown to have difficulty communicating with her eager interlocutor. These instances suggest that medieval imitators of *Consolation* were aware of the difficulties that Philosophy encounters when she attempts to communicate her knowledge to Boethius in prison. In each of these imitations, the author draws on the Menippean elements of *Consolation* to explore both the extent and limitations of the powers of a personification.

The reason for the continuation of the Menippean elements of *Consolation* in medieval literature may be easily accounted for. In the Middle Ages, Boethius was not considered the same sort of authority as a figure like Augustine or Jerome, whose words had the weight of incontestable truth almost equivalent with the authority of Scripture. Despite his literary contribution, Boethius earned his place among the learned as the translator and interpreter of Aristotle's logical works, not as a theologian or an expounder of Scripture. Boethius himself was partially responsible for transmitting to the Middle Ages a distinction between a limited reason and an unlimited faith. In *De trinitate* he says that "[w]e should of course press our inquiry only so far as the insight of man's reason is allowed to climb the height of heavenly knowledge."[4] In *Consolation* 5.4 and 5.5, Philosophy herself distinguishes between rational understanding and divine intelligence. Boethius was often associated with the secular reason that was not sufficient to appreciate theological truths. On this account, Otloh of St. Emmeran (1010–1070) condemns the practice of monks who place the study of Boethius before the study of Scripture.[5] Since in an academic arena the separation of faith from reason was the separation of philosophy from theology, it is probable that at least some of those who imitated *Consolation* were concerned that they should properly assimilate limited pagan philosophy into a Christian system. While the aptness for imitation of an authority like Augustine was beyond question, imitations of Boethius's Philosophy can be expected to vary according to the degree to which their authors believe that pagan philosophy can be assimilated into Christian experience.

Consider Dante's strategy for assimilating Boethius's brand of philosophy into the Christian scheme in *Paradiso*. Boethius is placed in the circle of lights in canto 10, where the strong current of medieval rationalism, culminating in Aquinas, is represented. There is no question that Dante believes that Boethius belongs here. He tells us that his philosophy "makes the fallacious world manifest to any who listen well to him" (10:125–26). Yet there is a hint here that one must carefully look through Boethius's work if one is not to be led astray. The danger is apparent in the character of another of the ten lights, Siger of Brabant, a heretic, who was the chief proponent of

Latin Averroism. Siger and the Latin Averroists held, following the lead of Boethius, that faith and reason could not be reconciled. Siger subscribed to the doctrine of the double truth. Pagan reason was considered self-sufficient and self-consistent, pointing to truths that were inconsistent with the tenets of the faith, such as the eternity of the world and the doctrine that immortality is collective, rather than of the individual. The Latin Averroist argument was based on the claim of Aristotelian demonstrative science to lead to truths through an inexorable chain of arguments.

Among those in Dante's circle of lights, Siger is the only other philosopher on whose death Dante concentrates, and his death can be contrasted with Boethius's death. Dante seems to suggest that Siger has fallen into error, because he has lived too long (10:135). The gift of long life allowed logic to take him too far into the exploration of worldly things. Dante says that he has "syllogized invidious truths."[6] By contrast, Boethius has been killed at a young age, before he can be led astray by the self-consistent arguments of syllogistic logic, which ultimately lead to the fallacy of the world. Boethius is kept from error, but not by his focus on the natural world, which is fallacious. Instead, he is saved because he concentrates on "the good." Dante reconciles Boethius's brand of pagan philosophy with the Christian scheme by emphasizing his Platonic concentration on "the good," rather than the technical, self-consistent Aristotelian logic of the Latin Averroists, which led Siger into error. The concentration on the good acts as an alternative and superior truth condition to that offered in the syllogism.

It is in this struggle to assimilate philosophy into a Christian context that the Menippean elements of *Consolation* appear in medieval allegories. Allegorical personifications who imitate Philosophy are frequently given limited powers. For instance, the character of Nature in *Complaint of Nature* attributed to Alan of Lille distinguishes her manner of operating from the manner in which God operates.[7]

His operation is simple, mine is multiple; His work is complete, mine is defective; His work is the object of admiration, mine is the subject of alteration. He is ungeneratable, I was generated; He is the creator, I was created; He is the creator of my work; I am the work of the creator; He creates from nothing, I beg the material for my work from someone; He works by his own divinity, I work in his name; He, by his will alone, bids things come into existence, my work is but a sign of the work of God. You can realize that in comparison with God's power, my power is powerless; you can know that my efficiency is deficiency; you can decide that my activity is worthless.[8]

In respect to the divine, Nature is limited. Her vocabulary is not theological, but philosophical. The difference between God and Nature is found in the contrast between God, who operates mystically (*numine*) and Nature, who operates on names (*nomine*). Nature's emphasis on names points us to the fact that Nature operates on rational universals, which are the subject of philosophical discourse. Nature shows her limitations as she clearly echoes Anselm's notion of *fides quaerens intellectum,* telling the dreamer that "I establish the truths of faith by reason, she [Theology] establishes reason by the truths of faith. I know in order to believe, she believes in order to know."[9] However, her assertion *Ego scio ut credam* reverses the priority of faith to reason, a fact that points to her distinct limitations. Despite these limitations, *Complaint of Nature* considers the extent to which reason can penetrate in matters of faith. For example, a shift from the waking world to the dream world allows the mind to shift its perspective toward human sexuality. The shift is explained in terms of act and potential. The dreamer begins considering sexuality as an act. However, Nature educates the dreamer so that he shifts his perspective toward sexuality to the consideration of the universal species, rather than gendered sexuality. This use of the mind's potential "has the power to transform man into a god."[10] The Aristotelian shift from act to potency prepares the way for the final coming of the mystical vision at the end of the poem. Yet Nature, whose perspective is rational rather than divine, does not directly contribute to the coming of the mystical vision, which she has not foreseen, at the end of the work.

The Menippean elements from *Consolation* are minimized in *Complaint,* but are not absent. Nature has difficulty expressing herself at times. The author plays on the philosophical conflict between the particular and the universal. Being a character who takes the rational perspective, which attempts to view everything under its universal perspective, Nature has difficulty understanding or sympathizing with the perspective of individuals. She anathematizes those "who delight in individualising their mode of action, try by every means to be individualistic in a crowd, separate in a class, to disagree amid universal agreement, to manifest diversity amid unity."[11] As an individual, the dreamer wishes to clarify his own situation and asks Nature to explain the human motivations of love. Nature replies that she will try, but the task tests the limits of reason:

> Either by describing with reliable descriptions or defining with regular definitions, I will demonstrate the indemonstrable, extricate the inextricable, although it is not bound in submission to any nature, does not abide an investigation by reason and thus cannot be stamped with the stamp of any one description.[12]

Demonstration, in the scholastic tradition of *Posterior Analytics,* is the consistent method of logical argument that moves the mind to a scientific knowledge of the domain of nature. She explains that desire, being the characteristic of the individual, cannot be signified according to the stamp of reason. Despite the limitations of the character of Nature, in the end *Complaint of Nature* offers a serious message, even as it confronts the Menippean elements of *Consolation.* We can elevate our minds through reason—though reason is differentiated from religious revelation—by looking at sexuality in a more rational manner. Alan downplays the Menippean elements of *Consolation,* though he clearly seems to imitate them at some moments.

Yet such an embrace of reason was not the only possible stance in the Middle Ages. Jean de Meun's *Roman de la Rose* features the personification of Reason, who, like Boethius's Philosophy, descends from above to lead a Lover out of error. However, Reason fails to present a convincing argument, and the Lover continues in his sexual quest. The exchange exaggerates the Menippean elements of *Consolation.* The Lover's debate with Reason is less a search for clarification than an outright attempt to lay bare her weaknesses. For her part, Reason is more petulant and more easily frustrated than Boethius's Philosophy. Her argument is weak and unconvincing. The key to understanding the limitations of Jean's Reason is again to recognize the medieval distinction between the disciplines of Philosophy and Theology. Reason clearly states that she is not a *devin* (l.4403), a member of the theological faculty. Instead, she is a member of the liberal arts faculty, which, at the time the poem was written, was forbidden to treat theological matters at the University of Paris because of the inadequacy of the methodologies of the liberal arts to treat theological subjects. Reason herself does not recognize any such limitations. She claims she is the daughter of God and speaks without hesitation of her own works—the naming of things—as though they were divine things. She does not recognize, as does Alan in the *Complaint*, that there is a difference between operating *numine* and *nomine*.

Even within the limited realm of the liberal arts, Reason's ability to communicate divine truths is tested. Her arguments are tainted with contradiction. Just as Boethius's Philosophy dismisses the Muses, only to render her teachings in verse, Reason promises to show the Lover the true nature of love without resorting to *fable* (l.4279), only to resort later to telling the Lover the story of the birth of Venus in order to make a point. Reason falls into contradictions because she fails in her attempts to transcend the limitations of the liberal arts. For instance, she believes that the Lover would never have fallen in love if he knew love as she knows it. However, she is not able to communicate numinous truths using the liberal arts. Like Nature in *Complaint*, she tells the Lover that she will demonstrate something that cannot be demonstrated (ll.4279–80: "Or te demonterrai senz fable / Chose qui n'est pas demontrable").[13] Rather than offer a scientific description of love, she describes it in a series of oxymoronic pairs: love is light and heavy, bitter and sweet. The description leaves the Lover confused and demanding further explanation.

Once Reason leaves the strategy of using rational demonstration to make her point, she becomes involved in a dialectical debate with the Lover, in which argument is not restricted to the purely rational. The debate is clearly modeled on the scholastic debates of the time, with the Lover often interrupting Reason to ask for points of clarification. While the Lover retains his equanimity throughout the argument, Reason becomes frustrated by his interruptions. At one point, when the Lover asks for proof of something she has said, Reason becomes impatient and tells him that she will offer proof if only he will just be quiet (l.5534: *Or te tais donc endementiers*).

Despite her inability to communicate a satisfactory answer to the Lover, Reason continues to try to find new ways to convince him that she offers him a morally superior course. Having already recognized a distinction between the secular and the holy—and having aligned Reason with the secular—Jean does not allow Reason to treat sacred things without failure. At the moment when Reason treats sacred matters, the *Roman de la Rose* exaggerates the Menippean elements of *Consolation* to the level of farce. After having used the word *coilles* (ll.6929, 6966), a vulgar term for testicles, in discussing the castration of Saturn, Reason becomes embroiled in a discussion with the Lover on the meaning of terms. Reason maintains that nothing that God made can be vulgar. God gave Reason the right to name things, and when she called testicles *coilles,* she was simply naming something divine.[14]

In the end, the Menippean elements of *Consolation* explode forth, as the *Roman de la Rose* becomes a paean to the unbridled release of sexual energy, to which feeble Reason offers no obstacle. The author takes special care to tell the reader at strategic points in the poem that everything he has done has been accomplished without reason. The God of Love speaks of Jean de Meun as "he who shall have no use for reason" (l.10572: *Qu'il n'avra cure de Raison*). We are told that those who read the poem will no longer believe in Reason (l.10653). At the end of the poem, the Lover tells us, when it came time to thank those who had helped him gain the object of his sexual desires, "I did not remember Reason" (l.21760: *de Raison ne me souvint*). Yet, despite the immorality of the sexual quest described in the *Roman,* the poem reverses one of the dilemmas of *Consolation.* Even Reason eschews the Stoic doctrine of suicide, which, with the death of Socrates, looms over the conversation between Philosophy and the prisoner. The Christian faith held the individual to be the object of salvation, and only Christ himself was worthy of and necessary for sacrifice. Like Boethius's Philosophy, however, Reason is unable to offer a solution whereby the individual might be saved. To follow the advice of Reason, to refrain from sex, would lead not only to the death of a single person but to the extinction of the entire species. *Roman de la Rose* solves the prisoner's dilemma of *Consolation* by rendering the allegorical teacher ridiculous, unworthy of being followed. The entire species is saved by rejecting the advice of Reason; the suffering individual of *Consolation,* released from the deadly arguments of Philosophy, is transplanted into a sexual paradise, a Garden of Delight.

Roman de la Rose points to the real uncertainty in medieval thought about the possibility that the pagan instrument of reason could peer into matters of faith. In the opposition between the worldly and the divine, even rationalism falls in the same worldly camp as boundless Epicureanism. Thus, when the *Roman* is finished, the authority of philosophy in respect to the divine is entirely undermined. The only path for the active life is one of pure sensuality. This leaves the problem—posed by the Menippean elements of *Consolation* and not entirely resolved by the ending of the work— of whether we should merely remain silent in divine matters and passively resign ourselves to our own annihilation in order to remain holy, or whether there is some way to communicate the divine. This problem is taken up in *Piers Plowman*, in which William Langland explores another strategy for reconciling pagan instruments of knowledge with Christian faith. As in *Consolation*, we meet an allegorical personification early on who attempts to teach a wayward individual, but Langland adapts the Menippean elements of *Consolation* differently than Jean. The difficulties that Jean's Reason has in explaining herself may be explained by the fact that she is a secular figure, who can not fully comprehend divine matters. Langland's Menippean character, however, is not secular at all. Instead, Langland's imitation of Philosophy is none other than the personification of Holy Church.

Although she is undoubtedly a sacred figure, Holy Church has difficulty communicating with Langland. The difficulties come about as she, like Jean's Reason, attempts to express the role of the worldly in religious matters. At first, she seems to assert such a role confidently. Where *Roman de la Rose* opposes the delight in the senses and the use of reason to contemplate the sacred, Holy Church suggests that even the senses can play a role in the worship of God. Man has been given his "fyue wittes" (I 15) for worship.[15] The moral problem comes from using the things of this world "out of reson" (I 25). Holy Church tells Will that there is indeed a use for the things of this world, as long as one does not indulge in them for their own sake. The three needful things—clothes, food, and drink—are only to be used "in mesurable manere" (I 19).

The moral here seems to be unexceptionally Christian. One should use the things of the world only insofar as they offer subsistence. Holy Church cites Matthew 22.21, which suggests that we render unto Caesar that which belongs to Caesar, while we should render the things of God to God. Yet there are problems of differentiating each sphere. For instance, Holy Church emphasizes her reliance on "reson" (I 22) in describing those things that are needful and tells Langland that "rightfully reson sholde rule yow alle" (I 54). The refrain of Holy Church's speech is her thrice repeated dictum that "[w]han alle tresors arn tried treuthe is the beste" (I 85). She imparts to Langland a sense of the urgency of being able to discern the truth properly. Speaking of Satan, "fader of falshede" (I 64), she tells Langland that those "[t]hat trusten on his tresour bitrayed are sonnest" (I 70). Holy Church's emphasis on testing the truth leads Langland to question her further. He does not feel she has adequately taught him to test the truth. He asks for her to provide a method for discerning the truth: "'Yet haue I no kynde know-ynge,' quod I, 'ye mote kenne me bettre / By what craft in my cors it coms-eth, and where'" (I 138–39).

Holy Church never answers this question to the dreamer's satisfaction. On the one hand, she seems to promise the dreamer that there is a method by which the truth may be discerned. She speaks of reason and "lawe" (I 161). She responds to his request for a method by telling him he has not studied enough in school: "Thow doted daffe! . . . dulle are thi wittes. / To litel latyn thow lernedest, leode, in thi youthe" (I 140–41). She tells the dreamer that learned men know that truth is best (I 136: "letred it knoweth") and that it can be approached through the method of reading texts (I 134: "by sighte of thise textes"). These pronouncements might seem to suggest that secular means suffice to teach divine things.

Yet Holy Church cannot communicate a method to him. From the point of view of logic, she does not propose any argument that is sufficient to achieve a demonstrable truth. She attempts to present truth, but when she attempts to communicate the truth to the dreamer directly, her language is laden with metaphor. She speaks of love as a "triacle of heuene" (I 148), as a "plante of pees" (I 152), and as a "myght" that comes into the heart (I 163–65). And, of course, she speaks of truth as a "tresor" (I 208). Despite the fact that she seems to point the dreamer toward testing the truth, in logical termi-nology, her constant repetition that when "all treasures are tried truth is best" is a tautology that proves nothing. The inability of Holy Church to ex-press the truth in philosophical terms represents the presence of the Menip-pean element of *Consolation* in *Piers Plowman:* the teacher who has difficulty expressing a truth. Although Holy Church cannot provide the sort of method for discerning the truth that Will seeks, her teaching is not under-mined, as Reason's is in *Roman de la Rose.* Even though the metaphors used by Holy Church are impenetrable to secular methodologies, she offers theo-logically sound metaphors. Nevertheless, the dreamer remains bewildered by this promise of method and his failure to penetrate to the truth of which Holy Church speaks. The sense of urgency she imparts for discerning truth sends him on a quest for a method of discerning truth. Later in the poem, when conversing with Holy Writ, the dreamer speaks of the folly of using secular methodologies to apprehend divine truths. Holy Church herself condemns the greatest teachers of secular learning (X 388–94):

Aristotle and [Solomon]—who wissed men bettre?
Maistres that of goddes mercy techen men and prechen,
Of hir wordes thei wissen vs for wisest as in hir tyme,
And al holy chirche holdeth hem bothe in helle!
And if I shal werche by hir werkes to wynne me heuene,
That for hir werkes and wit now wonyeth in pyne,
Thanne wroughte I vnwisly, whatsoeuere ye preche!

The only saying of Solomon in which the dreamer professes any confidence is Solomon's declaration in Ecclesiastes 9.1 (X 436): "Sunt iusti atque sapientes, et opera eorum in manu Dei sunt" [There are just men and wise men, and their works are in the hand of God]. This Holy Church glosses as, "Ther are witty and wel libbynge ac hire werkes ben yhudde / In the hondes of almyghty god, and he woot the sothe" (X 437–38). The truth ("sothe") may not be known by human means. And Learning has already quoted approvingly the words of Gregory the Great (X 257): "Fides non habet meritum ubi humana racio prebet experimentum" [Faith has no merit when human reason offers proof].[16]

Yet in the passages that follow, teachers appear who tell the dreamer the manner in which human reason might yield divine truths. In Passus XI, he meets the emperor Trajan, a pagan who has been saved by good works. Trajan believes that secular methods may sometimes prove spiritually efficacious, telling the dreamer that "love and lewtee [lawfulness] is a leel [trustworthy] science" (XI 167). But he continues (XI 171–73):

"Lawe withouten loue," quod Troianus, "ley ther a bene!
Or any science vnder sonne, the seuene arts and alle—
But thei ben lerned for oure lordes loue,

       lost is al the tyme . . ."

Learning that is not in the spirit and service of the divine is labor lost, but learning directed towards the proper end with the proper frame of mind may lead somewhere.

With the renewed possibility that human reason might lead to divine understanding, the dreamer soon meets the personification of Reason. The dreamer is raised above the earth and glimpses the animal world. Each creature functions as it should. Unlike Reason in *Roman de la Rose*, who claims a divine authority but relies on arguments about universals and names to lead the mind to God, the works of this Reason are presented through a tableau of the rationally ordered natural world. The dreamer's response to this vision is to rebuke Reason for neglecting to order mankind.[17] Langland's Reason, who is male rather than female, responds that the time of Reason is not yet at hand. He emphasizes personal humility and personal suffering, rather than a hope that the general human world should be ordered by reason. He tells him that "[s]uffraunce is a souerayn vertue" (XI 379) and asks, "Who suffreth moore than god?" (XI 380). This Reason quotes both secular sources and Holy Writ as the basis of his authority. He suggests that "Holy writ . . . wisseth men to suffre" (XI 383). He also can quote secular authorities to support his case. His last words in passus II are a quotation from *Disticha Catonis*, "Distichs of Cato," which suggests that no man is without sin.[18] Upon hearing this secular quotation the dreamer becomes ashamed, and his sense of shame wakes him up from the dream in which he had confronted Reason.

When he awakes, he is greeted by the character of Imagination, who rebukes him for arguing with Reason. If he had not argued with Reason and Clergy, says Imagination, he would have learned more. He then adapts *Consolation* 2.7.20 and speaks in Latin (XI 416): "Philosophus esses si tacuisses" [You would have been a philosopher, if you had remained silent].[19] This is the only quotation from *Consolation* in all of *Piers Plowman*. It points to one of the characteristically Menippean moments, in which Philosophy attempts to quiet the objections of Boethius and lead him to understand truth (2.7.19–20):

But you mortals—you do not know how to act honorably except in response to flitting vulgar favors and empty gossip; you have abandoned the excellence of your conscience and your virtue and demand your rewards from the idle chatter of outsiders. Hear now how wittily someone mocked the shallowness of this sort of presumption. Once one man upbraided and insulted another because the latter had clothed himself in the name of philosopher falsely: not because of his practice of true virtue but because of vainglory and pride. The one added, "Now I will know whether or not you are a philosopher if you endure the injustice I've done you mildly and with forbearance." The other played at forbearance for a time, took the insult, then said with a taunt, "Now do you know that I am a philosopher?" The first snapped viciously and said, "I would have known it, had you kept your silence."[20]

The irony of the moment for Boethius's prisoner is that he is being taught that he must withdraw from public life and leave his family behind to suffer for the sake of Philosophy. Yet the withdrawal from public life is a withdrawal from one of the most important forums for the exercise of philosophy. Despite his otherworldly idealism, in *Republic* Plato had hoped that philosophy could become the instrument of the redemption of human society. Boethius is asked to suffer privately, in silence, and accept the death, the absolute withdrawal from all worldly concerns, that Philosophy demands. The dreamer in *Piers Plowman* need not face such an absolute choice.

The motif of opposing otherworldly silence to worldly speech found in this passage from *Consolation* is repeated in the personification allegories of the Middle Ages. In each allegory it appears differently. In *Complaint of Nature*, logic and grammar, the worldly instruments governing speech, have some efficacy in leading the mind to divine expression. In *Roman de la Rose*, rational speech is worldly, and Reason's insistence on trying to express the divine through rational speech leads her to vulgarity rather than genuine divine expression. The message in *Piers Plowman* is that the division between the worldly methods of human reason, which governs the art of speech, and the divine is not entirely absolute. It is true that silence is associated with the divine, while speech is associated with the worldly. As Imagination tells the dreamer (XI 417–19),

> Adam, whiles he spak noght, hadde paradis at wille,
> Ac whan he mamelede [spoke] about mete, and entremetede
> to knowe
> The wisedom and the wit of god, he was put fram blisse.

Adam fell from paradise because he inquired too deeply of God. Yet Imagination also tells the dreamer that Christ saved the woman taken in adultery by writing characters on the ground. "Forthi lakke thow neuere logik, lawe ne hise custumes," he concludes (XII 97). The worldly methods of ordering and understanding the world may now prove effective in spiritual matters.

This breaking down of the absolute division between the worldly and the absolute helps to explain the Menippean presentation of Holy Church as a character modeled on Philosophy and Jean de Meun's Reason. According to a strict understanding of human logic, Holy Church cannot provide a method for understanding the divine and so develops a nonsensical, tautological argument. Langland's dreamer goes off in search of such a method, but ends up believing that Holy Church has established an absolute barrier between divine wisdom and the human wisdom of such figures as Aristotle and Solomon. However, he learns from Imagination that reason can reveal things to him if he will only suffer in silence and be taught. Holy Church's words now make more sense. The senses and things of this world can be used within the guidance of reason and can provide insights into spiritual matters if one remains silent and does not question the teachings of Reason. This new, nonmethodological way of interpreting reason does not entirely negate the Menippean element in Holy Church's presentation. Despite the fact that her perspective is on a higher plane than the dreamer's, Holy Church still has a limited perspective. She fails to realize that the dreamer cannot bridge the gap between the worldly and the otherworldly. He does not rely on a deeper understanding, as she does. Thus she, too, continues to speak to a man whose mind is unprepared for the sort of method for discerning truth that she advocates. Langland merely disarms the extraordinary comic possibilities of the Menippean elements of *Consolation* that are exploited in *Roman de la Rose*. But the dreamer is sent on his quest to search for a method of learning the truth, because Holy Church cannot provide this method at the outset of the poem.

The recognition that *Consolation* contains elements from the genre of Menippean satire, a genre that did not play an important role in the Middle Ages, should not be ignored in our understanding of the role of *Consolation* in shaping medieval literature. The Menippean elements of a teacher who has difficulty explaining subject material to a pupil and the interrupted trains of argument as the teachers cannot adequately understand or address their pupils have prominent and important roles in these allegories. Although *Consolation* was the source of popular imagery of the Wheel of Fortune, the poem was not simply blindly copied by its medieval imitators, but its Menippean subtleties seem to have been imitated, exaggerated, or deliberatlely discarded by various authors.

Perhaps the most important legacy of the Menippean Boethius in the Middle Ages is the manner in which he allows authors to explore psychological and intellectually complex arguments. Rather than presenting an ignorant individual and a dogmatic allegorical personification, the imitators of the Menippean Boethius often explore the interplay of two limited perspectives in their allegorical dialogues. The final judgment about the truth is held at bay. Attitudes toward Boethius and his Philosophy are as varied as medieval attitudes toward classical philosophy. In each case treated in this chapter, Boethius's medieval imitators concern themselves with the limits of secular philosophy. Each author has a different strategy for dealing with the limits of philosophy, which is a chief concern of Boethius himself. None follows Boethius exactly. Our understanding of the rich medieval literature that imitates *Consolation* can only be enhanced by this recognition.

Chapter Nine

The Wisdom of Boethius

There are many ways to speak of religion, and many ways in which to write a religious book. That this text does not speak explicitly of the Christian God is no disqualification for its Christian status; after all, *Consolation* ends with a quotation from Esther, the book that in Hebrew never mentions God at all, the book that Luther wished had never been written. Boethius would know of Esther through Jerome's Vulgate, in which the Greek additions to the Hebrew text, frequently printed these days among the Apocrypha, were tacked on to the end of the canonical book as if they were an appendix. Thus, for the Latin reader, the book gains its God in the end, and Boethius, in having Philosophy quote from the last of these chapters (16.4), could bring to our mind two things: the context of Artaxerxes' letter to his governors, in which he complains of the evils done to the innocent by corrupt politicians—by which we infer a rebuke to those who betrayed Boethius[1]—and the nature of the Book of Esther itself, in which a tale of unexpected survival after court intrigue and the threat of annihilation finally gets around to acknowledging the God who is the guarantor of justice, beyond human actions. Because *Consolation* refuses to let the matter of the political injustices done to the prisoner drop, a refusal that stems from the prisoner himself and not from Philosophy, who had originally hoped to strip him of such concerns, we can see Esther as well as Job at work in its construction, and necessary for its interpretation.

When we consider the value of the quotation from Wisdom 8.1 at *Consolation* 3.12.22,[2] and of the quotation from Esther, and of the presence of Job, we can say that Boethius the author has an interest in Wisdom literature, and that he has given us his own version of Wisdom. To speak of other biblical genres, we can say Boethius has avoided apocalyptic, with the prisoner's refusal to take Philosophy's hand and journey to the promised homeland; nor does he prophesy. Certainly he attempts no historical record (remember Philosophy's contemptuous reception of his apology at 1.4), nor does he show step by step the purposes of God being acted out in the world of his own actions, although the repeated image of the journey to the true home could make us think of Exodus. And here too we would find another religious parallel for the lack of explicit religion in *Consolation*: it is the hallmark of Wisdom literature that it asserts that the experience of everyday life is a path to the understanding of God. To the extent that one can speak of secular Hebrew literature, one can say that secular stories are the core of Wisdom (the ancient story of Job, who is not an Israelite; the popular, national story of Esther). Because *Consolation* is Boethius's personal text, whose prisoner is not some abstracted Everyman but the philosopher who used to write Aristotelian commentaries, we can say that it is about the discovery of God through the prisoner's and the author's personal experience of Philosophy. And the topics of *Consolation*, both in its moral and its philosophical dimensions, are those of Wisdom as well: "retribution, the theory that good will be rewarded and evil will be punished; concern for origins (creation) and ends (death); and the issue of the incomprehensible in life."[3]

This study has reached the conclusion that the thematic essence of *Consolation* is that of the philosopher keeping himself from the glimpse of his true, supernal homeland by confining Philosophy to the realm of question-and-answer; he thus gains a view of the earth, his temporal home, and his place within it. There is a remarkable confluence of causes here: its doctrines are Platonic in essence, yet its morality is part Stoic (the contemplation of death, the rejection of the supernatural journey); its literary structure is part Cynic (the *catascopia*, the Olympian vision) and part Aristotelian; and its religious aspirations are Christian, longing for humble access to God through prayer. This reading of *Consolation* rests on five fundamental assertions: (1) that the work does belong to the genre of consolation, though it frustrates the desire for transcendent proof of the meaninglessness of death; (2) that Philosophy appears to the narrator as a death figure as well as a doctor; (3) that the prisoner attempts to derive a Christian truth from Philosophy's knowledge, although that specific truth comes as a painful surprise; (4) that the concluding two books are digressions, movements away from Philosophy's original intent; (5) that the Philosophy who delivers the concluding sermon is not consubstantial with either the prisoner or the author. Ultimately, Philosophy has in her hands life and death; the reader awaits the outcome of the narrator's choice, and the narrator chooses life. Now I state this fact a little unfairly, echoing the language of Deuteronomy 30:19, but if we shall be satisfied that ultimately *Consolation* is a Christian work, it is more likely that we are to hear religious texts between the lines than, say, a reference to Ennius's contention between Life and Death (Quintilian, *Institutio oratoria* 9.2.36). Were we to accept the formulation, that *Consolation* is a non-Christian work that can be read in a Christian way, we would still need to try to say just what this Christian way would be;[4] but if it is Christian, then it is necessary to address its religious resonances, even if such an elusive book would require its readers to come to different conclusions and different readings.

Why did Boethius choose to write what could still be called uncharitably a crypto-Christian work? We could speak of a failure of nerve or of a crisis of faith if we felt that he chose to suppress his religion; or of a kind of intellectual inertia if we thought that he was unable, after all of his other Aristotelian endeavors, to talk about about God in any other way. But these suspicions founder on the fact that *Consolation* is an atypical philosophical work, and that Boethius is trying very hard to do something different and unexpected. *Consolation* is one of a number of literary experiments of late antiquity, taking its place alongside Augustine's *Confessions* and *Soliloquies* as a spiritual meditation, as an attempt to speak objectively about the life of the mind and its relation to God. We cannot say that it is not Christian because it is not a catechism; that would be to expect far too little of such a learned author and from such a complex book. Like Wisdom literature in general, which gains its religious dimensions by its placement in the religious context of the canons of Scripture, *Consolation* co-opts secular traditions for religious purposes.

Consolation also serves as an intertext for *Crito,* and we see the temptation of the philosopher and the rejection of escape. Yet further behind *Crito* is Achilles in his tent in *Iliad* 9. Socrates explicitly thinks of himself as an

Achilles, who will on the third day his fertile Phthia reach (*Crito* 44b; cf. *Iliad.* 9.363). Achilles listens to the pleas of those who want him to come out and fulfill his destiny in what he knows is death; subverting the code by which he has lived his warrior's life, he decides that his honor is not dependent on the opinions of others, for he has found favor in the eyes of Zeus alone (9.608). Socrates knows what Achilles does not, that Achilles will not escape the war alive. Though we may speak of Achilles' mistake and his heroic inability to live by the heroic code,[5] Socrates sees their bond in death and in their willingness to heed a voice other than that of the society about them. Boethius aligns his prisoner with Socrates and Achilles; imminent death forces the examination of principles; a realignment with higher principles occasions the discovery of the self.

It is difficult to resist the temptation to examine the author's motives, because we see that Boethius has been trying to examine them himself; and if we have ultimately to be content to say that *Consolation* is the work that he wrote to analyze his life and his soul and not to know exactly why he wrote it the way that he did, it is still proper to imagine some more positive motivations. I propose a genuine religious honesty. The prisoner has been much concerned to assert a hope that the same divine will will have sway on earth as it does in heaven. Klingner was correct to see the presence of the Lord's Prayer in all of this,[6] and the thrust of the conclusion of *Consolation* has been to assure the prisoner that there is both reason and a need to pray. Simply put, Philosophy assures the prisoner that there is prayer, without teaching him how to pray, without being able to tell him what to pray. And if we remind ourselves of the context of the Lord's Prayer in Matthew, we can claim that that Boethius the author has been trying in these five books to represent a recreation not of the process of thought, but of the process of prayer.

> 6.5. And when ye pray, ye shall not be as the hypocrites that love to stand and pray in the synagogues and corners of the streets, that they may be seen by men: Amen I say to you, they have received their reward. 6. *But thou when thou shalt pray, enter into thy chamber and, having shut the door, pray to thy Father in secret:* and thy Father who seeth in secret will repay thee. 7. *And when you are praying, speak not much,* as the heathens. For they think that in their much speaking they may be heard. 8. Be not you therefore like to them: for your Father knoweth

what is needful for you, before you ask Him. 9. Thus therefore shall you pray: Our Father who art in heaven . . . 14. For if you will forgive men their offences, your heavenly Father will forgive you also your offences. 15. But if you will not forgive men, neither will your Father forgive you your offences.

The solitude of the prison provides the means for proper prayer; the prisoner who falls silent has learned that it is not by his speech that he recommends himself to God; he has also learned not to dwell on the wrongs done to him. Philosophy speaks, but the prisoner does not. Their voices are not united. Whatever is in his mind is his alone, whether prayer or thought or silence. We do not hear the prisoner's prayer; it is not submitted to or made for our approval; it is directed to the Father who sees in secret.

The text is essentially religious, not philosophical, insofar as these terms may be disentangled. Olmstead makes the nice point that by its very "parsimony" *Consolation* may be revealing about just what it is that religious discourse is. Because Boethius's prisoner (a term Olmstead doesn't use) is divorced from the world and from all spheres of action, he works with spare resources to rediscover the cosmos and its order from a purely individual level:

> Boethius' text may offer much to us precisely because it, in a sense, requires us to believe less, to be more tentative with respect to particular actions and ways of life and still to achieve an attitude of tranquility unruffled even by seemingly terrible circumstances. It provides a way for the solitary individual to overcome his isolation and understand himself to be in relation to all else that is.[7]

We may pursue the text's desire for silence and secrecy still further. The prisoner, originally outside of the order of things, had not called on Philosophy. She comes to him to put him into this order, and it is for her own purposes that she comes. Her history of philosophers represents one such order and purpose, and the ladder on her dress represents another; the theodicy, a third, but this does not serve her purposes, though it does serve the prisoner's.[8] The prisoner calls on God at 1.m.5, begging him to rule mortals as he rules the physical world; at 5.3 he expresses his horror at the prospect of not being able to pray to God; at 5.m.3 he gives eloquent expression to his doubts

about the ability of the human intellect to see the truth.[9] In the course of
Consolation God has gone from being an obvious reality to being a problem,
and by the end of *Consolation* the prisoner is ready to approach God on his
own, and in a new way; the fact that the book has been written shows that
he has chosen not Philosophy's path but God's. The prisoner was never a
skeptical, but a passionate, inquirer; the goal that has been achieved is a personal and a private one; the publication of this process and this book is the
moral act of one who has found his path to God.[10] Boethius the author does
not take into account his own theological tractates and has the prisoner proceed as if he had never written them. We are not to see the religious nature
of *Consolation* as the logical outcome of such studies. It is hardly a deathbed
conversion, but it does present itself as a deconversion: the prisoner, and the
author, have learned to let go of Philosophy.

It is the very writing of *Consolation* that is the most problematic element
in any interpretation of it. It is surely not full of a martyr's self-justifications;
as it is addressed to no one, not even to his sons, it is not within the traditional limits of instructional literature.[11] If the writing of the text is a personal recreation of a crisis and its resolution, then Philosophy's occasional
invocations of a plurality of readers or of guilty government officials may in
some sense ask us all to take the example of the prisoner to heart. I think
that for all of Boethius's willingness to depict himself in a self-deprecatory
fashion as a bad poet, as a misguided self-consoler, as a student who has forgotten his lessons, his work is a work of some pride. I say this not just because of Philosophy's claims that the prisoner is the last true philosopher,
and that after his death all will be silence and philosophy will be no more.[12]
Rather, the prisoner makes a discovery in the course of *Consolation*, and this
spiritual discovery is treated with both the secrecy and the pride that New
Testament parables would lead us to expect.

I have claimed that *Consolation* does not point to a reuniting or assimilation of the prisoner and Philosophy. There is a parting of the ways at the
end: the prisoner prays, and Philosophy addresses the multitude. The prisoner has fallen silent, not because he has been browbeaten into submission,
or because there is just nothing left to say; silence is a response to Philosophy's downward vision. Remember, Philosophy wanted him to look down
from the heights and laugh at the fates of tyrants and the lives of his assail-
ants; now the prisoner looks down to see himself. He does not laugh: he has
been granted a glimpse of the world in which he is both observer and ob-

served. This jaw-dropping realization is not the vision that Philosophy thought she was preparing for the prisoner, with the ascent that comes through death. It is a vision of the world of the living, to which the prisoner belongs.

Philosophy, whose function has changed from leading to pointing, is not divine. She had been willing from the first to speak of "our leader" (1.3.13, *nostra dux*); she frequently speaks of God, though never in explicitly Christian terms; and at the end she handles the prisoner's objection about the necessity involved in human actions by claiming that it would take a theologian to understand it (5.6.25, *diuini speculator*). She is explicitly reticent about explaining the divine operation of the world; the problem is the frequently encountered one of words and their limitations (4.6.54): "Bút it is hárd to explaín all these thíngs as if Í were a goddess," she says, appropriating Homer's own words (*Iliad* 12.176); "No, and it is forbidden to mortals either to grasp all of the machines of the divine operation in the acuity of their minds or to unfold them in the words of their mouths."[13] The prisoner has not been instructed by God; there is no notion in the text that half of the author's self is divine. The Philosophy that teaches the prisoner how to pray, and who in some sense is the other half of the author, is not reunited with the prisoner; this leaves us with the question of whether it is the reunited author, or the instructed prisoner, who writes the text that we read.

The prisoner has chosen to stay alive and has redirected Philosophy, who hoped to take him to what she thought was his true home. He saw a possibility of a Christian truth in her Christian language, in her teasing quotation from Scripture near the end of book 3. He did not know how he would end once he started; but Philosophy knows, at least from the beginning of book 5, that the conclusion will come as quite a surprise to him, for the prisoner will have to give up his superiority and accept the divine justice of all that happens. And it should satisfy us that the prisoner, as a philosopher, pursues to its end his insight and his desire. The philosopher is not to be content with Philosophy's guided tour. The prisoner has made a discovery, and the text is devoted to the preservation of this discovery.

The philosophical exemplum of the buried gold "accidentally" discovered is the ultimate metaphor for the action of *Consolation*. And it too has its Christian overtones, for the common folk-tale motif of the hidden treasure-trove is one of the parables of the kingdom (Matthew 13.44): "The kingdom of heaven is like unto a treasure hidden in a field. Which a man having found, hid it: and for joy thereof goeth and selleth all that he hath and buyeth that field."[14] If book 5 lets us think of the discovery of gold in this way—that the prisoner may find in the words of Philosophy what Philosophy did not realize was buried there—then there is no need to restrict our appreciation of the exemplum to Aristotle and those many pagan commentators who appeal to it. It was a folklore motif before Aristotle appropriated it; and it has other Christian resonances of relevance to *Consolation*, particulary in the "Egyptian gold" of the apologists, the treasure that the Israelites took with them from Egypt in Exodus, and that Augustine would point to as an image of how the Christian believer may take what is necessary from pagan learning and appropriate it for Christian use, leaving useless or harmful things behind.[15]

The sequence of events in Jesus' parable is as follows: the treasure was hidden, and was found by someone not looking for it, on land belonging to someone else; the treasure is then rehidden, the finder sells all that he has, buys the field in exultation, and claims the treasure as his own. It is a difficult parable, for the suspicion is that the treasure does not rightfully belong to the finder, but is appropriated to his benefit in violation of the law; he gives up all of his possessions in order to break the law and claim a greater treasure. The finder is wily and stealthy, and we sympathize with him because he sees clearly the value of what he has found. These details are not universal in folk tales of treasure troves, particularly in selling all that one has; in these details we may achieve an understanding of the writing down of the book *Consolation*. To take the parable as an allegorical key: the prisoner has found by accident a treasure that Philosophy did not know she had; he takes possession of this treasure by giving up his usual goods, those of philosophy. But it is the retrospective author of the whole of *Consolation*, not the engaged prisoner, who has hidden the treasure after the discovery, to be rediscovered and claimed after the dialogue is over and only memory remains. The writing of the text is the surreptitious laying claim to the treasure that was revealed, and purchased at great price, in the course of the dialogue. And in the face of death, the author proudly reveals what he has done.[16] But to speak of the kingdom here as "Jesus' chosen expression for the act or experience wherein and whereby God's dominion is manifested and accepted on earth"[17] would seem clearly beyond the realm of talking about what is clearly indicated in the text. At what point must discussion of *Consolation* leave its text behind? *Consolation* is designed to raise questions, and not to supply absolute answers. The reader is left to make sense of a silence and to try to fill it in; to ask how the prisoner has been consoled; to evaluate the differing aims of Philosophy and the prisoner; to contemplate how the text came to be written, and who wrote it. I have tried to suggest answers to these questions.

AND AT THIS POINT we may finally bring our thoughts back to Menippean satire and to *Consolation*'s rightful place within its definition and its history.[18] Its title is eccentric and creates generic expectations that are fulfilled only in unexpected ways; it begins with a self-absorbed bad poet whose nonsense must be stopped by a figure of authority; it implies a journey to heaven; it represents a dialogue in which the authority figure is deflated by the questioner; there is a debate with a Muse and struggle for control of the text that is before the reader's eyes; its general medium is a sort of academic self-parody; one of its topics is how the present text has come to be written; its end is a surprising repudiation of the importance of a good deal of the antecedent material; it assumes a relation to academic materials not consistent with that seen in the author's other works; it implies a heaven that it does not describe; it asserts the value of life on this earth over metaphoric journeys to other worlds; it is composed not only of a mixture of prose and verse, but of a mixture of many another work and genre; in its themes and in its construction it attempts a vision of the totality of the world; it creates an Olympian vision; the presence of human beings within this world is a surprise. What *Consolation* has done is insert a number of religious texts and symbols as substrata: Job is here, in the story of the innocent who learns the value not of his innocence, but of God's transcendence, and then falls silent; the Psalms lurk behind the composition of some of the poems; the prisoner prays according to the injunctions of the Sermon on the Mount and finds his buried treasure and buries it again. The medieval texts that build on Boethius may take a serious route and assert that only theology can make up for the deficiencies in philosophy's ability to explain the place of human beings in the order of the world; or they may take a more playful route and describe an authority figure who must be turned away from her own view of the totality of things to accommodate the human perspective. These elements and these influences do not only mark *Consolation* as a Menippean satire; they also show what Boethius has done in Christianizing the genre. *Consolation* is about prayer and the willingness to overlook the logical strictures that would label all action necessary; it rejects Philosophy's attempt to lead an exile up to God's heaven and chooses rather to look down to God's earth. Boethius has created not a series of programmatic truths about the world, but a myth about where truth may be found. This myth is reenacted by each reader, just as it was reenacted by its author.

Appendix 1

Latin Texts
Consolation 4.1; 5.1; 5.6.44-48

These Latin passages are to accompany the translations and discussions of chapter 2. The text is that of Bieler 1984; the text of Moreschini 2000 differs only in insignificant matters of orthography (primarily the use of consonantal *v* and lack of assimiliation in compounds; e.g., *admiratione* for *ammiratione*) and punctuation (rather overabundant commas).

Introduction to Book 4

4.1.1. Haec cum Philosophia dignitate uultus et oris grauitate seruata leniter suauiterque cecinisset, tum ego nondum penitus insiti maeroris oblitus intentionem dicere adhuc aliquid parantis abrupi et: 2. O, inquam, ueri praeuia luminis, quae usque adhuc tua fudit oratio cum sui speculatione diuina tum tuis rationibus inuicta patuerunt, eaque mihi etsi ob iniuriae dolorem nuper oblita non tamen antehac prorsus ignorata dixisti. 3. Sed ea ipsa est uel maxima nostri causa maeroris quod, cum rerum bonus rector exsistat, uel esse omnino mala possint uel impunita praetereant; quod solum quanta dignum sit ammiratione profecto consideras. 4. At huic aliud maius adiungitur; nam imperante florenteque nequitia uirtus non solum praemiis caret, uerum etiam sceleratorum pedibus subiecta calcatur et in locum facinorum supplicia luit. 5. Quae fieri in regno scientis omnia, potentis omnia, sed bona tantummodo uolentis dei nemo satis potest nec ammirari nec conqueri. — 6. Tum illa: Et esset, inquit, infiniti stuporis omnibusque horribilius monstris si, uti tu aestimas, in tanti uelut patris familias dispositissima domo uilia uasa colerentur, pretiosa sordescerent. 7. Sed non ita est; nam si ea quae paulo ante conclusa sunt inconuulsa seruantur, ipso de cuius nunc regno loquimur auctore cognosces semper quidem potentes esse bonos, malos uero abiectos semper atque imbecilles, nec sine poena umquam esse uitia nec sine praemio uirtutes, bonis felicia malis semper infortunata contingere multaque id genus, quae sopitis querelis firma te soliditate corroborent. 8. Et quoniam uerae formam beatitudinis me dudum monstrante uidisti, quo etiam sita sit agnouisti, decursis omnibus quae praemittere necessarium puto uiam tibi quae te domum reuehat ostendam. 9. Pennas etiam tuae menti quibus se in altum tollere possit adfigam, ut perturbatione depulsa sospes in patriam meo ductu, mea semita, meis etiam uehiculis reuertaris.

Introduction to Book 5

5.1.1. Dixerat orationisque cursum ad alia quaedam tractanda atque expedienda uertebat. 2. Tum ego: Recta quidem, inquam, exhortatio tuaque prorsus auctoritate dignissima, sed quod tu dudum de prouidentia quaestionem pluribus aliis implicitam esse dixisti re experior. 3. Quaero enim an esse aliquid omnino et quidnam esse casum arbitrere. — 4. Tum illa: Festino, inquit, debitum promissionis absoluere uiamque tibi qua patriam reueharis aperire. 5. Haec autem etsi perutilia cognitu tamen a propositi nostri tramite paulisper auersa sunt, uerendumque est ne deuiis fatigatus ad emetiendum rectum iter sufficere non possis. — 6. Ne id, inquam, prorsus uereare; nam quietis mihi loco fuerit ea quibus maxime delector agnoscere. 7. Simul, cum omne disputationis tuae latus indubitata fide constiterit, nihil de sequentibus ambigatur. — 8. Tum illa: Morem, inquit, geram tibi, simulque sic orsa est: Si quidem, inquit, aliquis euentum temerario motu nullaque causarum conexione productum casum esse definiat, nihil omnino casum esse confirmo et praeter subiectae rei significationem inanem prorsus uocem esse decerno. Quis enim cohercente in ordinem cuncta deo locus esse ullus temeritati reliquus potest? 9. Nam nihil ex nihilo exsistere uera sententia est, cui nemo umquam ueterum refragatus est, quamquam id illi non de operante principio sed de materiali subiecto hoc omnium de natura rationum quasi quoddam iecerint fundamentum. 10. At si nullis ex causis aliquid oriatur, id de nihilo ortum esse uidebitur; quodsi hoc fieri nequit, ne casum quidem huius modi esse possibile est qualem paulo ante definiuimus. — 11. Quid igitur, inquam, nihilne est quod uel casus uel fortuitum iure appellari queat? An est aliquid, tametsi uulgus lateat, cui uocabula ista conueniant? — 12. Aristoteles meus id, inquit, in Physicis et breui et ueri propinqua ratione definiuit. — Quonam, inquam, modo? — 13. Quotiens, ait, aliquid cuiuspiam rei gratia geritur aliudque quibusdam de causis quam quod intendebatur obtingit casus uocatur, ut si quis colendi agri causa fodiens humum defossi auri pondus inueniat. 14. Hoc igitur fortuito quidem creditur accidisse, uerum non de nihilo est; nam proprias causas habet, quarum inprouisus inopinatusque concursus casum uidetur operatus. 15. Nam nisi cultor agri humum foderet, nisi eo loci pecuniam suam depositor obruisset, aurum non esset inuentum. 16. Hae sunt igitur fortuiti causae compendii, quod ex obuiis sibi et confluentibus causis, non ex gerentis intentione prouenit. 17. Neque enim uel qui aurum obruit uel qui agrum exercuit ut ea pecunia repperiretur intendit, sed, uti dixi, quo ille obruit hunc fodisse conuenit atque concurrit. 18. Licet igitur definire casum esse inopinatum ex confluentibus causis in his quae ob aliquid geruntur euentum. 19. Concurrere uero atque confluere causas facit ordo ille ineuitabili conexione procedens qui de prouidentiae fonte descendens cuncta suis locis temporibusque disponit.

Conclusion of *Consolation*

5.6.44. Quae cum ita sint, manet intemerata mortalibus arbitrii libertas nec iniquae leges solutis omni necessitate uoluntatibus praemia poenasque proponunt. 45. Manet etiam spectator desuper cunctorum praescius deus uisionisque eius praesens semper aeternitas cum nostrorum actuum futura qualitate concurrit bonis praemia malis supplicia dispensans. 46. Nec frustra sunt in deo positae spes precesque, quae cum rectae sunt inefficaces esse non possunt. 47. Auersamini igitur uitia, colite uirtutes, ad rectas spes animum subleuate, humiles preces in excelsa porrigite. 48. Magna uobis est, si dissimulare non uultis, necessitas indicta probitatis cum ante oculos agitis iudicis cuncta cernentis.

Appendix 2

Boethius, *In de interpretatione*[2] 3.9, 221.27–227.12 Meiser

The following passage comes from Boethius's massive second commentary on Aristotle's *On Interpretation*. The two commentaries were written between 513 and 516 and cost Boethius much sweat. He ends on a rare note of resignation: "And so, if I have brought to completion with zeal and painstakingness the task I set before myself, it will be a very useful thing for all those who are gripped by the desire to understand these things through reason; but if I have fallen short of my task, to untie the very obscure passages of this book, it does not condemn my labor as something which will harm them, even if it does not help them." The passage below is from the commentary on *De interpretatione* 9, on future contingents, perhaps the most notorious passage in Aristotle's logical works and one that Boethius brings to bear on the relation of divine foreknowledge to human free will in book 5 of *Consolation*. Aristotle's three-and-a-half pages of Greek receive sixty-five pages in the *Second Commentary*, the whole of book 3; this selection deals with divination, rewards and punishments, the limitations of God's knowledge, and the impiety of anyone who would strip God of his free will or his foreknowledge. It is directly related to *Consolation* 5.3 ff.; parallels are given in the notes.

The following translation is not primarily designed to allow Aristotle's Greek to shine through, but to demonstrate Boethius's thoughts about these topics, primarily through preserving his metaphors. The primary difficulty lies in his terms *consiliari* (representing Aristotle's βουλεύεσθαι) and *negotiari* (πραγματεύεσθαι). Ackrill 1963 offers the translations "deliberate" and "take trouble"; this path is followed in the translation of Blank and Kretzmann 1998, which should certainly be consulted in conjunction with what I offer below. The Greek is even more neutral than the English, with root meanings of "exercise the will" and "do a thing." But as Boethius glosses *negotiari* with *actum incipere atque negotium gerere*, "enter upon an action and carry out a business," "take trouble" will not do. *Negotiari* is a businessman's term, and *consiliari*, from *consilium*, is a word of practical wisdom, not nearly as abstract as βουλεύεσθαι. I suggest "engage in, or do, business" for *negotiari* and "business" or "engaging in business" for *negotium*; and "take counsel" for *consiliari*, with *consilium* and *consiliatio* as "counsel" or "taking counsel." Such commercial terms in *Consolation* and its language of prayer have been noted by Mohrmann 1976 and related to Christian liturgical language; it is salutary to see them at work elsewhere in Boethius.

I have tried for some consistency in language (*esse* regularly, exist; *facere*, do; *fieri*, become, happen; *evenio/provenio*, occur, turn out, be the case that). When alternate conditions and outcomes appear in hypotheses as *hoc . . . hoc . . . hoc*, I have translated X . . . Y . . . Z. *Homo* is "person," as are the masculine forms of pronouns used to designate a single speaker: *unus, alter, ille*, etc.

(221.27) For if necessity were to exist in things, whether someone were to do X or not, what would have to exist would occur. For this reason, that which happens by reason of taking counsel does not happen by the violence of necessity. However, he has joined "nor do business" to "taking counsel," and the order is as follows (18b31–36): "For this reason no one will be obliged to take counsel, since (in taking counsel) if we do X, Y will be, but if we do Z, it won't—for nothing prevents one person from saying that something will exist a thousand years in advance, and another from denying it. And for this

reason whichever of their statements was true to say at that time will necessarily be—nor to do business," that is, to enter upon an action and to carry
out a business.[1]

(222.9) For taking counsel is first and engaging in business is second, but
he put engaging in business (directly) after taking counsel, and after the in-
terposition of engaging in business he appended all the things that needed
to be added concerning the nature of taking counsel. It is this way: if, he
says, necessity compels all things, there is no need to take counsel, since in
taking counsel if we do X, Y will occur for us, but if we do Z it will not. For
nothing keeps one person from saying something in vain, and another from
denying such a speaker; if we do X, either Y will be or it will not. For that
which is going to occur will happen, whether one by counsel conjectures
that X can happen (regardless of what else this person shall do), or whether
another denies that X can happen (regardless of whether this person should
do what he said).[2] For whatever was the true thing that one of them said will
of necessity be. For if there is no need at all to take counsel, there will be no
need to do business either; that is, to enter upon any business. For whether
one enters upon it or not, that which is of necessity will doubtless occur.

(222.26) And for this reason one human being will be not at all different
from another. For we judge people to be better to the extent that they are
more effective in taking counsel. But when taking counsel is in vain because
necessity does all things, people too in no way differ among themselves.
Now it makes no difference whether this counsel is good or bad, since the
necessity of the outcome lies in the administration of fate. For this reason,
if people of good counsel deserve praise, and people of bad counsel deserve
blame—in no other way will this situation exist justly unless evil action and
evil counsel (and conversely, good action and counsel) are in our power and
not in fate. For when the outcome of a thing is bound by no necessity, then
too is the exercise of the will free, so that it is not subservient to the necessity of fate.

(223.12) Therefore, those who have posited simple causes and effects of
things[3] in this world are not to be approved; and those who have it that
there are not also mixed causes of events in the mixed mass of this world are
likewise to be rejected. For neither do those think correctly who say that all
things come about by chance, nor are those who pretend that all things
come about by the violence of necessity considered to be of sound mind, and
it is clear that not all things exist by free will; rather, for all these things

both the causes and the outcomes are mixed. For some things exist by chance and other things exist by necessity; and we see that some things are in the realm of free decision.[4] And within us exists at least the willing of our own actions.

(223.23) For somehow or other our will is the master of our actions and of the rationale of our entire life,[5] but the outcome is not also similarly within our power. For when we do something for some other reason of our own free will a chance occurrence coming from the same causes butts in.[6] As when someone lays down a trench to plant a vine—should that person find a treasure chest, to be sure, the laying down of the trench comes of free will, but it is chance alone that brings the discovery of the treasure chest, albeit the chance has the same cause that the will brought.[7] For if the person had not dug the trench, the treasure chest would not have been found. Now certain events come to the aid of our free will, and a certain violent necessity obstructs others. For just as eating and reading and other things of this sort exist of our own free will, so too does their outcome often depend on our free will. But if a Roman should wish to rule over the Persians—the decision of the will is certainly in him, but a harsher necessity holds the outcome in check and prevents its being brought to completion. Therefore chance and will and necessity—each rules over all things,[8] nor is there one of these that can be posited alone in all things, but the power[9] of the three of them is mixed together.

(224.19) So it happens that the intention of sinners is taken into account rather than the outcome, and the intention is punished, not the completion, because our will at least is free, but the sequence of events leading to the completion[10] is at times held in check. For if all things were to happen either by chance or by necessity, praise would not be appropriate for those who do well, nor would punishment be appropriate for those who fail, nor would any laws be just which would fix[11] rewards for the good or punishments for the bad.[12]

(224.27) Now I come to that question which is asked in many ways, whether divination remains if in things not all things happen by necessity.[13] For the same things exist in knowledge which exist in true prediction; and just as when someone predicts the truth, that which is truly predicted necessarily exists, similarly what someone knows will exist necessarily will exist. But divination does not pronounce that all things will exist as if by necessity, and for this reason divination is frequently of this sort, which is easily recognized in the books of the ancients: X will indeed occur, but if Y happens it will not occur, as if it could be interrupted and then come about in another way.[14] If this is so, then it does not occur by necessity.

(225.9) But whether it is necessary that all things be, if God knows all future things—let's inquire as follows. Were someone to say that God's knowledge of future things follows the necessity of events, such a person would certainly state the converse,[15] that it is not possible that God knows all things, if all things do not happen by necessity. For if the necessity of events follows the knowledge of God, should there be no necessity of events, divine knowledge is destroyed. And who could in mind be put to the rack by such blasphemous reasoning as to dare to say these things about God?

(225.17) But perhaps one might say that, since it can't be the case that God does not know all future things, it therefore is the case that all things exist by necessity, because it is blasphemous[16] to remove from God the knowledge of future things. But whoever would say this would have to take care lest, while struggling to make God know everything, he argue that God is ignorant of everything.[17] For were someone to claim to know that the number two is odd, he would not *know*; rather, he is ignorant. Therefore, that which is not in the realm of possibility to know,[18] is rather in the realm of impossibility to think to know. Therefore, whoever says that God knows all things and that for this reason all things will exist out of necessity, says that God out of necessity believes that those things will occur which do not occur out of necessity. For if God knows that all things will occur out of necessity, he is deceived in his knowing. For not everything occurs out of necessity; some things happen contingently.[19]

(226.7) Therefore, if he should know that those things will occur out of necessity which will occur contingently, he is deceived in his own foreknowledge. For God knows the things that will exist not as occurring out of necessity, but as occurring contingently, in such a way that he is not unaware that it could become something else, but all the same he knows what it does become by reasoning from the people themselves and their actions.[20] Therefore, whoever says that all things happen out of necessity, must necessarily snatch away from God his goodwill.[21] For his generosity brings forth nothing, inasmuch as necessity administers all things, with the result that God's very kindness exists somehow or other out of necessity and not out of his own will. For if some things do happen out of his will, so that he is himself constrained by no necessity, then not all things happen out of necessity.

Therefore: Who is so blasphemously wise[22] as to constrain God too by necessity? Who would say that all things happen out of necessity if the violence of that impossibility[23] will occur as well?

(226.22) For this reason, it must be posited that in things some things are possible by chance and some things are made by will, \<nor\> are they constrained by necessity; and the reasoning which undermines either of these two is to be judged impossible.[24] And so Aristotle not implausibly leads to this impossible reasoning[25] in saying that possibility and chance and free will are lost, which cannot happen, if of all future statements one is always definitely true and the other is always definitely false.[26]

(227.2) For there follows upon the truth and falsehood of these statements a necessity which secretly banishes[27] chance and free will from things. And so it is that now too, repeating the same thing, he says (18b33–34): "Nor does it make any difference whether someone should affirm or another deny a thousand years in advance that something will exist." For it is not in accordance with affirming or denying that all things are to be done or are not to be done; rather, if it is necessary that things which are also affirmed or denied follow upon the one who affirms or the one who denies, then the things which were necessary to occur as they were speaking necessarily occur even if they were not speaking. He puts it this way . . .[28]

Appendix 3

Maximian, *Elegy* 3

The text is from Baehrens's Teubner edition (*Poetae Latini Minores*, Leipzig, 1883, 5:332–36) with modifications only in matters of capitalization. Baehrens's text is also used for the commentaries of Agozzino 1970 and Spalstenstein 1983. The following translation tries to preserve the imagery of the Latin, though in the highly formulaic language of erotic elegy this is frequently impossible. Other English translations of Maximian are Ashton-Gwatkin 1975 and Lind 1988, which are less and more reliable, respectively. The notes are selective, pointing primarily to parallels within *Consolation* and to Maximian's other elegies. For a discussion of the *Third Elegy* in the context of Maximian's other elegies, see here chapter 7, pp. 101–7. For a discussion of Maximian as a source for the seemingly Boethian character of Pandarus in Chaucer's *Troilus and Criseyde*, see J. A. Mitchell 2003.

Nunc operae pretium est quaedam memorare iuuentae
　　atque senectutis pauca referre meae,
quis lector mentem rerum uertigine fractam
　　erigat et maestum noscere curet opus.
captus amore tuo demens, Aquilina, ferebar　　　　　　　5
　　pallidus et tristis, captus amore tuo.
nondum quid sit amor uel quid Venus ignea noram,
　　torquebar potius rusticitate mea.
nec minus illa meo percussa cupidine flagrans
　　errabat, tota non capienda domo.　　　　　　　　　　10
stamina, pensa procul nimium dilecta iacebant:
　　solus amor cordi curaque semper erat.
nec reperire uiam, qua caecum pasceret ignem,
　　docta nec alternis reddere uerba notis;
tantum in conspectu studium praestabat inane,　　　　　15
　　anxia uel solo lumine corda fouens.

me pedagogus adit, illam tristissima mater
　　seruabat tanti poena secunda mali:
pensabant oculos nutusque per omnia nostros
　　quaeque solet mentis ducere signa calor.　　　　　　20
dum licuit, uotum tacite compressimus ambo
　　et uaria dulces teximus arte dolos.
at postquam teneram rupit uerecundia frontem
　　nec ualuit penitus flamma recepta tegi,
mox captare locos et tempora coepimus ambo　　　　　25
　　atque superciliis luminibusque loqui,
fallere sollicitos, suspensos ponere gressus
　　et muta nullo currere nocte sono.
nec longum: genitrix furtiuum sensit amorem;
　　et medicare parans uulnera uulneribus　　　　　　　30
increpitat caeditque: fouentur caedibus ignes,
　　ut solet adiecto crescere flamma rogo.
concipiunt geminum flagrantia corda furorem,
　　et sic permixto saeuit amore dolor.
tunc me uisceribus per totum quaerit anhelis,　　　　　35
　　emptum suppliciis quem putat esse suis.

And now it is worth my while to bring to mind certain events of my youth and to tell a few stories about my old age, so that the reader may lift up a mind that is broken by the maelstrom of the world[1] and take the time to get acquainted with this lugubrious poem. By your love was I captured, Aquilina; I was mad, I wandered pale and pathetic; by your love was I captured. I had no idea yet what love was, or volcanic Venus; no, what tortured me was my own naïveté. And she was no less knocked senseless by love for me; she wandered in a daze; she was on fire; she could not be kept within the confines of her house. (11) The day's wool, the spun thread: much loved once, they lay unused apart; dear to her heart were only love and ever its anxiety. She knew not how to find a way to feed the sightless flame within, nor to send words back and forth in secret messages; she would only exhibit in my presence an empty-handed fondness, tending to her distraught heart by sight alone.[2]

(17) My teacher came to me asking questions, and her most unsympathetic mother, a second punishment in the midst of our woes, was keeping a close eye on her. They carefully observed our eyes and our gestures for all of the signs that a brain on fire is apt to produce. While we could we both suppressed in silence the vows we made, and in many a clever scheme we fashioned sweet dissimulations. But after shame burst asunder our delicate composure, and the fire that we had deep within us could no longer be concealed, we both immediately began to steal moments, to find places, and to speak with our eyebrows and our eyes, to disguise the eagerness of our feet, to walk on tiptoe,[3] to run off in the middle of the night without a sound. (29) It didn't take long: her mother sniffed out our secret affair, and, intending to cure her wounds with still more wounds,[4] she screamed at her and beat her; her fires grew with the beatings, just as flames mount higher when the fuel is tossed on. Her burning heart conceives a double passion, and that's the way grief rages when love is an ingredient.[5] Then she tries to find me everywhere,[6] hot to the marrow,[7] she who thinks she bought me, her beatings the price she paid.

nec memorare pudet turpesque reuoluere caedes,
    immo etiam gaudens imputat illa mihi.
"pro te susceptos iuuat" inquit "ferre dolores:
    tu pretium tanti dulce cruoris eris.   40
sit modo certa fides atque inconcussa uoluntas:
    quae nihil imminuit passio, nulla fuit."
his egomet stimulis angebar semper et ardens
    languebam, nec spes ulla salutis erat.
prodere non ausus carpebar uulnere muto;   45
    sed stupor et macies uocis habebat opus.
hic mihi, magnarum scrutator maxime rerum,
    solus, Boethi, fers miseratus opem.
nam cum me curis intentum saepe uideres
    nec posses causas noscere tristitiae,   50
tandem perspiciens tacita me peste teneri
    mitibus alloquiis pandere clausa iubes:
"dicito, quando nouo correptus carperis aestu!
    dicito et en dicti sume doloris opem.
non intellecti nulla est curatio morbi,   55
    ut magis inclusis ignibus antra fremunt."
Dum pudor est tam foeda loqui uitiumque fateri,
    agnouit taciti conscia signa mali.
Mox ait: "Occultae sat pestis prodita causa est.
    Pone metum: ueniam uis tibi tanta dabit."   60
Prostratus pedibus uerecunda silentia rupi,
    cum lacrimis referens ordine cuncta suo.
"Fac" ait "ut placitae potiaris munere formae."
    Respondi "pietas talia uelle fugit."
Soluitur in risum exclamans "pro mira uoluntas!   65
    Castus amor Veneris dicito quando fuit?
Parcere dilectae iuuenis desiste puellae:
    impius huic fueris, si pius esse uelis.
Vnguibus et morsu teneri pascuntur amores,
    uulnera non refugit res magis apta plagae."   70
Interea donis permulcet corda parentum
    et pretio faciles in mea uota trahit.
Auri caecus amor natiuum uincit amorem:
    coeperunt natae crimen amare suae.
Dant uitiis furtisque locum, dant iungere dextras   75
    et totum ludo concelebrare diem.

(37) She's not ashamed to tell of her awful beatings,[8] and to tell them again; in fact, she's even happy when blaming them on me. She says, "I'm glad to suffer such a burden of sorrows, since I got them because of you; you will be the pleasant price for all this blood.[9] Just let your faith be unwavering and your will unbent; the passion which violated nothing was no passion at all." With these whips I was perpetually tortured; though on fire, I went limp; there was no hope of salvation.[10] I did not dare to reveal it;[11] I was torn to pieces in voiceless wounds; but shellshock and starvation were like a voice.[12] (47) It was at this point that you alone, Boethius, loftiest investigator of all lofty things, took pity on me and brought me aid.[13] For when you would see me, again and again, bent over in worry, and were not able to discover the cause of my sorrows, nevertheless, because you sensed that I was in the grip of some silent disease,[14] in sympathetic conversation you bade me to lay open what was locked up inside me. "Speak to me, since you have been torn to pieces, in the throes of some unknown agitation! Speak to me, and look! You can then receive some help for the sorrow that you speak of. There is no cure for a disease that is not understood,[15] just as the moanings come louder and louder from caves that have volcanic fires shut up inside them."[16]

(57) And while I was ashamed to speak of such foul things and to admit to my failings,[17] he recognized the telltale signs of a silent evil.[18] Soon he said, "The cause of your hidden plague is sufficiently betrayed.[19] Don't be afraid;[20] its great violence will afford you some pardon."[21] I threw myself at his feet and burst through my shamefaced silence,[22] telling him everything in order through my tears. He said, "See to it that you get the enjoyment of the beauty that has so pleased you."[23] I answered, "My scruples make me shy away from even wanting things like that."[24] He burst into helpless laughter and said, "What an amazing act of will! Tell me, when was the love of Venus ever a continent thing? You're a young man—stop wanting to spare the girl you love. You'll never do right by her, if you want to do right. Innocent loves are fed by bites and scratches;[25] a thing that is more suited for violence does not run away from the shedding of blood."[26] (71) In the meantime he softened the hearts of her parents with bribes; with money he drew them easily over to my heart's desire.[27] The blind love of money overwhelmed their parental affections, and they began to love the delinquency of their daughter. They furnish us a place for our sins and our secrets, and they let us hold hands and make holiday, all day long, in our sport.[28]

Permissum fit uile nefas, fit languidus ardor:
  uicerunt morbum tabida corda suum.
Illa nihil quaesita uidens procedere, causam
  odit et illaeso corpore tristis abit.   80
Proieci uanas sanato pectore curas
  et subito didici quam miser ante fui.
"Salue sancta" inquam "semperque intacta maneto,
  uirginitas, per me plena pudoris eris."
Quae postquam perlata uiro sunt omnia tanto   85
  meque uidet fluctus exsuperasse meos,
"Macte" inquit "iuuenis, proprii dominator amoris,
  et de contemptu sume trophaea tuo.
Arma tibi Veneris ceduntque Cupidinis arcus,
  cedit et armipotens ipsa Minerua tibi."   90
Sic mihi peccandi studium permissa potestas
  abstulit atque ipsum talia uelle fugit.
Ingrati, tristes pariter discessimus ambo:
  discidii ratio uita pudica fuit.

(77) Once permitted, it becomes a cheap and unspeakable act; passion goes limp; my wasted heart had overcome its illness.[29] And she, seeing that the thing she desired was making no progress, despised the very cause of it and went home depressed, her body intact.[30] And from my chest, which was now healed,[31] I cast forth all of my empty anxieties,[32] and I suddenly learned[33] just how wretched I had been before.[34] And I said, "Hail, holy virginity; may you ever remain whole and untouched! Because of me, you shall be full of modesty."[35] (85) And after news of all this had been brought back to that great man, and he sees that I had emerged atop the waves that would drown me, he says, "Congratulations, my boy! You are now the master of your own love.[36] Raise high the trophy that comes from your despising! The weapons of Venus, the bow and arrow of Cupid, now yield to you; Minerva herself, with the weapons she wields, yields to you as well."[37] The free opportunity, once it was granted to me, stole away my eagerness for error, and the very desire for such things bolted and ran.[38] Unsatisfied and depressed alike we both departed[39]—the cause of the divorce was a life of chastity.

Appendix 4

Agathias Scholasticus,
Greek Anthology, 11.354

The text below is that of Beckby, *Anthologia Graeca* 3.718.[1] The notes given here are selective; for a fuller discussion the reader is directed to my article "Agathias Scholasticus (*A.P.* 11.354), the Philosopher Nicostratus, and Boethius' *Consolation*" (Relihan 1990a); see also here chapter 7, pp. 99–100.

Ἄλλον Ἀριστοτέλην, Νικόστρατον, ἰσοπλάτωνα,
   σκινδαλαμοφράστην αἰπυτάτης σοφίης,
τοῖα περὶ ψυχῆς τις ἀνείρετο· "Πῶς θέμις εἰπεῖν
   τὴν ψυχήν; θνητήν, ἢ πάλιν ἀθάνατον;
σῶμα δὲ δεῖ καλέειν, ἢ ἀσώματον; ἐν δὲ νοητοῖς   5
   τακτέον, ἢ ληπτοῖς, ἢ τὸ συναμφότερον;"
αὐτὰρ ὃ τὰς βίβλους ἀνελέξατο τῶν μετεώρων,
   καὶ τὸ περὶ ψυχῆς ἔργον Ἀριστοτέλους,
καὶ παρὰ τῷ Φαίδωνι Πλατωνικὸν ὕψος ἐπιγνούς,
   πᾶσαν ἐνησκήθη πάντοθεν ἀτρεκίην.   10
εἶτα περιστέλλων τὸ τριβώνιον, εἶτα γενείου
   ἄκρα καταψήχων, τὴν λύσιν ἐξέφερεν·
"Εἴπερ ὅλως ἔστι ψυχῆς φύσις (οὐδὲ γὰρ οἶδα),
   ἢ θνητὴ πάντως ἐστὶν ἢ ἀθάνατος,
στεγνοφυὴς ἢ ἄϋλος· ὅταν δ' Ἀχέροντα περήσῃς   15
   κεῖθι τὸ νημερτὲς γνώσεαι ὡς ὁ Πλάτων.
εἰ δ' ἐθέλεις, τὸν παῖδα Κλεόμβροτον Ἀμβρακιώτην
   μιμοῦ, καὶ τεγέων σὸν δέμας ἐκχάλασον·
καί κεν ἐπιγνοίης δίχα σώματος αὐτίκα σαυτόν,
   μοῦνον ὅπερ ζητεῖς τοῦθ' ὑπολειπόμενος."   20

Good Nicostratus,[2] our Aristotle the Second, Plato's equal,[3] a split-hair speaker of the steepest wisdom,[4] was once quizzed on the soul. "How does one properly denominate the soul? Is it mortal? Or, contrariwise, immortal? Should you call it corporeal, or incorporeal? Shall we place it among things intelligible, or things perceptible, or both together?" But he read the books of things stratospheric from beginning to end,[5] and, after reading Aristotle's essay *On the Soul* and the Platonic loftiness[6] found in the *Phaedo,* he clothed himself on every side with every accuracy.[7] And then, with a flourish of his cape, stroking the end of his beard,[8] he laid the solution out:[9] "If the soul has a nature in an absolute sense (I'm not sure about this), it is either completely mortal or completely immortal, either of a constipated nature or immaterial.[10] But when you pass over Acheron, there you will learn, as Plato learned, the incontrovertible truth.[11] But if you want to, follow the example of Cleombrótus, the young man from Ambracia:[12] cast your body down from the rooftop, and then, separated from your body, you would immediately 'Know thyself,'[13] leaving behind only this, the very thing that you are looking for."[14]

Notes

Chapter One. The Ironic *Consolation* and Its Reception

1. Sharples 1991, 41–46, is perhaps the simplest introduction to the issue of the sources, doctrines, and influence of the crucial final books, particularly on the relation of divine foreknowledge and human free will, and the question of determinism. As Sorabji 1980, 124–25, points out, Boethius's formulation holds the field until Aquinas modifies it by speaking not of God's foreknowledge (which does imply irrevocability) but simply of knowledge. For the eternal now of God's vision see also Sorabji 1983, 108–13; Mignucci 1987; Leftow 1990. Marenbon 2003, chapters 6–7, 96–145, offers a subtle analysis of the dialogue that reveals both the virtues and the shortcomings of Philosophy's presentation of these issues; I follow his arguments here in chapter 2.

2. Relihan 1984; Claassen, forthcoming, also speaks of Ovid reasserting himself in the course of *Consolation*, the attempted dismissal of the Muses in *Consolation* 1.1 mirroring the functions of Elegeia and Tragoedia in *Amores* 3.1.

3. See Relihan 1993, 203–10, for a translation of the prologue of *Mythologies*, and pp. 152–63 for discussion. Cherniss 1987, 37–38, has some helpful comments; see Hays 1996, 142–79, for a discussion of Fulgentius's sources in the body of *Mythologies* and his debts to earlier mythical allegoresis. My working presumption was the common one, that *Mythologies* is prior to *Consolation*; but if the suspicion raised by Hays (1996, 7–12) is correct, that Fulgentius draws on *Consolation* in a number of ways (Philosophy as the model for the epiphany of Vergil in *Allegorical Vergil*; the setting of *Consolation* as the model for the setting of *Mythologies*), then the Fulgentian corpus may actually represent the earliest use of *Consolation* in the creation of texts that are ironic monuments to erudition. Ultimately, however, after suggesting that the parallels may be due to traditions common to epiphanies, Hays claims only that Boethian evidence cannot provide solid dates for Fulgentius. See Hays 2006 (forthcoming) for further thoughts on the language of Fulgentius. Here I consider further the possibility that *Mythologies* is a witness to the reception of *Consolation* (see chapter 7).

4. Marenbon 2003, 160–61, more willing than most to see Martianus's comic trappings as more than mere comic relief, acknowledges that part of the pedagogue's task in *Marriage* is to acknowledge the "pretensions and absurdities" of such pedagogy. Further on Martianus, see below, n. 15.

5. Cf. Relihan 1993, 13–17, for a translation of this passage and a discussion of its value in defining just what sort of a paradoxical mixture of opposites the Menippean genre is.

6. Literary interpretation precedes generic classification, at least when dealing with critically and historically established genres, but in *defining* a genre there is inevitably a circular process: as I have already admitted (Relihan 1993, 9), in all of the back-and-forth between work and genre, structural characteristics suggest that certain works belong together, and interpretation suggests the thematic unities that give meaning to the structures. I prefer, with Frye, to consider genres as literary realities; reception theory is less willing to do so. Cf. Martindale 1993, 14: "Genres need not be reified, but can be understood discursively, as part of the dynamics of social transaction and communication, and of artistic practice." There is a large element of discovery in the definition of Menippean satire, and if I cannot escape the fact that discovery is idiosyncratic and assertive, I would still claim that there was a reality to be discovered, and that the history of the genre outlined in *Ancient Menippean Satire* is a sort of validation of the definition of the genre there advanced. If not quite a scientific theory, it is at least an attempt to marshal and to account for a large body of data and evidence.

7. Marenbon 2003, 162: "The *Consolation* is not a work that rejects philosophy . . . , but it is one that—in the tradition of Menippean satire—explores its limitations." Marenbon argues that Philosophy is no goddess; her head-in-the-clouds portrait at 1.1.2 is a satiric portrayal of her pretensions.

8. Fortin 2004, 302–3, notes that after the last poem, 5.m.5, Philosophy abandons her attempts to motivate the prisoner to contemplate the heavens and "no longer calls for him to follow her plan."

9. The question is not just whether Philosophy is in any sense consoling; Fortin 2004 advances various ways in which we could claim that the narrator is consoled. For example, it is Boethius the author who offers consolation to the reader in the form of encouragement: evil will not prosper, and acceptance of Providence does not mean that one should cease to pursue justice in this life and in this world (307). Rather, it is a question of generic expectations, not emotional satisfaction.

10. It is this lack of a definition that leads Tränkle 1984 to claim that the work is unfinished; Boethius is elsewhere in his career quite a good definer of the nature of persons, as in his theological works; cf. Chadwick 1981, 180–85, on the originality of the tractate *Against Eutyches and Nestorius* in this regard. It can be argued that this question of definition is treated in passing, or that it is interwoven in other arguments: Astell 1994 (cf. here chapter 2, n. 9) sees it in the presentations of the heroic nature in the three mythological poems in the concluding books (*Orpheus*, 3.m.12; *Odysseus*, 4.m.3; *Hercules*, 4.m.7); Marenbon 2003, 111, in the argument that

every truly happy person is a God; Dougherty 2004, focusing on Philosophy's arguments (claimed to be Aristotelian in origin) that human beings can lose their natures, argues that Philosophy is trying throughout to keep the prisoner from losing his human nature.

11. Shanzer 1984, 362–66; Shanzer makes the point that *Phaedo* is one of the major texts behind *Consolation*, not because Socrates claims that he has been composing songs in prison (60c–61b), but because of the imminence of death.

12. Marenbon 2003, 162–63, working primarily from the philosophical details of the dialogue, argues that the philosophical inconsistencies of *Consolation* are crucial to its interpretation; finding the argument in my *Ancient Menippean Satire* too extreme, he still admits that Philosophy's limitations are explored, and that *Consolation* deals silently with the gap between her demonstration of the highest good and her inability to offer the prisoner a means by which to grasp it. Colish 2005, 274, a review of Marenbon, objects that there is an obvious way for the prisoner to grasp this good, by means of a good death. The presence of death in *Consolation* is explored here in chapter 5.

13. Cf. Curley 1986, 263: "The question of Boethius' personal allegiance to Christianity is probably unanswerable and is certainly in bad taste—it is just not done among gentlefolk to force simplistic statements of belief or unbelief from one another. What we do know, what Boethius allows us to know is that, confronted with death, he chose to practice philosophy and poetry."

14. In his book on writers who lose their faith in Christianity, Barbour 1994 offers four characteristics of deconversion, all of which are relevant to what I would call Boethius's deconversion from pagan philosophy: "intellectual doubt, moral criticism, emotional suffering, and disaffiliation from a community" (2). Further, Barbour distinguishes deconversion from secularization; the latter is merely a fading away; the former implies self-consciousness. "As a literary narrative, a version of deconversion represents a series of events arranged as a plot and a decision that the writer tries to justify" (2). The autobiographers that Barbour examines "revise their fundamental beliefs about their identity as they change their convictions about God, truth, the moral good, and the best literary form for narrating their lives" (6). It is *Consolation*'s preoccupation with its literary form, its worrying "How best can I say this?", that is particularly interesting in this regard. Note that Jerome's famous account of his deconversion from pagan literature (*Letter* 22), whether or not it is absolutely honest, is also cast in terms of how best to speak and write Latin, with advice given to Eustochium in these regards.

15. Shanzer 1997, in a review of Pabst 1994: "Pabst is more than outspoken about Relihan's deconstructionist readings of certain philosophico-didactic Menippeae as parodies (Martianus Capella, Ennodius, and Boethius, for example). Fine. In the case of Martianus, how reasonable is it to posit that a 300-page encyclopedia of evidently respectable content aims to undermine its own intellectual validity?" Marenbon 2003, 161, is sensible: "Although it seems far-fetched that the whole work

is designed to demonstrate the failure of the encyclopaedic enterprise in which it is engaged, Martianus does appear to go beyond merely providing comic relief during a dull pedagogical grind: he takes his enterprise as an educator seriously, and yet—in true Menippean fashion—encourages us to see that it has its pretensions and absurdities."

16. Pabst 1994, 1.3–4, taking bitter exception to my doctoral dissertation, views my interpretations of individual Menippean satires as special pleadings designed to make them fit my theory, and thus valueless. Pabst is more concerned with the didactic aspects of late classical philosophical and allegorical prosimetra and their influence. But *prosimetrum* is not used by the Middle Ages to designate ancient works, and I insist that there are considerable differences between the ancient and the medieval works, which Pabst's umbrella title *Prosimetrum* obscures. I proceed more cautiously, taking Menippean satire as a subset of classical and late classical prosimetric texts sharing certain structural and thematic devices; the late classical Menippean satires can be understood within the classical parodic traditions.

17. Payne 1981, 77–79, neatly describes the action of *Consolation* as involving a gradual loss of freedom by Philosophy, as she in her citadel comes under attack by the prisoner; and a gradual gaining of freedom by the prisoner, who comes out from under her control. Our fundamental disagreement is that I see a completely different set of specific actions to define this shift, and a Christian motive behind it. Cherniss 1987, 30–34, being too convinced of the practical value of Boethius's text, offers a much too harsh evaluation of Payne's search for an ironic *Consolation*.

18. Lerer 1985, 236: "Finally, there is the silence of prayer also characterized in the *Confessions*. Here, Boethius rejects articulated language altogether in favor of a form of communication which cannot be transcribed and which supplants the authority figures of the human judges or of Lady Philosophy with that of God." Lerer concludes his book (236): "The prisoner's final silence stands in sharp contrast to his opening speechlessness, and his final refusal to transcribe prayer or poetry differentiates him from the creature of lethargy possessed by the difficulty of beginning the text."

19. Dronke 1994, 5–6 (truth-testing); 83–114 (chapter 4, "The Poetic and the Empirical 'I' "); 22 (interplay of minds); 46 (radiant strength). Dronke largely follows Bakhtin here; the real value of his book lies not in its reading of *Consolation* but in its presentation of later, medieval prosimetric works that operate on Menippean principles (even if they can't be called Menippean satires) and belong to the history of autobiography.

20. See Relihan 1995, a review of Martindale 1993.

21. Chronology is not much of a determinant: Dante and Milton come between Vergil and me, but I read Vergil long before I read Dante or Milton, and to claim that these latter made up the climate in which I first read Vergil is far from conclusive.

22. Cf. Stock 1996, III; quoted here in chapter 3, n. 46.

23. Martindale 1993, 106, concludes on a religious note, alluding to Dante: "In such relationships (sc. dialogues between readers who accept their historicity and accept texts in all their multiplicity) who knows what could be found? Maybe only an absence. But there is always the possibility that, for some reader, somewhere, one day, it will prove to be the Love that moves the sun and the other stars."

24. See here the first two pages of chapter 8 for the fortunes of "close reading" in the criticism of medieval literature and *Consolation*.

25. See Relihan 1993, 179–97.

26. A nice discussion of the origins and implications of this phrase is Synan 1992.

27. For medieval dialogue forms, see here chapter 3, n. 23.

28. Dronke 1994, 75–76, with further references. At the court of Henry III in the 1040s, and at the cathedral school of Canterbury in the 1050s, a full performance of *Consolation* was staged with spoken dialogue and all thirty-nine poems sung. Dronke points out that the closest medieval parallel to these performances (singing in the midst of a prose narration) are *Aucassin et Nicolette* and the old French prose *Tristan*, which has songs assigned to the various characters. Alan William's modern production of *Consolation*, performed by the Great Canadian Theatre Company under his direction, and billed as a "free wheeling musical adaptation of the sixth-century spiritual classic by Boethius," can be said to belong to an accidentally comic reception of the text, if the review in *The Ottawa Citizen* is to be believed (Feb. 1996): "The plot is that the daughter of the lead character runs away to Las Vegas and leaves Dad at the bus stop to be consoled by Philosophy. . . . After that, Philosophy and the downcast Ian trade concepts in a dialogue that bases itself on the Boethius original and that diverts itself with bits of sixth-century text set to Marc Desormeaux's original music—most of it pleasant, if not particularly memorable."

29. Dwyer 1976, 29–32, concluding: "One effect of such juxtapositions is to return the *Consolatio* some distance along the road to satire as it was anciently understood by those authors . . . who allowed cynicism and obscenity to mingle with higher things in their medleys of prose and verse."

30. See the chapter "Boethian Lovers" in Astell 1994, 127–58, for a discussion of Abelard, Dante, and Chaucer's *Troilus and Criseyde;* the latter is discussed extensively in Payne 1981, 86–158; see also Dronke 1994, 107–14, for Dante.

31. Blanchard 1995, 77–107, in the chapter "Rabelais and the Comic Encyclopedia in the Sixteenth Century," follows up on Frye's idea of "anatomy" as a crucial part of the Menippean tradition, but Boethius does not appear in his excellent account of the influences on Renaissance Menippean satire. Unfortunately, Blanchard does not know the *Elegantiores Praestantium Virorum Satyrae* (Leiden, 1655), an anthology of ancient and contemporary Menippean satires; this omission also mars the discussion of Kirk 1980, though the text is mentioned in Riikonen 1987, 15; cf. Relihan 1996, 283–84. Included in this volume are nine *Prolusiones* of Octavius

Ferrarius (cf. Relihan 1996, 289–91); the first of these, *De Nuptiis Philologiae*, shows the influence of *Consolation*. An old man comes and makes the narrator, like Boethius, rise from his bed; he takes him on the back of a winged horse to witness Philology's wedding, an obvious use of Martianus Capella; the ascent to heaven on a fantastic animal comes to Ferrarius more through Lucian's *Icaromenippus*, I think, than through the dung beetle of Aristophanes' *Peace*, Lucian's immediate model. For Erasmus's *Praise of Folly* as a Menippean text, cf. Haarberg 1998.

32. Melissa Green 1990 offers a respectful poem, spoken by Philosophy. It begins: "I dreamt my love was lost, uncomforted. / He lay alone in Pavia, eclipsed / by fortune, by the catastrophic tides / of men. . . ." She sadly relates her lover's complaints, and the poem ends: "'I've lifted up my eyes and cannot see— / Sophia, where's salvation? Where's my crown?' / He read the silence of the earth and sky, / and died, because he did not know I'd come."

33. Sutherland 1992, 40: "Rubashov's tentative affirmation of eternity enables him to begin breaking out of time's destructive cycle and his conversion in this respect parallels the development of Boethius as Lady Philosophy leads him along at the end of book one and throughout books two and three."

34. Davies 1990 takes "translation" as the primary concern of prison writing, meaning the creation by the prisoner of new forms of discourse and communication when others had been denied. This is plausible; the chapter "The Consolations of Philosophy" (38–58) comes close to making the point that there are at work in *Consolation* two competing forces: one directed outward, to the preservation of what the prisoner knows; one inward, toward a revelation of "the hidden self and ultimately the hidden god" (40).

35. Toole 1981, chapter 5, 145–46.

36. Alan, *The Complaint of Nature*, prose 1, ll. 280–82 (Häring, 819): "Quid uero in caligis camisiaque, in superioribus uestibus consepultis, picture sompniaret industria, nulla certitudinis auctoritate probaui" [I had no authoritative source for discovering for certain what the efforts of adornment had dreamed up for the tops of her boots and the undergarments that lay buried in her outer robes]. The narrator goes on awhile to imagine, in a mildly sexually suggestive way, trees, herbs, flowers, and buds. *Complaint* is probably not by Alan; see here William Heise's arguments, 1911./.

37. Curley 1986, 211–14, describes *Consolation* as "little more than a historical curiosity" in the modern world, partly because the twentieth century cannot take Boethius seriously as a philosopher, partly because it does not know how to read poetry as philosophy.

38. To a great extent, books about *Consolation* are books about the influence of *Consolation*; cf. Payne 1981; Astell 1994. To the great work of Courcelle 1967 on the influence of *Consolation* we may now add the annotated medieval bibliography of Kaylor 1992.

39. Cf. Wetherbee 1972, 74–82, for a synopsis and discussion of *Consolation* that emphasizes its "dark side" (82): "reason and intuition give way to faith" in Phi-

losophy's final expositions on the nature of the world and of divine wisdom, for the prisoner and the reader, who see the difficulty of rejecting this life and transcending it, cannot fully endorse Philosophy's exhortations. According to Wetherbee, this somber *Consolation*, leavened with the fantasies of Martianus Capella, creates the poetic worlds of the texts of Bernardus Silvestris and Alan of Lille. Weinbrot 2005 argues against the inclusion of *Consolation* as a Menippean satire, but does describe the function of Menippean satire, both in antiquity and in the early modern period, as a means of dealing with two conflicting world views.

40. Habinek 2005, 191, is worth quoting at length: "[M]imetic play, perhaps especially the play of satire, becomes central to Roman culture. In a sense, there is no Rome without an incorporated other. Rome comes to be over and against Etruscan, Greek, Sabine, and other cultures. Rome is always both an agrarian community looking to an idyllic and isolated past and a city among cities, a center of trade and commerce, interconnected with Latium, Etruria, Italy, and the whole of the Mediterranean basin. In the latter context, the construction of Roman identity becomes a project not just of shoring up the frail masculine ego of an embattled élite, but also a project of continuing incorporation of the new, the threatening, the alien. Roman identity must be made secure, but it is an identity that is itself constantly evolving. As preparation and substitution for the performance of Romanness, play thus becomes a constant necessity. It performs throughout the ages the work of establishing psychic and social boundaries between inside and outside. Satire is the textualized trace of this widespread and essential practice, one that enacts both exclusion and assimilation, that compensates for loss and insecurity by celebrating difference, but also by seeking, however recklessly, to destroy the obstacles to love."

Chapter Two.   Two Digressions and a Pointed Conclusion

1. At 1.6.17, Philosophy labels the prisoner's lack of knowledge of who he is as the greatest cause of his illness; Tränkle 1984 is the now classic statement of the thesis that the absence of an answer in *Consolation* to this crucial discussion proves that the work is unfinished.

2. See Relihan 1990c for a presentation of this argument; see also here chapter 5.

3. This analysis of the argument of *Consolation* follows closely the details of Marenbon 2003, chapters 6–7, 96–145.

4. See Dougherty 2004 for a discussion of the question of how human beings are said in *Consolation* to be able to lose their natures; the prisoner needs more to regain his nature than to understand it.

5. Olmstead 1989 discusses *Consolation* as an exercise in religious minimalism, an attempt to see how little one has actually to believe, in a world in which the sphere of social action and interaction is denied to the prisoner.

6. This approach is an improvement over that advanced in his commentary on Aristotle's *De interpretatione,* in which Boethius argues that God has foreknowledge both of events and of the fact that they occurred contingently. See here appendix 2, esp. n. 20.

7. For an analysis of this pivotal poem and how its Timaean cosmology transforms the treatment of the natural world in *Consolation,* see O'Daly 1991, 163–65.

8. 3.12.35: "nullis extrinsecus sumptis . . . probationibus" [proofs . . . not a one of them adopted from something external to it].

9. O'Daly 1991, 188–207, contrasts the failure of Orpheus's ascent in 3.m.12 to Philosophy's account of a successful ascent to heaven in 4.m.1: only after one has properly scaled heaven can one look down and see that the tyrants are really the exiles. Astell 1994, 41–69, discusses this poem in connection with the other two mythological poems (4.m.3, on Ulysses and Circe; 4.m.7, on the homecomings of Agamemnon, Ulysses, and Hercules) as providing the key to the definition of a human being that *Consolation* requires: the first shows the mortal, the second the rational, and the third the immortal part. For Astell's interpretation of *Consolation* as an epic, whose story is the hero's discovery of his true nature, see here chapter 6.

10. "perfectly appointed house": *disposit issima domo.* The adjective is related to the verb *dispono,* "to arrange"; this is the key word for describing the order imposed on the world by God, appearing first and frequently in the key section 3.12 (3.12.7, 12, 14, 17, 22; cf. also 4.6.9, 4.6.21). It reappears as the last word of the introduction to book 5 (5.1.19), and then as the last word of the next prose section as well (5.2.11). The obsession with asserting the order of the world is the hub of the discussion in the final books.

11. To 4.1.9 ("ut perturbatione depulsa *sospes in patriam* meo ductu, mea semita, meis etiam uehiculis *reuertaris,*" translated above). Compare 3.12.9: "Cum haec, inquit, ita sentias, paruam mihi restare operam puto ut felicitatis compos *patriam sospes reuisas*" [Then she said: Since such is your understanding, I think that I have only a little work remaining so that you can return to your fatherland fully recuperated, the master of your happiness].

12. Consider the conclusion of the central poem, 3.m.9, *O qui perpetua,* in which Philosophy describes the vision of God in these terms: "their (pii, 'those who are holy') goal is to see you; / You are their source, their conveyance, their leader, their path, and their haven" [te cernere finis, / principium, uector, dux, semita, terminus idem (3.m.9.27–28)]. If we were thus to equate Philosophy as divine wisdom with God, then we could claim with Varvis 1986 that in that equation is a Christian presence. But I think that Philosophy and God are to be kept separate.

13. 4.6.7: "Tunc uelut ab alio orsa principio ita disseruit." Note that the fifth prose section consists of the exile's request for information on this new topic, so that the real beginning of the substantial part of the second half of the book falls here.

14. 4.7.22: "In uestra enim situm manu qualem uobis fortunam formare malitis; omnis enim quae uidetur aspera, nisi aut exercet aut corrigit, punit." Note that at

the end of book 5 Philosophy similarly addresses a moral exhortation to a plurality, leaving the reader to puzzle out its unfortunate implications for the prisoner.

15. The poem ends: "Ite nunc, fortes, ubi celsa magni / ducit exempli uia. Cur inertes / terga nudatis? Superata tellus / sidera donat" (4.m.7.32–35) [Forward, strong men all, where this great example, / Where this high road leads! Shoulder now your burden, / Now without delay, for the earth, once conquered, / Gives you the fixed stars]. The specific reference is to the ascent of Hercules to heaven along the Milky Way.

16. 1.5.2: "sed quam id longinquum esset exsilium, nisi tua prodidisset oratio, nesciebam."

17. Note that, in Philosophy's own abbreviated account of the history of philosophy at 1.3.4–10, it is a quick jump from Socrates (the paradigmatic philosopher) and Plato to the Stoics and Epicureans; Philosophy has an interest here only in praising martyrs and reviling those schismatics who have destroyed the unity of philosophy. Aristotle finds no place on either account; to the extent that we keep Philosopy's interests in mind, we judge Aristotle's appearance in book 5 to be an unexpected thing, despite the general presence of Aristotelian thought in *Consolation*.

18. "The old philosophers" are the pre-Socratics, as the following sentence tries to make clear.

19. Philosophy is actually confused in her Aristotelian reference; see Sharples 1991 ad loc. for an account of the debate about possible sources of the confusion. Her reference is to *Physics* 2.4–5, 195b31–197a36, a discussion of chance and spontaneity, but the actual example of the discovery of the buried gold is from *Metaphysics* 5 (Δ), 30, 1025a16–19. This is a standard example, found often in many commentaries and contexts; it is brought into Boethius's *Second Commentary* at 3.9, 194.8 ff. Meiser.

20. 2.m.5.27–30:

Woe is hím! Whó wás that invéntor
Who uneárthed thése treácherous treásures,
Thé deád weight of góld covered óver,
Thé jéwels that lónged to lie hídden?

For the thematic implications of the passage for the interpretation of *Consolation* as a whole, see here chapter 9, 133–35.

21. "Est igitur summum, inquit, bonum quod regit cuncta fortiter suauiterque disponit."

22. "Attingit ergo a fine usque ad finem fortiter et disponit omnia suauiter." The Advent Antiphon *O Sapientia,* modeled on this passage, includes words a little closer to Boethius's text: *fortiter suauiterque disponens omnia.* For a discussion see Gruber 1978 ad loc.

23. 3.12.23: "Quam, inquam, me non modo ea quae conclusa est summa rationum, uerum multo magis haec ipsa quibus uteris uerba delectant, ut tandem aliquando stultitiam magna lacerantem sui pudeat!" Haarberg 1998 (95–96) takes this

as an instance of personification, Folly playing a minor role in the conflict of Philosophy and Fortune, seen as parallel to Prodicus's contention of Virtue and Vice. He translates, "At last Folly whose profession it is to tear up the great truths is ashamed." For the interesting implications of the reading *latrantem* "barking" for *lacerantem* "clawing at," see here chapter 3, n. 9. But tearing figures largely in *Consolation:* Philosophy, wearing robes torn by schismatic philosophers, expresses the hope at the beginning of book 4 that the conclusions that she and the prisoner previously reached have not been torn apart (4.1.7; translated above). She longs for unity; primarily, the unity of herself and the exile.

24. Chadwick 1981, 237–38.

25. "Sed uisne rationes ipsas inuicem collidamus? Forsitan ex huius modi conflictatione pulchra quaedam ueritatis scintilla dissiliat. — Tuo, inquam, arbitratu" ["But do you want us to smash the arguments themselves into each other? Perhaps from a striking of this sort some beautiful spark of truth may fly out." "As you think best," I said]. We think that Philosophy means that she will push her own arguments so far as to create a paradox, but for the possibility that the *rationes* that collide will prove ultimately to be philosophy and revelation, see here chapter 6, 82–83.

26. Reading *Quisue* for *Quis* at line 18; see the commentary of Sharples 1991 ad loc.

27. The influence of the Alexandrian Neoplatonist Hierocles and his *On Providence* has been noted (cf. Photius, codex 251, 465a, said to be from the tenth chapter of the third book; translation in Wilson 1994, 225–28). Hierocles defends the same complex of ideas as *Consolation* presents at its conclusion: free will, Providence, prayer, and the value of the system of law, reward, and punishment.

28. Payne 1981, 17; accepted largely by Curley 1986, 215–16.

29. Sharples 1991, 215, commenting on 5.1.19.

30. 5.6.25: "Hic si dicas quod euenturum deus uidet id non euenire non posse, quod autem non potest non euenire id ex necessitate contingere, meque ad hoc nomen necessitatis adstringas, fatebor rem solidissimae ueritatis, sed cui uix aliquis nisi diuini speculator acceserit" [Now if you should say at this point that what God sees will happen cannot *not* happen, and that what cannot not happen is contingent by necessity, and if you bind me tight to this word 'necessity,' then I will admit that it is indeed a thing of the most steadfast truth, but one that scarcely anyone but a contemplator of the divine has approached].

31. Even Theiler 1966, 324–25, generally discussing the similarities that Christian and Neoplatonic language share in speaking of the approach to God, and therefore generally denying the relevance of the question of whether *Consolation* is Christian or anti-Christian, is impressed by the use of the probably Christian terms *humilitas* and *gratia* at 5.3.34 and the phrase *inaccessa lux* ("the inaccessible light"), which may well reflect 1 Timothy 6.16. Further, see here chapter 6, n. 29.

32. *stabili . . . gradu* can be a military term, a place on which you can "stand your ground"; thus my published translation "Soldiers who fell never had stable ground on which to stand." But *gradus* is a step and the proper term for a rung in a ladder;

the iconography of Philosophy's dress suggests my translation here, and much of *Consolation* is about rising up to the heights.

33. We can see similar concerns in Boethius's *Second Commentary on On Interpretation* 224.19–26: "So it happens that the intention of sinners is taken into account rather than the outcome, and the intention is punished, not the completion, because our will at least is free, but the sequence of events leading to the completion is at times held in check. For if all things were to happen either by chance or by necessity, praise would not be appropriate for those who do well, nor would punishment be appropriate for those who fail, nor would any laws be just which would fix rewards for the good or punishments for the bad." See further here in appendix 2, 144.

Chapter Three.   Universality and Particularity

1. Lerer 1985, 14–93, in a discussion of *Consolation* and a number of works that have influenced it: Cicero's *Tusculan Disputations*, Augustine's *Soliloquies*, Fulgentius's *Allegorical Content of Vergil*.

2. "Haecine est bibliotheca, quam certissimam tibi sedem nostris in laribus ipsa delegeras, in qua mecum saepe residens de humanarum diuinarumque rerum scientia disserebas?"

3. Cf. Relihan 1993, 153–58 (Fulgentius), 13–16 (Martianus Capella, Lucian).

4. Reiss 1981 claims that the historical content of *Consolation* is of purely allegorical value and that there is no proof that it is Boethius's final work or that it was written with death impending. Basilius, Opilio, and Gaudens (1.4.16–17), the *delatores* named in the prisoner's apology, are said to represent by etymology power (Greek, βασιλεία), wealth (*ops*), and physical delight (*gaudium*). The objections to this reasoning in Shanzer 1984 are powerful, and the parallels to *Phaedo* and *Crito* do assure us that *Consolation* is to be read as a final work. However, as with the Bible, so also here: historical matter is not present because it is true, but because that truth makes a further point; here, about the prisoner's distracted frame of mind. We must read *Consolation* from the inside, not the outside.

5. Frye 1957, 311–12, speaking of "its creative element of exhaustive erudition," assigns *Consolation* to the genre of Menippean satire, which he prefers to rename "anatomy," after Burton: the "pervading tone of contemplative irony" is a nice appreciation of the value of the multifarious learning to be found within *Consolation*.

6. Note the introduction to *De ordine*, in which the Liberal Arts erect a platform from which one leaps into the divine world; it is clear from the *Tractates* that Boethius limited pagan philosophy's contribution to Christian theology largely to linguistic matters and the question of precision in definition. Cf. Chadwick 1981, 250–51, commenting on the similarites and differences between Boethius and Augustine: "Boethius' vision of the cosmos is of a single great whole kept from disin-

tegration by the goodness and power of providence, and one might expect him to affirm an optimistic view of the concord of faith and reason. In actuality there is more more of this kind of optimism in Augustine than in Boethius."

7. See Alfonsi 1955, and the eloquent expositions of Curley 1986 and 1987.

8. Cf. 1.5.2 (translated here in chapter 2, p. 25 and n. 16) and 1.5.3: "Sed tu quam procul a patria non quidem pulsus es sed aberrasti ac, si te pulsum existimari mauis, te potius ipse pepulisti; nam id quidem de te numquam cuiquam fas fuisset" [How great the distance is! Yet you have not been driven out of your fatherland; no, you have wandered away on your own or, if you prefer to think of yourself as driven out, it is rather you yourself who have done the driving—for such a power over you could never have been granted to anyone else].

9. 1.5.1: "Haec ubi continuato dolore delatravi" [When I was through barking all this out in my protracted lamentation]. The compound verb *delatro* is attested only once elsewhere. The Cynic implications of this dog speech become obvious when we connect the imagery of the prisoner's cell to the tomb, and Philosophy herself to Death, come to take the prisoner away home (see here chapter 4). Menippus was also thought of as a dog in the land of the dead; see Relihan 1990b. The point is this: we would not expect a Cynic dog to be housebroken by Philosophy, but to maintain an independence. At 3.12.23, some read *latrantem* "barking" for *lacerantem* "clawing at" when the narrator finally feels ashamed of the stupidity that "claws at great things"; see here chapter 2, p. 28 and n. 23.

10. 1.2.6: "Sui paulisper oblitus est. Recordabitur facile, si quidem nos ante cognouerit; quod ut possit, paulisper lumina eius mortalium rerum nube caligantia tergamus" [He has forgotten himself for a time, but he'll remember easily enough, since he knew us once before. And so that he can remember, let us just wipe his eyes for a time, eyes clouded with the cataracts of the human world]. Philosophy speaks in the plural, but is this only to refer to herself and her Muses (cf. 1.1.11)? Given the equivalence of the prisoner and Philosophy that is implied here (see here chapter 4), one almost hears the language of God creating Adam in his own image (Genesis 1.26).

11. So I would oppose Cherniss 1987, 42, who speaks of the practical value of *Consolation* this way: "Boethius means the *Consolation* to be read as a literal account of the process by which a particular human being, about whom specific biographical details are supplied, overcame his existential despair and learned to understand and accept his condition through the agency of philosophy." It is possible to learn through one's experience with Philosophy the importance of something that Philosophy does not feel competent to teach.

12. Cf. 1.3.13–14. "Qui si quando contra nos aciem struens ualentior incubuerit, nostra quidem dux copias suas in arcem contrahit, illi uero circa diripiendas inutiles sarcinulas occupantur. At nos desuper irridemus uilissima rerum quaeque rapientes securi totius furiosi tumultus eoque uallo muniti quo grassanti stultitiae aspirare fas non sit" [And if this army should ever array itself against us and attack

us with all its might, our leader withdraws all her forces into her own citadel, leaving the others to occupy themselves with the plundering of useless baggage. 14. But we laugh at them from on high as they snatch at each and every worthless thing— we are safe from all their maddened riot, protected by a wall that marauding stupidity is forbidden to assault]. This feminine general is probably Philosophy herself; her Olympian laughter is a reflex of the Cynic *catascopia*, the view of the world from an impossible height; see Relihan 1993, index s.v. "*catascopia*," esp. 114–16.

13. We speak too easily of *Consolation* as taking place in prison; the author may have written the book in prison, but his images of imprisonment are quite different. When Philosophy comes to visit him, he says, "to this, the solitude of our exile" (1.3.3: in has exsilii nostri solitudines). He is silently awaiting execution, not trial: "But now! At a remove of nearly five hundred miles, without voice and without defense, I am condemned to death and confiscation because of my overzealous concern for the Senate. Would that no one could be convicted of such a crime ever again, Senators—you have earned it!" (1.4.36: nunc quingentis fere passuum milibus procul muti atque indefensi ob studium propensius in senatum morti proscriptionique damnamur. O meritos de simili crimine neminem posse convinci!); he is certainly not in his library (1.4.3). The point is not so much that he is in prison as that he is alone with Philosophy. It is strange to me that the recent volumes devoted to the study of private life in antiquity have overlooked the privacy afforded by prison.

14. Olmstead 1989 offers a nice interpretation of *Consolation* as a religious text in which Philosophy, using "the most sparing of resources," reconciles the prisoner "to a universe in circumstances where he is not able to participate in community or in dialogue with friends. His sphere of action is gone; his chance to affect the course of the world is gone" (35).

15. After his impassioned poem (5.m.3, discussed here in part in chapter 2, 29–30) the prisoner has nothing to say; the objection *minime* which appears twice in the last prose section (5.6.19, 5.6.40) is certainly spoken by Philosophy herself (cf. Lerer 1985, 229–30); the objections assigned to the prisoner at 5.4.8 and 5.4.16 could similarly be put in Philosophy's mouth. Curley would claim that by the end of the book the two speak the same language, and that the dialogue, patterned so as to represent the processes of human thought, dramatizes the emergence of order (Curley 1986, 260–61).

16. Cf. Plato, *Phaedo* 81a: μελέτη θανάτου. The body is itself a tomb, as the Pythagoreans and Plato would have it: σῶμα/σῆμα. Some of the implications of the death imagery in the appearance of Philosophy to the prisoner in book 1 are worked out in Relihan 1990c, 192–94.

17. Plotinus VI 9 (9) 11, the last words of the *Enneads*. Cf. Corrigan 1996 for an attempt to get around the narcissistic implications of this sort of mysticism; Corrigan argues that μόνος (alone) in the Greek phrase has to do with "being truly what one is," separated from dross and accretions in the material world, and is not to be taken as an expression of isolationism. See also Payne 1981, 77–80, for themes

in *Consolation* of the freedom to be gained from the rejection of Philosophy's abstractions and constructs.

18. The prisoner was not able to get to heaven on his own, as we learn in book 1; cf. 1.m.1.21–22, with the image of the fall from the ladder ("Qui cecidit, stabili non erat ille gradu; see here chapter 2, p. 32 and n. 32) and 1.m.2.6–7, with its imagery of failed flight ("Hic quondam caelo liber aperto / suetus in aetherios ire meatus" [Tíme was when hé would ascénd to heáven unboúnded, / Freé to proceéd in the tráck of stárs in their coúrses]). This latter suggestion of Daedalus and Icarus (or of Phaethon) is as ominous here as it is in the title of Lucian's *Icaromenippus*.

19. See Brown 1988, 404–8, for Augustine's analysis of the defects of the human will (detected in the frequent incompatibility of will and sexual desire) that are the true consequence of Adam's fall. Brown quotes *Confessions* 10.30.41–42 on the subject of erotic dreams; we may compare a portion of this passage to the prisoner's experience on his bed with the pagan Muses in book 1 (*Confessions* 10.30.41): "et tantum ualet imaginis illius inlusio in anima mea in carne mea, ut dormienti falsa uisa persuadeant quod uigilanti uera non possunt. numquid tunc ego non sum, domine deus meus? et tamen tantum interest inter me ipsum et me ipsum intra momentum, quo hinc ad soporem transeo uel huc inde transeo!" [And in my soul, in my body, so great is the deception of that image that visions that cannot impress themselves upon me when real, when I am awake, can impress themselves upon me when false, when I am asleep. But, O Lord my God, surely it was not the case that I was not myself then? And yet there is so great a gap between myself and myself within the split second when I pass from here to sleep, or when I pass from there back here again!].

20. When the prisoner delivers an inadequate definition of the word *homo* at 1.6.15 as "a rational and mortal animal" and says that he knows himself to be this much and no more, Philosophy claims that he does not know himself. To Philosophy, the exile is *homo*; but the prisoner may not wish to have his self-definition so limited.

21. 1.m.5.46–48:

Ó hélmsman, make cálm the swíft-running seá swell,
Máke stáble the eárth in the sáme cóncórd
Wíth which you pílot the límitless heávens.

2.m.8.22–30:

Hé [Love] hólds nátions togéther toó
Wíth invíolate treáties boúnd;
Hé joíns márriage's sácred rítes
Ín immáculate bónds of lóve;
Fór thé lóyal and faíthful friénds
Hé láys dówn what is ríght and wróng.
Ó hów háppy the mórtal ráce,
Wére Lóve kíng over áll your heárts,
Lóve thát heáven accépts as kíng!

It is not hard to see Boethius the husband and father, Boethius the honest politician and man of integrity, behind Philosophy's words; here, the prisoner would not
be Everyman but the ideal that other mortals could not attain.

22. Kennedy 1980, 178, takes the lack of address to Theoderic as further evidence
of a decline in the status of civic rhetoric in late antiquity: rhetoric cannot sway
hearts or events, and Boethius "turns away from speech to pursue the eternal life."
The panegyric of Theoderic that Boethius delivered in 522 on the occasion of the
installation of his two sons as consuls in Rome does not survive; cf. Chadwick
1981, 46.

23. There is no doubt that *Consolation* is a model for the medieval teacher-
student dialogue, styled in German Unterweisungsgespräch (cf. von Moos 1971–72,
C 186, T 1044 ff.); but such Hermetic works as *Poimandres* typically have the student
being told to write down what has been learned for the benefit of others; cf. Fowden
1993, 156–7. Cherniss 1987, 11–12, 28, 35, details some of the parallels between *Poimandres* and *Consolation*.

24. Cf. Lewis 1964, 90, commenting on Gibbon's objections to the inadequacy
of *Consolation* as a consoling work (Gibbon's text is quoted here at the beginning
of chapter 4): "But no one ever said it would have subdued Gibbon's [heart]. It
sounds as if it had done something for Boethius."

25. For such implications in the title of *Consolation* itself, see here chapter 4,
52.

26. The author was in fact canonized as St. Severinus, a witness to orthodoxy
against the Arians; see Gruber 1978, p. 13 and n. 95, for references.

27. Gruber 1978, 414–15, comments on the concluding sentences of *Consolation*
and their call to ethical conduct as an allusion to Boethius's apology at 1.4 and his
political determination to do right regardless of cost.

28. See O'Donnell 1993, in a review of Moorhead 1992: "I do not see that Moorhead asks the question, or that anyone has seriously asked the question, just *who*
Boethius and his friends would have liked to see on the Italian imperial throne.
But perhaps to ask this question in this context as I have just done is to make explicit the suspicion to which Moorhead gives, brilliantly or unwittingly I cannot
tell, rise: did no one then dream of Boethius *augustus*? If not Boethius, who? If
Symmachus, then Boethius as son-in-law and heir is scarcely less important. It is
ironic that in our great reverence for the cloistered intellectual, we may have
blinded ourselves to his true role in history."

29. The introduction of Mitchell 1992 speaks of a Job who, like the prisoner,
must struggle to find his voice, and who then loses it in the end, in awe-struck submission; and, like Job, the prisoner will dare to say what is true, even if orthodoxy
will not allow it (see xvi–xvii, on God as the author of evil; cf. the prisoner in
book 5, on the necessity imposed on human actions by divine foreknowledge). Further on Job, see here chapter 4, p. 58 and n. 47; chapter 6, 81.

30. Mohrmann 1976 points out that the terms *commercium, deprecari, supplicandi
ratione, praesidium, mereor,* and *porrigere* (cf. 5.3.34 and 5.6.47–48) can be found in the

collects of early Latin sacramentaries. Chadwick 1981, 251, is not very impressed by the parallels.

31. Reitz 1990.

32. Quacquarelli 1989, 485–87. Within a Christian ambit for these symbolic letters, he draws attention to Cassian's fourteenth *Conference*, which speaks of the progress of spiritual knowledge from the practical (moral correction) to the theoretical (contemplation of the divine). Quacquarelli considers this a close parallel to the framework of *Consolation*. See also Varvis 1986, who argues that Christianity is to be seen in the divinity of Philosophy herself: Philosophy is from God, and order is brought to the prisoner's mind by an invitation to participate in the divine order.

33. Augustine, *Enarrationes in Psalmos* 2.19; cf. Magee 1988.

34. Howlett 1995, 49–54, analyzes the central poem of *Consolation, O qui perpetua* (3.m.9), as an example of this. The author notifies me that a similar analysis of *O stelliferi conditor orbis* (1.m.5), taken as an adaptation of Psalm 18 (*Caeli enarrant gloriam dei*) is forthcoming in *Pillars of Wisdom: Irishmen, Englishmen, Liberal Arts* (Dublin: Four Courts), in a chapter entitled "The Bible and Boethius."

35. Though Quacquarelli 1989 takes these final words seriously as a Christian and religious exhortation to humility and to virtuous action in this world, a practical application of Christian ethics to complement the theoretical *Theological Tractates.*

36. Modern scholarship applies the label "apocryphal", but Boethius could only have known the Vulgate Esther without entertaining any doubts about its authority or applicability. Similarly, the crucial Book of Wisdom, quoted by Philosophy herself at 3.12.22 (see here chapter 2, p. 28 and nn. 21, 22), would not have raised questions about its biblical authority.

37. "Rex magnus Artaxerxes ab India usque Aethiopiam centum viginti septem provinciarum ducibus ac principibus, qui nostrae iussioni oboediunt, salutem dicit. 2. Multi bonitate principum et honore, qui in eos collatus est, abusi sunt in superbiam; 3. et non solum subiectos regibus nituntur opprimere, sed datam sibi gloriam non ferentes in ipsos qui dederunt moliuntur insidias. 4. Nec contenti sunt gratias non agere beneficiis et humanitatis in se iura violare, sed Dei quoque cuncta cernentis arbitrantur se posse fugere sententiam. 5. Et in tantum vesaniae proruperunt, ut eos, qui credita sibi officia diligenter observant et ita cuncta agunt ut omnium laude digni sint, mendaciorum cuniculis conentur subvertere, 6. dum aures principum simplices et ex sua natura alios aestimantes callida fraude decipiunt. 7. Quae res et ex veteribus probatur historiis et ex his quae geruntur cotidie, quomodo malis quorundam suggestionibus regum studia depraventur. 8. Unde providendum est paci omnium provinciarum."

38. For a good, if speculative, account of Boethius's downfall, see Barnish 1990, 28–32.

39. A good point made by Walsh 1999, xviii.

40. She has one universalizing detail, however; her talk of hopes and prayers (*spes, preces*) corresponds to the prisoner's fear of the loss of the ability to hope and to avoid things by means of prayer (5.3.34: *commercium . . . sperandi ac deprecandi*). The prisoner wants to pray for deliverance, possibly the avoidance of the death sentence; Philosophy just tells him to pray.

41. Unless of course the prisoner writes *Consolation* as a moral act.

42. Best argued by Tränkle 1984; but the work of Reitz 1990 makes it clear that all of book 5 is in language and style inconsistent with the preceding books, while the symmetrical arrangement of the poems throughout *Consolation*, shown by the balancing of the various meters (see the chart of correspondences in Gruber 1978 between pages 19 and 20), demonstrates that book 5 is highly structured. Book 5 was planned to be different.

43. Brown 1967, 427–33, the eloquent last chapter.

44. Possidius, *Life of St. Augustine*, 31.1–3; Brown 1967, 432; see also O'Donnell 1996, his review of Stock 1996, *Augustine the Reader*. His privacy was interrupted only by those who brought him meals and by the occasional visit of a doctor. When Philosophy the doctor visits Boethius, it is to make him abandon his tearful writing, rather than to prolong a tearful reading.

45. Reichenberger 1954 is still a useful description of the various generic presences in Boethius; but I do not limit what is Menippean about the text to this notion of the mixture of genres.

46. Stock 1996, 23–121, examines the role of reading in *Confessions* 1–9 and Augustine's account of his progress in self-awareness and conversion. Boethius does not attempt Augustine's intellectual complexities in *Consolation*'s attempt at confession and autobiography. Cf. Stock, 111: "Our understanding of our lives is inseparable from the stories by which we represent our thoughts in words. Every understanding, therefore, is a reading of ourselves, every genuine insight, a rereading, until, progressing upwards by revisions, we have inwardly in view the essential source of knowledge, which is God."

47. Dronke 1994 shows the way by demonstrating the influence of *Consolation* on medieval prosimetric autobiographical texts; see the review by Relihan 2005.

48. The phrase "hidden author" I borrow from the title of Conte 1996; *Consolation* and *Satyricon* have much in common; see here chapter 5, 60–61. As to autobiography, Boethius is not mentioned in Stock 1996; nor in Humphries 1997, who is worth quoting at length (136): "Writing represents a practical strategy; this is evident in both Marcus' *Meditations* and Augustine's *Confessions*, where the distinction resides not in the act of writing itself but in what is written. Marcus collects and inscribes codes of behavior in order to take care of the self in everyday life. The Delphic injunction, 'know thyself' (γνῶθι σεαυτόν), is of little concern for the Stoic philosopher who, like the Gnostic, already knows the self. This writing practice becomes a form of *paideia* designed for self-cultivation, not self-disclosure. For Augustine, on the other hand, the self remains hidden, dispersed in the infinite depths of the memory. One must search, collect, and organize these disparate bits

of memory in order to render the self present unto itself. Furthermore, this activity is no longer a private matter; writing becomes *publicatio sui*, a confessional strategy by which the self draws itself out of amnestic solitude and lays itself bare to public gaze."

49. Curley (1986, 242–43) claims that by the end of the dialogue the prisoner has reached the point at which he may enter Philosophy's homeland; and that the author does not attempt to represent this world of true being out of a Platonic respect for the limits of language and thought. I have argued that it is common for Menippean satires in general not to seek to represent the other worlds that the authors would point to as authoritative, for the genre is uncomfortable with the dramatization of absolute truths. Julian's Neoplatonic heaven is not in evidence in his *Caesars;* Martianus Capella's Olympus is not the place where the Ineffable Father resides. Cf. Relihan 1993, 89 (Seneca); 126 (Julian); 143 and 148 (Martianus Capella).

Chapter Four.   *Consolation* and the Genre of Consolation

1. *The Decline and Fall of the Roman Empire*, chapter 39.

2. Socrates says at the beginning of *Crito* (44a–b) that he learned of his imminent death from a woman who appeared to him in a dream. Crito tells him that he had been letting Socrates sleep; Socrates then assigns the vision to this recent sleep, so that the dialogue begins in effect with a sleeping Socrates. The prologue to Fulgentius's *Mythologies* includes a poem that the narrator seems to have composed in his sleep (13.6 ff; translation in Relihan 1993, 209); the anonymous prologue to Alan's *Complaint* picks up on this as well and has the narrator of *Complaint* fall asleep before the work starts; see Hudry 1989.

3. Surely Gibbon would not have us think of the Pythagorean *Golden Verses*, the medieval *Legenda Aurea*, or the *Golden Book* of the Venetian Nobility. The *Golden Book* of the shadowy Greek Themistagoras, surviving in three fragments on etymological speculations, is out of the question; so is the equally shadowy *Liber Aureus de contemptu mundi*, attributed to Isidore, which, if it existed at all, was a digest of Isidore's *Synonyma*, about which more later (see here chapter 7, 107–10).

4. *Academica* 2.44.135: "Legimus omnes Crantoris ueteris Academici de luctu: est enim non magnus uerum aureolus et, ut Tuberoni Panaetius praecipit, ad uerbum ediscendus libellus" [We all read *On Grief,* by Crantor of the Old Academy; it is not a big book but a golden one; and as Panaetius says to Tubero, it is a book to be learned by heart]. Panaetius and his disciple Tubero appear again in Cicero, *De finibus* 4.9.23; cf. van Straaten 1946, fr. 137 and fr. 138. Chadwick 1981, xv, and Synan 1992, 477, miss the literal meaning of the phrase. Kassel 1958, 101–3, discusses the use of Servius Sulpicius's famous consolatory letter to Cicero (*Ad familiares* 4.5) in the third chapter of the fifth book of Sterne's *Tristram Shandy* (1759–67), appearing some twenty years prior to Gibbon.

5. Kassel 1965 makes only the brief statement that Boethius's *Consolation* had great medieval influence.

6. Nor are Boethius and his *Consolation* mentioned in Favez 1970. Buresch 1886 speaks of Boethius as one above the topic of death; Johann 1968 seems to mention him not at all; Marenbon 2003, 97–98, treats consolation only as a well-known type of philosophical discourse.

7. Von Moos 1971, 1.32, C 35. Courcelle's work on the influence of *Consolation* has little to do with von Moos's late medieval genre, "weil die *Consolatio Philoso-phiae* keine Tröstung über den Tod darstellt und ihre Abhängigkeit von der para-mythetischen Gattung überhaupt sehr schwach ist (d. h. sich allgemein auf den aus Cicero und Seneca bekannten Grundgedanken der *consolatio sui* beschränkt)." The Middle Ages knew it and used it for its consolatory content; Dante found con-solation after Beatrice's death in it: but it is mostly a matter of individual motifs and the use of 1.m.1 and 2.m.7 on Death the Leveler. Von Moos 1971–72 notes an im-portant exception (C 1095–1136): a description of an *imitatio boethiana* by Laurentius Dunelmensis (Lorenz von Durham), *Consolatio de morte amici* (ca. 1141); von Moos speaks of Lorenz as *rara auis in terra nostra*.

8. Scourfield 1993, *Consoling Heliodorus*, 16 n. 68. Scourfield 1996 finds room for *Consolation* in his *Oxford Classical Dictionary* entry on the genre; Favez 1970 did not. The most current complete study of classical and Christian consolation is Gregg 1975; see pp. 1–50 for an overview of the development of the genre.

9. Shanzer 1984, 362–66.

10. For example, Seneca's *Consolatio ad Polybium* is not so much on the death of Polybius's brother as it is an attempt by an exiled Seneca to find an intercessor be-fore the emperor (Gregg 1975, 41–42).

11. Cf. Relihan 1993, 12–13, on the paradox inherent in Varro's name of "Me-nippean satires" or "Cynic satires." For the proper form and implication of Petro-nius's title, see Branham and Kinney 1996, xxii–xxiv. Seneca's *Apocolocyntosis* and Lucian's *Icaromenippus* and *Necyomantia* also need to be kept in mind.

12. Marenbon 2003, 162, would seem to reject this approach: "The *Consolation* is not a work that rejects philosophy (as if its title had to be pronounced with ironic emphasis: 'that's the *consolation* you gain from *philosophy*!'), but it is one that—in the tradition of Menippean satire—explores its limitations."

13. Favez 1970 refers to Seneca, *Epistles* 63 and 81, on ingratitude. Juvenal's *Thir-teenth Satire* may be thought of as a hard-edged consolation against financial loss.

14. Cf. Gruber 1978, 19–24, and chart between p. 16 and p. 17 for a demonstration that the poems are carefully arranged, framing both by symmetry of content and meter this central poem.

15. Courcelle 1948, 285, sees this description of the structure of *Consolation* as a representation of the life of the soul. Curley's description of it as a representation of the process of thought is an appropriate complement (Curley 1986, 1987).

16. Klingner 1921, 33–34; Payne 1981, 69, speaks of Philosophy's argument in the last four books of *Consolation* as falling into four parts, each with distinctive tone

and manner of argument: Cynic (book 2-book 3, prose 9); Platonic (book 3, meter 9-book 4, prose 5); Aristotelian (book 4, prose 6-book 5, meter 1); and Augustinian (book 5, prose 2, to end). See also McMahon 2006, 214–26, for a four-fold division based on cognition: sensation, imagination, reason, understanding.

17. Alfonsi 1942–43; the interpretation is pursued further in Alfonsi 1955. These two articles together form one of the most valuable modern interpretations of *Consolation*.

18. Klingner 1921, 1–3 (book 1); 22–24 (book 2); 83–84 (book 3); 84–85 (book 4); 93–95 (book 5).

19. Seneca affords some nice examples: cf. the consolatory letter *Ad Marciam*; the *De providentia*; and particularly *Epistle* 99, in which Seneca asserts his own authority as consoler by telling Lucilius to read the appended letter that Seneca himself once wrote to one Marullus on the death of the latter's son. Another example: near its conclusion, pseudo-Plutarch, *Ad Apollonium* (120e–121e), quotes as authoritative Plato, *Gorgias* 523a–524b, the myth concerning Zeus's appointment of the judges Minos, Aeacus, and Rhadamanthys, and the fate of the good on the Isles of the Blest.

20. The obvious parallel in *Consolation* is the narrator's statement at 4.6.7 that Philosophy now begins to speak as if from another starting point (see here chapter 2, 20; p. 24 and n. 13. If Boethius knew the *Axiochus*, he would have found the transition from Socrates as consoler to Philosophy a very easy one to make, for Boethius makes Philosophy herself speak of Socrates as the true philosopher of her own unitary self, before sectarians divided her (1.3.6); here she says that Socrates earned the victory of undeserved death as she stood by his side (*Socrates iniustae uictoriam mortis me astante promeruit*); for the Christian tone of this phrase, see Gruber 1978 ad loc., with reference to 1 John 5.4 and Apocalypse 17.14.

21. In Cohoon's introduction to his Loeb text and translation of this discourse (2:395–98) he catalogues suggested referents for these two characters: Antisthenes or Dio himself for the morose man; Cleanthes for the peasant, unless this character be a fiction altogether.

22. The trustworthiness of the tradition is in doubt, though it makes little difference here whether Antiphon the Sophist is the referent of the story. See Laín Entralgo 1970, 97–105; Guthrie 1969, 290–91.

23. Cicero, *De consolatione*, fr. 1, claims to be the first to have consoled himself *per litteras*; defended by Kassel 1958, 34–35, even though earlier authors may have done so without this specific intent. It is a great loss that this work does not survive; we should have liked to see Cicero at work as a pioneer and an innovator in generic matters.

24. Consolatory dialogue is another variation, but is primarily a medieval phenomenon, with an embodiment of wisdom instructing the *consolandus*. Von Moos 1971, 1 C 186, notes that the Platonic-Socratic notion of dialogue as common search for the truth disappears in the Middle Ages (as it does in patristic literature) to be replaced by the *Unterweisungsgespräch*; cf. also 3 T 1044 ff. Augustine's *Soliloquies* and Boethius's *Consolation* make available the principle of "progressive insight,"

but Boethius's particular art of accommodating to the physical status of the *consolandus* the various resources of the dialogue shall not be found again in such full form.

25. This is approximately the same structure as in Martianus's *Marriage*, in which the vision of the world of ultimate truth (books 1 and 2) precedes the exposition of the encyclopedic material, which takes place in the comic, Olympian heaven. For the two heavens of the *Marriage*, see Relihan 1993, 148.

26. He apostrophizes his friends in the opening poem (1.m.1.21), but this is a mere rhetorical flourish: "Quid me felicem totiens iactastis, amici?" [Tell me, my friends, why you boasted so often that I was so blessèd]. Kennedy 1980, 178, makes the excellent point that Boethius does not try to address Theoderic or his own court friends; like Cassiodorus and Gregory, he "turns away from speech to pursue the eternal life;" see here chapter 3, p. 40 and n. 22. This is a silent use of the anti-rhetorical topos.

27. *Anicii Manlii Severini Boethii Philosophiae Consolatio*, according to Bieler's text. Of course, the manuscripts have their variations, often adding others of the author's official titles. But because the manuscripts label the individual books rather than the whole, we get an extra genitive form: . . . *Boethii Philosophiae Consolationis Liber Primus*.

28. Blumenthal 1986 raises this point and entertains the possibility that it is Boethius who, through poetry, consoles the bedraggled Philosophy by showing her that she still does have one true disciple left, laying his poetry like roses at her feet. Similarly Fortin 2004, 305–6, who concludes: "Philosophy does console the prisoner once she accedes to his agenda and purpose, once she realizes that she is at his service and he is not at her service. Ironically the prisoner becomes a consoler of Philosophy herself even as he works through with Philosophy the proper response to his situation." We could call this a consolation in the face of death (for Philosophy's relation to the Land of the Dead, see here chapter 5), for if there is a Christian truth implicit in *Consolation*, then the opportunity that the author gives to Philosophy to contribute her bit to the prisoner's redemption could be a demonstration of why *she* need not fear death.

29. Cf. Scourfield 1993, 15: "The barriers erected between individuals in consequence of personal enmity or social difference or any other circumstance that tends to separate are readily broken down." He gives the good example of Achilles and Priam in *Iliad*, book 23.

30. For the motif in general, cf. Schmid 1956.

31. Cannata Fera 1989 suggests that there is at least a genuine Plutarchan core of material in *Ad Apollonium*.

32. Cf. Schmid 1976, 368–69.

33. This concludes: ἀποκλείεται δὲ πενθοῦντος ὁ νουθετῶν καὶ παραμυθούμενος φιλόσοφος [and as he mourns, the sympathetic and consoling philosopher is shut out].

34. In the Aristotelian *Problems* (30.1) the question is raised, "Why is it that all those who have become eminent in philosophy or politics or poetry or the arts are clearly of an atrabilious temperament?"

35. See Toohey 1990, 145: the passage is from Caelius Aurelianus's Latin translation of Soranus's *On Acute Diseases and Chronic Diseases*.

36. *peregi* means "brought to completion," not just "wrote." The reader infers that the present text is a last work, for these opening words mirror the famous false introduction to the *Aeneid*: "Ille ego qui quondam gracili modulatus auena / Carmen" [I who once did sing my song to the tune of the slender shepherd's pipe]. Cf. also Vergil, *Georgics* 4.564–65 (Bieler's apparatus).

37. Cf. the beginnings of Lucian's *Jupiter Tragoedus, Menippus,* and *Icaromenippus;* and, in Latin, Martianus's *De Nuptiis.*

38. Cf. Relihan 1990c, 185–86; see also Relihan 1993, index s.v. "personifications of genres." Fulgentius's *Mythologies,* following the beginning of Ovid's *Metamorphoses,* shows the author's plans were changed by a divinity, and his genre as well. Cherniss 1987, 42, in a good discussion of symbol-allegory and personification-allegory, claims that Philosophy "stands for an abstract idea—perfect, ideal philosophical inquiry," and insists that *Consolation* is not an allegory because "the literal level of the drama is of primary importance."

39. Cf. Waterfield and Kidd 1992, 363, in reference to Plutarch's *Ad uxorem* 608e–f.

40. Part of her plan is to make certain that the prisoner is not left alone, according to consolatory precept: cf. Seneca, *Epistle* 10.2: "lugentem timentemque custodire solemus, ne solitudine male utatur" [Typically we keep watch over someone who is in mourning and afraid, to make sure that he does not abuse his loneliness]. Cf. also Seneca, *De beneficiis* 2.14.2.

41. Cf. Cherniss 1987, 17 and 21. See further here chapter 5, 63–65.

42. Also in accordance with Menippean satire, which has an interest in the presentation of abnormal psychic states, as Bakhtin has pointed out; in the Latin tradition, Varro's *Bimarcus* ("Double Marcus," the author split in two) is a very influential text. Cf. Relihan 1993, 7 (Bakhtin), 62–65 (Varro).

43. Cf. von Moos 1970–71, T 1023–1024, on music as a consoler. Boethius, *De musica* 1.1 (Friedlein 181. 23, trans. Bower 1989): "Why is it that mourners, even though in tears, turn their very lamentations into music?" It is considered a particularly feminine habit ("quod maxime muliebre est"). See Gruber's comments on 1.m.1.2.

44. *Ad uxorem* 610b, quoting Euripides, *Andromache* 930.

45. For example, he knows that there is no chance in the universe and that God regulates all, but he cannot say how he does so.

46. I would argue against Payne 1981, 157–58, that the end of *Troilus and Criseyde* does not borrow Boethius's Menippean vision, but that it is true to the old Cynic conventions that Boethius transforms. Chaucer's narrator contrasts contemptible earth and glorious heaven; *Consolation* asserts the value of the earth.

47. Cf. Mitchell 1987, xxviii, on the end of Job, and the words by which he acknowledges his ignorance of the ways of God: "From this point of vision, the idea that there are accidents or victims is an optical illusion. This statement may seem cruel. Certainly it is a difficult statement. How could it not be? Paradise isn't handed out like a piece of cake at a Sunday school picnic. But the statement is not cruel. It is the opposite of cruel. Once the personal will is surrendered, future and past disappear, the morning stars burst out singing, and the deep will, contemplating the world it has created, says, 'Behold, it is very good.' Job's comfort at the end is in his own mortality." Frye 1976, 188, speaking of the end of the *Fairie Queene,* offers what is in effect a suggestive reading of the end of *Consolation:* "At the end of the poem the poet identifies himself with God's contemplative vision of the model created world, and the last line reads: 'O that great Sabbaoth God graunt me that Sabaoths sight!' There is a pun on Sabbath and Sabaoth, 'hosts', as the liberated subject, no longer a subject, contemplates the objects, no longer objects, in all their infinite variety. Spenser thus passes on to his reader *the crowning act of self-identity as the contemplating of what has been made,* including what one has recreated by possessing the canon of man's word as well as God's. . . . real silence is the end of speech, not the stopping of it, and it is not until we have shared something of this last Sabbath vision in our greatest romance that we may begin to say that we have earned the right to silence" (my italics). Lerer's view of the end of *Consolation,* that its silence is the silence of prayer, may be emended in this light.

48. *Consolation* 3.12.25; see here chapter 2, p. 28 and n. 25; and chapter 6, 82–83.

Chapter Five.   Death and Meditation

1. "Tamen abiit ad plures. Medici illum perdiderunt, immo magis malus fatus; medicus enim nihil aliud est quam animi consolatio." So says the dreary and sententious Seleucus at Trimalchio's banquet about the good Chrysanthus.

2. Relihan 1993, 96–97.

3. Tacitus, *Annals* 16.18–19; see Branham and Kinney 1996, ix–xiii, for a discussion. Petronius was well known in late antiquity; there is no reason to doubt that the traditions concerning his death were known as well.

4. 1.4.25: "Cuius rei seriem atque ueritatem, ne latere posteros queat, stilo etiam memoriaeque mandaui" [A continuous account of this affair and the truth of the matter I have entrusted to my pen and so to public memory, so that it cannot be hidden from those who come after me]. We know nothing more about this work, whether it was written or was ever really intended to be written. It is a curious fact that *Consolation* as a prosimetric text comes to be a model for autobiography in the Middle Ages (cf. Dronke 1994, esp. 83–114; and Relihan 2005); consider

also the prosimetric and self-parodic autobiography of the thirteenth-century grammar-teacher and cleric Elias of Thriplow, *Serium Senectutis*, available in Hillas 1987, who translates the title *Grave Thoughts in Old Age*.

5. Gersh 1986, 2.651–54, lays the material out most conveniently.

6. Klingner 1921, 5–6, sees it in the narrator's demand at 1.m.5.45–48 that the same peace rule on earth as rules in heaven, reminiscent of the Lord's Prayer; pp. 95–96, in the specific contrast of free will and divine foreknowledge in book 5 (however, Courcelle 1967, 208–21, reveals the Neoplatonic commentaries of Ammonius and Simplicius behind this); p. 101, in the approach to God through humility. So also Mohrmann 1976, 54–61, endorsed by Chadwick 1981, 250–51, who concludes that *Consolation* is a humanist work with only a Christian subtext. See here chapter 3, 41–42.

7. Brown 1971, 132, is refreshingly honest: "He still puzzles us by the tranquillity with which a staunchly Christian Roman aristocrat of the sixth century could reach back for comfort, in the face of death, to the pre-Christian wisdom of the ancients."

8. For text and translation of this passage, see here chapter 3, n. 10.

9. Cherniss, 1987, 17 and 21.

10. Lerer 1985, 237–53 (Appendix: Seneca's Plays in *The Consolation of Philosophy*).

11. For example, the *De remediis fortuitorum*, an inner dialogue contrasting seeming loss and real possession; see Newman 1988 and here chapter 6, 69–70. I have argued similarly in the case of the satires of the Stoic Persius that we have a dramatic presentation of conflicting halves of the author's self; cf. Relihan 1989.

12. Bower 1989, xxxvii, on Boethius *De Musica* 1.9.

13. Similarly, or so I would argue, we can say that the last of Persius's satires, in which he speaks of enjoying his wealth and his status on his country estate, is his resolution of the conflict between his two warring halves, who speak on the one hand of the inevitable thralldom to passion and vice, and on the other of the application of the sternest Stoic ethics: what cannot be resolved logically in satires 1–5 is consigned to the past in satire 6, in which the satirist has come to terms with his wealth and status.

14. *Anecdoton Holderi*, ed. Usener, 3–4.

15. Opening poems in other Menippean satires function similarly: consider the opening of Lucian's *Jupiter Tragoedus*, the reaction of the narrator's son to the narrator's poem in Martianus Capella, and the narrator's two poems in Fulgentius's *Mythologies* (Relihan 1993, 18–19; 142; 155–57).

16. "quis dedit ut pleno fertilis anno / autumnus grauidis influat uuis / rimari solitus atque latentis / naturae uarias reddere causas: / nunc iacet effeto lumine mentis / et pressus grauibus colla catenis / decliuemque gerens pondere uultum / cogitur, heu, stolidam cernere terram."

17. See the reference to Ptolemy at *Consolation* 2.7.4, and Chadwick 1981, 102–7.

18. "Talis habitus talisque uultus erat, cum tecum naturae secreta rimarer, cum mihi siderum uias radio describeres, cum mores nostros totiusque uitae rationem ad caelestis ordinis exempla formares?" [Was this my appearance, was this my countenance, when I would investigate with you the hidden things of nature, when you would with your measuring rod plot out for me the paths of the stars, when you would mold both my actions and the principles of life in general in accordance with the model of the heavenly order?]. So the usual interpretation, but the first five words do not make clear whose clothes and face he means. Philosophy's robes are torn, and her face resembles a sooty death mask; the prisoner could be upset that Philosophy is not her glorious self in his hour of need.

19. For Boethius's prolixity and contemporary reactions to it, see Chadwick 1981, 120.

20. The primary metaphor of book 1 is the recovery of sight, of the parting of clouds, of looking up to the heavens. Cf. O'Daly 1991, 104–38, for the nature imagery of book 1, esp. 107–12, 119–22, 136–38.

21. So too in Boethius's immediate Menippean models narrators confront their Muses in the form of genres: Martianus Capella and Satura; Fulgentius and Calliope, who brings Satyra in her train.

22. "praeceptor eius Socrates iniustae uictoriam mortis me astante promeruit" [His (Plato's) teacher Socrates won the victory of an unjust death while I stood at his side]. The Christian language of Philosophy's rapturous description has already been noted here, chapter 4, n. 20.

23. 1.1.4: cf. Chadwick 1980; Chadwick 1981, 225–27.

24. Relihan 1990, 186–88; the comedies in question are the *Pytine* ("The Chianti Bottle") of Cratinus, in which Comedy appears to complain of the author's drunkenness; and the *Chiron* of Pherecrates, in which Mousike appears to lament before Justice and Poetry her treatment at the hands of modern musicians. Lucian compounds similar fantasies in *Bis Accusatus*. The author (the "Syrian Rhetorician") is attacked in court by Rhetoric and Dialogue, and various philosophers are remanded to the custody of those who successfully argue for their possession: Drunkenness and the Academy argue about Polemon, Pleasure and the Stoa for Dionysius the Renegade, Excess and Virtue for Aristippus.

25. Colish 2005, in a review of Marenbon 2003, objects to Marenbon's claim (162–63) that Philosophy offers no way for the prisoner to gain the highest good of which she speaks; death is precisely the way.

26. The prisoner could, like Socrates in his *Apology*, speak of going off to death fearlessly, but he does not.

27. See the excellent article of Newman 1988, which argues for Senecan authorship.

28. Courcelle 1967, 208–21, draws attention to the importance of these commentaries.

29. Cf. 4.7; 11.18.11–13; 11.36; 12.25. Cf. Payne 1981, ix–x, for this point as essential to Menippean satire in general.

30. All translations are from Grube 1963. There is a difficulty in the text here, and the translation follows Farquarson's transposition, accepted in the edition of Dalfen 1979.

31. This is a point to which I shall return in chapter 6 in speaking of the epic nature of the prisoner's journey in *Consolation*.

32. Cf. Birley 1987, 213: "There can be no doubt that Marcus wrote for himself alone, in his tent 'among the Quadi' as in Book 2, or 'at Carnuntum,' as Book 3 is headed, in the camp of the legion XIV Gemina, and wherever else he found himself in the years from 172–180."

33. Φαντάζου πάντα τὸν ἐφ᾽ ὁτινιοῦν λυπούμενον ἢ δυσαρεστοῦντα ὅμοιον τῷ θυομένῳ χοιριδίῳ καὶ ἀπολακτίζοντι καὶ κεκραγότι· ὅμοιος καὶ ὁ οἰμώζων ἐπὶ τοῦ κλινιδίου μόνος σιωπῇ τὴν ἔνδεσιν ἡμῶν· καὶ ὅτι μόνῳ τῷ λογικῷ ζώῳ δέδοται τὸ ἑκουσίως ἕπεσθαι τοῖς γινομένοις, τὸ δὲ ἕπεσθαι ψιλὸν πᾶσιν ἀναγκαῖον. The words καὶ ἀπολακτίζοντι καὶ κεκραγότι resemble Philosophy's description of her own abduction by the philosophical sects at 1.3.7 (*reclamantem renitentemque*); even if this is the common language of Stoics speaking of necessity compelling the unwilling, it is curious that Philosophy describes herself in such unphilosophical terms. Farquharson takes τὴν ἔνδεσιν ἡμῶν not as the object of οἰμώζων but, together with καὶ ὅτι . . . δέδοται κτλ, as the object of a missing, or unexpressed, ἐπινόησον δέ.

34. Cf. Brown 1987, 289: The monk in the desert inhabits an image of Paradise, "the first, the true home of humankind, where Adam and Eve had dwelt in full majesty, before the subtle and overpowering onset of the doublehearted cares of human life in settled society, before marriage, physical greed, the labor of the earth, and the grinding cares of present human society robbed them of their original serenity." I do not suggest that *Consolation* is about a Christian monk in his cell, for if Christianized to this extent the work should certainly include some of the beatific vision vouchsafed to hermits.

35. *Meditations* 12.24.3–4, quoted here in chapter 6, p. 79 and n. 11. Philosophy's poem at 4.m.1 is on this same theme.

36. Text and translation here in chapter 3, n. 12. For a Stoic view of the citadel of Wisdom, cf. *Meditations* 8.48.3: διὰ τοῦτο ἀκρόπολίς ἐστιν ἡ ἐλευθέρα παθῶν διάνοια [and it is for this reason that the mind, when it is free of the emotions, is a fortress].

37. Ἀναχωρήσεις αὑτοῖς ζητοῦσιν, ἀγροικίας καὶ αἰγιαλοὺς καὶ ὄρη· [εἴωθας δὲ καὶ σὺ τὰ τοιαῦτα μάλιστα ποθεῖν]. ὅλον δὲ τοῦτο ἰδιωτικώτατόν ἐστιν ἐξὸν ἧς ἂν ὥρας ἐθελήσῃς εἰς ἑαυτὸν ἀναχωρεῖν· οὐδαμοῦ γὰρ οὔτε ἀπραγμονέστερον ἄνθρωπος ἀναχωρεῖ ἢ εἰς τὴν ἑαυτοῦ ψυχήν, μάλισθ᾽ ὅστις ἔχει ἔνδον τοιαῦτα, εἰς ἃ ἐγκύψας ἐν πάσῃ εὐμαρείᾳ εὐθὺς γίνεται· τὴν δὲ εὐμάρειαν οὐδὲν ἄλλο λέγω ἢ εὐκοσμίαν. συνεχῶς οὖν δίδου σεαυτῷ ταύτην τὴν ἀναχώρησιν καὶ ἀνανέου σεαυτόν· βραχέα δὲ ἔστω καὶ στοιχειώδη, ἃ εὐθὺς ἀπαντήσαντα ἀρέσκει εἰς τὸ πᾶσαν αὖ τὴν ‹δυσαρέστησιν› ἀποκλύσαι καὶ ἀποπέμψαι σε μὴ δυσχεραίνοντα ἐκείνοις, ἐφ᾽ ἃ ἐπανέρχῃ.

Chapter Six.   The *Odyssey* of *Consolation*

1. *Liber de deo Socratis* 35.14–23 Thomas: "nec aliud te in eodem Ulixe Homerus docet, qui semper ei comitem uoluit esse prudentiam, quam poëtico ritu Mineruam nuncupauit. igitur hac eadem comite omnia horrenda subiit, omnia aduersa superauit. quippe ea adiutrice Cyclopis specus introiit, sed egressus est; Solis boues uidit, sed abstinuit; ad inferos demeauit et ascendit; eadem sapientia comite Scyllam praeternauigauit nec ereptus est; Charybdi consaeptus est nec retentus est; Circae poculum bibit nec mutatus est; ad Lotophagos accessit nec remansit; Sirenas audiit nec accessit."

2. See Pépin 1991, 234, for "Ulysses as the symbol of the soul which is not resigned to its fall" in the Neoplatonic tradition; Pépin also points to Maximus of Tyre (*Philosophoumena* 11.10.h, ed. Hobein), who speaks of Ulysses swimming toward Phaeacia in a similar way, saved when Philosophy throws her cloak about him (reading ὑποβαλοῦσα for ὑπολαβοῦσα, with Kindstrand). For Neoplatonic readings of the *Odyssey* in general, see Lamberton 1986, 221–32; for Homer's presence in *Consolation* in general, see Lamberton 1986, 274–79, who observes that only Philosophy, and not the prisoner, cites Homer. For the prisoner, Homer is only a childhood author, learned in excerpts in general education (Lamberton 1986, 275; cf. the presence of *Iliad* 24.527–28 at *Consolation* 2.2.13: "'And surely you learned as a boy what Homer says lies on Jupiter's threshold?' 'Twó járs, óne full of goód things and óne full of évil.'"). Lamberton could have compared the disparaging way in which Augustine recalls his childhood Vergil in *Confessions* 1.13 (21). Thomas Taylor (1823, 241–71) presents in an appendix his own *On the Wanderings of Ulysses*.

3. Another curious connection between *Consolation* and *Aeneid* is suggested by Fulgentius, through his *Allegorical Content of Vergil*. Vergil is made to say that the shipwreck in book 1 of *Aeneid* is to suggest birth, and that the hero's initial speechlessness and inability to recognize his mother reflect the stages of infant development (*Expositio Vergilianae continentiae* 91.6–9, 92.7–93.19 Helm). This is not unintelligent as a reading of *Aeneid*; the speechless prisoner who does not recognize Philosophy at first and the prisoner's well documented search for voice in *Consolation* have epic ramifications.

4. In *Iliad*, Athena takes off this handmade cloak in order to put on armor. See Gruber 1978 ad loc. for further Neoplatonic interpretations; one simple point to make is that Philosophy is not dressed for war when she comes to the prisoner, even though she speaks in military language.

5. Astell 1994, 41–69, in a chapter entitled "Boethius and Epic Truth," details the frequent appearances of Homeric material in *Consolation* and describes the action generally as a heroic pursuit of self-knowledge. But the connections that Astell draws between *Consolation* and Job, as thematically linked works that become medieval patterns of epic, are not the connections that I make here.

6. So does Courcelle 1974, 181–229, in a discussion of the use of this precept in the fifth and sixth centuries.

7. For the presence of Homer's *Odyssey*, in the company of Old Comedy and Platonic myth, as one of the three subtexts of Menippean satire, see Relihan 1993, 30–34.

8. See Relihan 1996 for an exploration of the fortunes of Lucian's Menippus.

9. ἡ δὲ διάνοια, ταῦτα πάντα ἡγησαμένη σμικρὰ καὶ οὐδέν, ἀτιμήσασα πανταχῇ πέτεται κατὰ Πίνδαρον "τᾶς τε γᾶς ὑπένερθε" καὶ τὰ ἐπίπεδα γεωμετροῦσα, "οὐρανοῦ θ' ὕπερ" ἀστρονομοῦσα, καὶ πᾶσαν πάντῃ φύσιν ἐρευν-ωμένη τῶν ὄντων ἑκάστου ὅλου, εἰς τῶν ἐγγὺς οὐδὲν αὐτὴν συγκαθιεῖσα. Translation by Waterfield 1987, 69.

10. οὐδὲν ἀθλιώτερον τοῦ πάντα κύκλῳ ἐκπεριερχομένου καὶ τὰ νέρθε γᾶς, φησίν, ἐρευνῶντος καὶ τὰ ἐν ταῖς ψυχαῖς τῶν πλησίον διὰ τεκμάρσεως ζητοῦντος, μὴ αἰσθομένου δέ, ὅτι ἀρκεῖ πρὸς μόνῳ τῷ ἔνδον ἑαυτοῦ δαίμονι εἶναι καὶ τοῦτον γνησίως θεραπεύειν. θεραπεία δὲ αὐτοῦ καθαρὸν πάθους διατηρεῖν καὶ εἰκαιότητος καὶ δυσαρεστήσεως τῆς πρὸς τὰ ἐκ θεῶν καὶ ἀνθρ-ώπων γινόμενα. Translation by Grube 1963, 15; text is from Dalfen 1979.

11. εἰ [ἄνω] μετέωρος ἐξαρθεὶς κατασκέψαιο τὰ ἀνθρώπεια καὶ τὴν πολυ-τροπίαν, ὅτι καταφρονήσεις συνιδὼν ἅμα καὶ ὅσον τὸ περιοικοῦν ἐναερίων καὶ ἐναιθερίων· καὶ ὅτι, ὁσάκις ἂν ἐξαρθῇς, ταὐτὰ ὄψει, τὸ ὁμοειδές τὸ ὀλιγο-χρόνιον· ἐπὶ τούτοις ὁ τῦφος. The most poignant expression of the Cynic *catasco-pia* is perhaps to be found at the end of Lucian's *Charon* (whose subtitle is Ἐπισκοποῦντες, or "Those Who Look Down from a Great Height"; the dialogue is more formally known by the Latin translation of this, *Contemplantes*): from the top of a pile of mountains Charon and Hermes survey the sixth-century world of book 1 of Herodotus and sadly conclude that inquiry into human affairs does little good, and keeping to oneself is the only way to lead a reasonable life. Further dis-cussion in Relihan 1993, 114–16.

12. Adapting *Somnium Scipionis* 9.3: *ille discessit, ego somno solutus sum*. Cf. Cher-niss 1987, 34–37, for a discussion of parallels between *Somnium* and *Consolation*.

13. I would refer to Frye 1957, 224, speaking of Swift's *Modest Proposal*: "Hence satire is irony which is structurally close to the comic: the comic struggle of two societies, one normal and the other absurd, is reflected in its double focus of mo-rality and fantasy. Irony with little satire is the non-heroic residue of tragedy, cen-tering on a theme of puzzled defeat."

14. Mitchell 1987, xxv–xxviii, is an eloqent presentation of the end of Job; see here chapter 4, n. 47.

15. For further discussion, cf. Relihan 1993, 139–40.

16. Asztalos 1993 concludes: "He seems to have come quite unprepared to both the *Isagoge* and the *Categories*, unarmed with proper translations and unfamiliar with the work he was commenting on. Boethius is indeed an epitome of the ex-pression *docendo discimus*."

17. We know that the gods have redirected Ovid's plans for the work because the second line is not the expected elegiac, but a hexameter line which reveals that the author is now writing unaccustomed epic. For the presence of Ovid in *Conso-lation* see Claassen 2007 (forthcoming).

18. Fulgentius's narrator had presented himself as a debunking scholar, about to write a handbook that exposes the inanity of myth: the mythical Calliope appears to make herself a coauthor, so that the resulting handbook speaks of the (albeit allegorical) value of myth. What is so clever about Fulgentius is that he consciously presents his narrator as an anti-Ovid, whose goals must be changed by his imperious Muse; in this he is exactly like Ovid, who begins the *Metamorphoses* with the brief account of how Apollo changed him from a writer of elegy to a writer of epic. Further in Relihan 1984.

19. See here chapter 5, n. 24. Fulgentius's Calliope is also in this tradition, appearing one step ahead of the vivisectionists of Alexandria.

20. "Nonne apud ueteres quoque ante nostri Platonis aetatem magnum saepe certamen cum stultitiae temeritate certauimus eodemque superstite praeceptor eius Socrates iniustae uictoriam mortis me astante promeruit?" For the Christian language of *uictoriam mortis,* see Gruber ad loc.

21. In Ovid, the poet is responsible for all once his goals are changed, and he claims to be singing a heroic song; in Fulgentius, the narrator is told to listen to (and, we presume, to write down) the handbook that Calliope dictates.

22. See Hadot 1993, 107–9, discussing what is chronologically the last of the *Enneads* (I 7).

23. Hadot 1993, 104–7, on the divine comedy that life can be seen to be; cf. Plotinus, *Enneads* III 2 (47) 15. This essay (*On Providence,* part 1) is full of positive assertions about the value of the physical world that do not find their way into Boethius's *Consolation.*

24. Barbour 1994; see the review by E. Ziolkowski 1996, who speaks of this as a "rough spiritual analogue to Sir Isaac Newton's third law of motion."

25. A passage from Hierocles, *On Providence,* states that laws are not in vain and that prayer is not useless even if Foreknowledge (πρόνοια) has dominion over all things: Photius, *Bibliotheca* cod. 251, translated in Wilson 1994, 225–28.

26. The adjective *efficax* is elsewhere in *Consolation* a logical term, describing propositions that lead to valid conclusions (4.4.11, 5.4.4; cf. also *In de interpretatione*², 466.26 Meiser).

27. "avenue of exchange," *commercium,* a business term. It does not seem to reflect a Greek patristic usage (the closest possible term is, I think, τὸ συμβόλαιον) or a Neoplatonic one; rather, it is a good Latin term, at home with the terms that Boethius adopted in his Aristotelian commentaries for πραγματεύεσθαι (*negotiari*) and βουλεύεσθαι (*consiliari*). See appendix 1.

28. "deserve the return of divine grace," *uicem diuinae gratiae promeremur.* Divine grace here surely has its Christian sense; cf. de Vogel 1972, 4 ff. (Gruber's reference); Mohrmann 1976, 55 ff. Gruber cites Theiler to the effect that there are Neoplatonic parallels to the phrase, but does not reproduce them, and says this is no argument for a Christian *Consolation.* But when the other Christian references in the passage combine with the Christian references in Philosophy's response to it at the end of *Consolation,* I think we can say that its provenance is Christian.

29. "inapproachable light", *inaccessae luci;* cf. the Vulgate of 1 Tim. 6.15–16: "Rex regum et Dominus dominantium, qui solus habet immortalitatem et lucem inhabitat inaccessibilem, quem nullus hominum vidit, sed nec videre potest" [the King of kings and Lord of lords: Who only hath immortality and inhabiteth light inaccessible: whom no man hath seen, nor can see]. Gruber ad loc. doubts the connection, given that Paulinus of Nola (*Carmina* 32.188–89) also uses the form of the adjective found in Boethius: *lucis inaccessae domus est sedesque potentis / sancta dei.* But note also the *Carmen de resurrectione* 85 (ca. 500; ed. Waszink, 193): *inaccessam habitans in saecula lucem;* and Rufinus's translation of Origen on Song of Songs (*Patrologia Graeca* 13.102.5): *inaccessam lucem . . . habitaret.* But this is denying the obvious: the habitation in the inaccessible light is a Christian and scriptural phrase; Bieler accepts the parallel in his *Index Locorum Sacrae Scripturae* without the usual asterisk to indicate a general rather than a strict parallel.

30. "have no force," *nihil uirium habere;* literally, "to have no strength." I believe that this phrase is answered when Philosophy speaks of prayers that cannot help but be effective. In William of Moerbeke's translations of Proclus, *inefficax* is regularly used for ἀδρανής, a word that in Neoplatonic writings passed from the meaning "weak" to "unreal"; see the indices in Boese 1960.

31. "Lord of the universe," *rerum principi.* This is not a particularly Christian formulation.

32. 5.3.33. igitur nec sperandi aliquid nec deprecandi ulla ratio est; quid enim uel speret quisque uel etiam deprecetur quando optanda omnia series indeflexa conectit? 34. auferetur igitur unicum illud inter homines deumque commercium, sperandi scilicet ac deprecandi, si quidem iustae humilitatis pretio inaestimabilem uicem diuinae gratiae promeremur; qui solus modus est quo cum deo colloqui homines posse uideantur illique inaccessae luci prius quoque quam impetrent ipsa supplicandi ratione coniungi. 35. quae si recepta futurorum necessitate nihil uirium habere credantur, quid erit quo summo illi rerum principi conecti atque adhaerere possimus? 36. quare necesse erit humanum genus, uti paulo ante cantabas, dissaeptum atque disiunctum suo fonte fatiscere. The final word, *fatiscere,* is elegantly chosen; it suggests a boat that has lost its caulking and lets the water in through the hull.

33. Lewis 1964, 90: "The work ends with Philosophia thus speaking; there is no return to Boethius and his situation, any more than to Christopher Sly at the end of *The Taming of the Shrew.* This I believe to be a stroke of calculated and wholly successful art. We are made to feel as if we had seen a heap of common materials so completely burnt up that there remains neither ash nor smoke nor even flame, only a quivering of invisible heat."

34. Lerer 1985, 230.

35. Weinbrot 2005, 6. He does not consider *Consolation* to be a Menippean satire.

Chapter Seven.   Models and Rewritings

1. Readers will have noticed that I do not discuss verse as a separate phenomenon in my interpretation. It is not truly separable; as I have indicated in the notes to my translation (Relihan 2001), the topics of the poems frequently change the course of argument and are not merely illustrative or decorative. A discussion of the twists and turns of the thought of *Consolation* does not require a separate discussion of verse per se; poems are treated as statements of particular points of view. But it remains true that the thorough mixture of verse and prose in *Consolation* is a sign that the text has a grand goal: to include within it all of the world as well as all of the literary traditions that have preceded it.

2. I treat these authors very briefly at the end of my discussion of Boethius in Relihan 1993, 191–94.

3. So we distinguish it from verse satire. A Horace may say something like, "What if a god should grant your request, what then?" (a motif generally referred to as *si quis deus*), but a Menippean satirist dramatizes such a thing and thus makes fun of it; he visualizes and puts on stage things that have no substance.

4. Those who abandon their earlier beliefs are said to run away: thus the term apostate. Lucian's dialogue Δραπέται (literally, "The Runaway Slaves") is discussed below as "The Fugitive Philosophers."

5. For Platonic myth as a subtext of Menippean satire, see Relihan 1993, 33; for the history of the involvement of Platonic thought and texts in the development of genre, see pp.179–87.

6. Kirk 1982 discusses Lucian's dialogues in general as a parallel to *Consolation*, but works rather schematically, arguing that such things as Lucian's parody of dogmatic philosophers made his prosimetric form appealing to Boethius. Payne 1981, 38–54, has a more profound analysis, though I disagree with its emphases; see here chapter 7, 99. For a treatment of Lucian's Menippean satires and their thematic relations to other, non-Menippean dialogues, see Relihan 1993, 103–18.

7. Titles of Lucian's dialogues are confusing and often need to be explained. The Greek title is Ἀναβιοῦντες ἢ Ἁλιεύς; the Latin title by which it is most commonly known, *Piscator*, only translates the second title; the first means roughly "The Resurrected," and "The Dead Come Back to Life" is a more transparent title. The philosophers who demand justice for the insulting treatment that Parrhesiades heaps upon them are the ancient philosophers, who need to return from the dead to press their claims.

8. Βίων Πρᾶσις, or "The Sale of Lives" (Latin, *Vitarum Auctio*); each philosophical school is thought of as offering its own distinctive way of life. Lucian's fantasy is that each philosopher is put on the auction block to see what he would fetch on the open market. Philosophy is so concerned with the exile's thoughts because she desires from him a particular way of life, one that accepts the philosopher's death.

9. Philosophy and her true supporters occupying the high ground, mocking the insane mob below, is paralleled at *Consolation* 1.3.13–14: "And if this army should ever array itself against us and attack us with all its might, our leader withdraws all her forces into her own citadel, leaving the others to occupy themselves with the plundering of useless baggage. But we laugh at them from on high as they snatch at each and every worthless thing—we are safe from all their maddened riot, protected by a wall which marauding stupidity is forbidden to assault."

10. Δραπέται; Latin, *Fugitivi*.

11. We will find a parallel to this in *Twice Accused*, in which the Academy and Drunkenness debate over the possession of Polemon; the Stoa and Pleasure (represented by Epicurus) contend for Dionysius; Luxury and Virtue for Aristippus; and finally Rhetoric and Dialogue attack the Syrian (a *porte-parole* for Lucian), and he speaks in his own defense. The Syrian's defense aginst these two accusers motivates the title (Δὶς κατηγορούμενος; Latin, *Bis accusatus*)

12. Ζεὺς Τραγῳδός, Latin, *Iuppiter Tragoedus*, often rendered in English as "Zeus Rants" or "Zeus the Opera Star"; Ζεὺς ἐλεγχόμενος, Latin, *Iuppiter confutatus*; both mean, "Zeus Proved Wrong."

13. Payne 1981, 45–47.

14. See my annotated translation of the prologue of the *Mythologies* in Relihan 1993, 203–10.

15. I reproduce here the material from Relihan 1993, 159: an address to a patron which claims that modern times do not support literature (*Expositio Vergilianae continentiae* 83.1–9, *Mitologiae* 3.1–9); the deprecation of the author's talents (*V.C.* 84.17–22, *Mit.* 3.9–20); reference to the task at hand as one that requires hellebore (*V.C.* 85.2–3, *Mit.* 15.4–5); address to the Muses in verse (*V.C.* 85.59, *Mit.* 7.5–8.5); introduction of a fabulous character (Vergil's ghost at *V.C.* 85.11–16; Calliope and the Muses (*Mit.* 8.6–8); character(s) drunk from the font of Hippocrene (*V.C.* 85.13, *Mit.* 8.6–8); character(s) carrying symbolic tools of an appropriate craft and looking absurd (*V.C.* 85.13–16, *Mit.* 14.6–20); character with a wrinkled brow, smelling something awful (Vergil at *V.C.* 85.17–19; Urania at *Mit.* 14.16–18); the narrator defining for the fabulous character(s) what the nature of the impending work will be and receiving the scorn of his guest(s) because his intentions are unsatisfactory (narrator demands trivialities of Vergil at *V.C.* 85.19–86.19; narrator proclaiming that he will not retell the old myths at *Mit.* 10.19–11.18); a fabulous character insulting the narrator (*V.C.* 86.6–10, *Mit.* 11.18–21); the narrator dull as a clod (*V.C.* 86.9; *Mit.* 15.12–15, in which the narrator is compared to an acorn eater); snoring as a sign of the narrator's stupidity (*V.C.* 86.9–10, *Mit.* 13.25–14.1); a fabulous character promising to teach what the narrator may not be able to understand, so that the narrator must open his ears (*V.C.* 86.16–19, *Mit.* 15.6–10).

16. See here chapter 1, 2–3.

17. Hays 1996, 7–12, ultimately decides only that the parallels cannot be used in the dating of Fulgentius the Mythographer. The possibility that the two rely on a

common tradition of epiphanies, rather than on specific texts, is quite strong; but there are verbal parallels, and I am now inclined to think that Boethius is prior to the Mythographer, especially given Hays's conclusion that the Mythographer is not the bishop (263–91).

18. I will refer to the latest edition of Maximian, Agozzino 1970.

19. Agozzino tries to rehabilitate him, claiming for him a serious didactic purpose in his suit of elegies. See the criticisms of Shanzer 1983, 188 and n. 4; but Barnish 1990 succeeds in uncovering the Boethian subtext of all of the *Elegies*.

20. For an account of this controversy, see Anastasi 1951.

21. Barnish 1990, 25 n. 40, argues against Shanzer's interpretation. But his general reading of the poem seems more consistent with a conclusion that shows the poet at odds with his mentor: "The whole story remains morally unresolved, the poet's verdict ambiguous. Boethius seems neither butt nor hero, but a figure deliberately introduced to perplex us."

22. Cf. the parallel passages cited by Agozzino 1970 (vv. 47–65).

23. It wouldn't make much difference if Ratkowitsch 1986 were right about dating the *Elegies* to the ninth century, for we could still say that there is a comic reception to *Consolation*, and it would be interesting to see it at work then. But the objections raised by Shanzer 1988 are still sufficient to overcome the rebuttal of Ratkowitsch 1990; and the article of Barnish 1990 lets us see Maximian's writing in the context of early sixth-century literature and culture, in which Boethius's work and memory are living things.

24. Barnish 1990, 21–28, especially p. 22: "Nonetheless, I believe that the whole corpus of the six elegies is the work of a poet steeped in the *Consolation*, rehandling its substance on other planes, poetic, comic, and ultimately tragic."

25. Cf. *Consolation* 2.4.2, the only passage from Boethius in the *Oxford Book of Quotations*: "in omni aduersitate fortunae infelicissimum est genus infortunii fuisse felicem" [in all of Fortune's adversities the most unhappy sort of misfortune is that one was happy once].

26. Barnish 1990, 25.

27. This apostrophe has its precedent in Petronius 132, in a poem of the impotent narrator Encolpius; discussion in Relihan 1993, 92–93.

28. "Conticuit tandem longo satiata dolore; / me uelut expletis deserit exequiis."

29. 5.151–52: "Ira breuis, longa est pietas, recidiua uoluptas, / et cum posse perit, mens tamen una manet."

30. *Cons.* 1.2.5. Cf. *Mit.* 8.10–11 Helm; when Fulgentius later has Calliope stroke the narrator's neck to persuade him that he needs her help for the book that he intends to write, the narrator objects that she did this more sensually than was proper (*Mit.* 10.8–10).

31. For the Latin text of Braulio's observations and a discussion, see Fontaine 1965, 168 and n. 15.

32. Fontaine 1965, 170.

33. If the *Synonyma* is written in response to *Consolation*, then we could take Isidore's use of Job in it as coming from a perception of the presence of Job in *Consolation*. But this, I think, could never be proven, and, given the enormous influence of Gregory's *Moralia in Job*, a simpler road to Isidore's Job can certainly be found.

34. I give the text of I.II here to convey some sense of the linguistic nature of this text, an ethical manual that presents to the reader the option of choosing an individual path through the text. The reader of Isidore is free to recast what is read by abbreviation or by rearrangement (*Patrologia Latina* 83:830b–c): "Testium et judicum falsa et crudeli sententia judicor. Testium falsa sententia ad necem innocens ducor. ex eodem concilio testes, ex eodem judices, ex eodem coetu accusatores. Improbos judices opponunt, falsos testes objiciunt, in quorum testimonio confidentia est. Nemo ab illis dissentit, nemo discordat, nemo consilium eorum repudiat. Cui dicam? cui credam? cui loquar? quem adeam? a quo consilium petam? in quo animum meum ponam? quem potissimum quaeram?"

Chapter Eight.   The Menippean Boethius in the Personification
Allegories of the Middle Ages, by William E. Heise

1. The arguments in this chapter are based on my dissertation, *Aristotle and the Allegorical Aesthetic: Poetry and the Limits of Philosophy from Alan of Lille to Edmund Spenser* (Heise 1996). In it, I attempt to show that the medieval Aristotelian philosophical tradition bred far more skepticism about religious matters than has been recognized in previous approaches to medieval literature.

2. Robertson 1962, 287.

3. Dronke 1994, 41.

4. *De trinitate*, introduction: "Sane tantum a nobis quaeri oportet quantum humanae rationis intuitus ad diuinitatis ualet celsa conscendere." Translation by Stewart, Rand, and Tester 1973, 5.

5. *Patrologia Latina*, vol. 146, col. 60.

6. Translation by Singleton 1970.

7. A full treatment of *De planctu naturae* is offered in Heise 1996. Since writing my dissertation, I have come to doubt that Alan of Lille is the author of *De planctu*. While Chaucer and Spenser point to Alan as the author, there is no contemporary evidence that he wrote this prosimetric text. On the other hand, many laud him as the author of *Anticlaudianus*. Secondly, and more importantly, the work is almost a poetic rendition of John of Salisbury's *Metalogicon*. John's work is sharply critical of the Platonic idealism of many twelfth-century thinkers like Gilbert of Poitiers, with whom Alan's philosophical work has been identified. John and Gilbert differ entirely over the important medieval question of whether universals lead the mind to understand the divine. John of Salisbury regarded universals as "fictions"— useful words for speaking about the similarities of things, but lacking actual

substance—while Gilbert sided with the Platonists, who believed that universals were in some sense "real." If *De planctu* was written early in Alan's career, as is often suggested, I find it difficult to posit a satisfactory explanation of such a radical change in his intellectual career. By the time that *De planctu* was written, the Platonism of Gilbert was on the wane, and the Aristotelianism of John was ascendant. If Alan had written the *De planctu*, he would have had to revert to an earlier, discredited position for the rest of his intellectual life, while both ignoring his earlier Aristotelian position and failing to counter it.

8. *De planctu* VI (Prose 3), 131–39; Häring 1978, 829; translation by Sheridan 1980, 124; (cf. also Wright 1872, 455): "Eius enim operatio simplex, mea operatio multiplex. Eius opus sufficiens, meum opus deficiens. Eius opus mirabile, meum opus mutabile. Ille innascibilis, ego nata. Ille faciens, ego facta. Ille mei opifex operis, ego opus opificis. Ille operatur ex nichilo, ego mendico opus ex aliquo. Ille suo operatur in numine, ego operor illius sub nomine. Ille rem solo nutu iubet existere, mea uero operatio operationis est nota divine. Et respectu diuine potentie meam potentiam impotentem esse cognoscas. Meum effectum scias esse defectum, meum uigorem uilitatem esse perpendas."

9. *De planctu* VI (Prose 3), 154–55; Häring 1978, 829; translation by Sheridan 1980, 125; (cf. also Wright 1872, 456): "Ego ratione fidem, ipsa fide comparat rationem. Ego scio ut credam, illa credit ut sciat."

10. *De planctu* VI (Prose 3), 60–61; Häring 1978, 826; translation by Sheridan 1980, 119; (cf. also Wright 1872, 451): "Illa [Ratio] hominem in deum potentialiter transfigurat."

11. *De planctu* XIV (Prose 7), 22–24; Häring 1978, 860; translation by Sheridan 1980, 186; (cf. also Wright 1872, 495): "Alii, suos actus specificare gaudentes, in multitudine singulares, in generalitate speciales, in uniuersalitate aduersi, in unitate diuersi, omnifariam esse laborant."

12. *De planctu* VIII (Prose 4), 269–73; Häring 1978, 860; translation by Sheridan 1980, 148; (cf. also Wright 1872, 471): "Siue certa descriptione describens, siue legitima definitione diffiniens, rem indemonstrabilem demonstrabo, inextricabilem extricabo, quamuis ipsa nulli nature obnoxialiter alligata, intellectus indaginem non expectans, nullius descriptionis posset signaculo sigillari."

13. The text is from the edition of Langlois 1914–24.

14. [See also Mann 2001 for an extended discussion of the use of the castration myth in Jean de Meun. Relihan's note.]

15. Quotations are from the edition of the B text of Kane and Donaldson 1975; the typography has been followed with the exception of the modernizations of the thorn, edh, and yogh and the elimination of editorial square brackets. Citations are by passus and line number.

16. Gregory the Great, Homily 26, *Homiliae XL in Evangelia*, in *Patrologia Latina*, vol. 76, col. 1197.

17. [The complaint that only human affairs are outside of the divine order of the world is of course the theme of the prisoner's poem, *Consolation* 1.m.5; see here chapter 3, pp. 39–40 and n. 21. Relihan's note.]

18. *Disticha* 1.5: "nemo sine crimine uiuit," [No one lives without transgression].

19. ["Or, you would be a philosopher now, if you had stayed silent then." Relihan's note.]

20. "Vos autem nisi ad populares auras inanesque rumores recte facere nescitis et relicta conscientiae uirtutisque praestantia de alienis praemia sermunculis postulatis. 20. Accipe in huius modi arrogantiae leuitate quam festiue aliquis illuserit. Nam cum quidam adortus esset hominem contumeliis, qui non ad uerae uirtutis usum sed ad superbam gloriam falsum sibi philosophi nomen induerat, adiecissetque iam se sciturum an ille philosophus esset si quidem inlatas iniurias leniter patienterque tolerasset, ille patientiam paulisper assumpsit acceptaque contumelia uelut insultans: 'iam tandem,' inquit, 'intellegis me esse philosophum?' Tum ille nimium mordaciter: 'Intellexeram,' inquit, 'si tacuisses.'" [I translate *populares auras* according to Servius's interpretation of the phrase at *Aeneid* 6.816, from which Philosophy borrows it, as "vulgar favors." The moral of the story is more reminiscent of Proverbs 11.12 ("He that despiseth his friend is mean of heart; but the wise man will hold his peace") than of classical parallels. See Gruber 1978 ad loc. Relihan's note.]

Chapter 9.   The Wisdom of Boethius

1. See here chapter 3, 42–43.

2. See here chapter 2, 28.

3. Bergant, 173. Cf. also Bergant, 179: "The wisdom tradition has been variously described as: a humanistic outlook on life; a world view for coping with reality; a search for the underlying principles of causality and order for the purpose of conforming to them; an attempt to organize an otherwise chaotic existence."

4. Chadwick 1981 offers two views: "The *Consolation* is a work written by a Platonist who is also a Christian, but it is not a Christian work" (249); "The book is an essay in natural theology apart from revelation; and the very possibility of that rests on Christian assumptions. The Christianizing readers have not been absolutely wrong" (251–52). But Chadwick, while speaking of the Christian language of the text, does not say what such a Christian reading of *Consolation* is, and in this I follow an amplification of Olmstead 1989, frequently referred to in the notes below, for reading *Consolation* as a religious text, specifically as a parallel to *Confessions*. Yet here too the specifics of a Christian reading are not presented as strongly as they could have been.

5. Griffin 1995, 25 28.

6. See here chapter 6, 87–88.

7. Olmstead 1989, 34–35.

8. Olmstead 1989 speaks of both *Confessions* and *Consolation* as being dialectical in the Platonic sense and of both acknowledging the limitations of the believer

in the process of defining the world at large, though she adds that Augustine includes himself more than Boethius does within the world that is to be understood. But I object to her conclusion (20): "Though Boethius' text is dialectically self-aware, it does not emphasize as consistently or as strongly as Augustine's the various ways the human inquirer influences and limits inquiry."

9. Olmstead speaks a good deal about the fact that Augustine begins *Confessions* by calling on God. "[T]he act of invocation is problematic," she says (22), generated by the speaker's desire to find out about his place in the whole. Olmstead says that in Boethius's case the question at issue is justification, and God is on trial, while "Boethius looks on, a troubled evaluator of 'what is'" (21).

10. I would modify the view of Olmstead 1989, 22: "Boethius never abandons his disengaged position, though he comes to see the limitations of his ideas. This disengaged attitude is much more appropriate to a spectator becoming reconciled to his life retrospectively than to a person choosing a way of life committed to God or to what he believes to be the whole of reality, and it results in an ethics that is, in some ways, less inclusive than that of Augustine."

11. LeMoine 1991 discusses father-son dedications in Latin literature in the context of establishing an author's didactic authority as a function of family and class and their obligations. But Boethius's two works with family dedications are in fact dedicated to his father-in-law Symmachus (*De sancta trinitate, De arithmetica*); this shows both changing traditions in late antiquity and Boethius's idiosyncrasies (365–66). For a discussion of the use of *munus* (obligation) in the preface to *De arithmetica*, see pp. 356–57; in *Consolation*, this term is once used in a way that suggests that the prisoner views instruction from Philosophy as her obligation within this didactic tradition (4.6.1): "Ita est, inquam; sed cum tui muneris sit latentium rerum causas euoluere uelatasque caligine explicare rationes, quaeso uti quae hinc decernas, quoniam hoc me miraculum maxime perturbat, edisseras" [I said: It is as you say. But since it is your function (*muneris*) to unfold the causes of things that are hidden and to reveal their principles, veiled in darkness, I beg you, please explain in full what is your judgment in these matters (i.e., the relation between chance and divine providence). For this supernatural occurrence confuses me most of all]. At 3.12.32–36 we may see a debate whether it is God's or Philosophy's obligation to explain the nonexistence of evil.

12. I discuss this sort of pride in connection with that evidenced by the emperor Julian in his Menippean satire *Caesars* (Relihan 2005, 119–21). Julian feels that he is the focal point of history; Boethius, the culmination. I would add now that Boethius thinks of himself not only as Rome's last poet, last philosopher, and last patriot, but also as its last satirist.

13. Cf. Lerer, 212.

14. See Crossan 1979 for an elaborate synchronic study of this verse in the context of Jewish treasure parables and world folklore. I follow Crossan's interpretation of the parable, which sees it as demanding first an abandonment of one's goods, then an abandonment of one's morality (93). This would correspond to what

I have termed Boethius's deconversion. Crossan's final point, that it demands an abandonment of the parable itself, is more problematic in terms of an interpretation of the parable per se, but quite appropriate to an interpretation of Boethius. Boethius is himself writing a parable, and this text too, about a leap to prayer over the voice of authority, would ask its reader to abandon the text in order to find its treasure.

15. Cf. Augustine, *De doctrina Christiana* 2.40.60–61 for the classic statement.

16. A parallel in the Vulgate Job offers an interesting possibility. Job 3.20–22: "Quare misero data est lux, et vita his qui in amaritudine animae sunt? Qui exspectant mortem, et non venit, quasi effodientes thesaurum. gaudentque vehementer cum invenerint sepulchrum" [Why is light given to him that is in misery, and life to them that are in bitterness of soul? That look for death, and it cometh not, as they that dig for a treasure: And that rejoice exceedingly when they have found the grave]. The words *qui expectant . . . sepulchrum* could however be translated quite differently: "And those who look for death are like those who dig up a treasure when death does not come; and mighty is their rejoicing after they have found the grave." Or, to find life instead of death is to find a treasure; afterward, death itself is a source of joy; this could serve as an interpretation of *Consolation*. Of course, modern scholarship sees quite another text (cf. Mitchell 1987, 14: "Why is there light for the wretched, life for the bitter-hearted, who long for death, who seek it as if it were buried treasure, who smile when they reach the graveyard and laugh as their pit is dug?").

17. Crossan 1979, 94.

18. Conte 1996, 140–70 (chapter 5: "The Quest for a Genre [or Chasing Will o' the Wisps?]") is a skeptial assessment of what in Petronius can be attributed to the Menippean genre. He concludes that only prosimetrum and parody are recognizable, and that both of these are hardly the exclusive property of the genre (163), and that *Satyricon* is not a "real Menippean satire" because Petronius "programmatically blurs the Menippean features of his work" (168). But similarities between the *Satyricon* and *Consolation* are worth drawing (see here chapter 5, 60–61. I note the following (Conte, 150–51): "It is not a matter of reaching for the heights of divinity in order to debase them with the corrosive power of paradox; Petronius does not degrade the sublime texts that are cited or parodied from time to time, and above all he does not debase divine, mythological, or heroic roles. Rather, he brings down to earth an ordinary humanity which had sought to scale heights to which it had no right. Moreover, unlike Menippean satire, Petronius has absolutely no intention of providing representations of universal or symbolic value. So the entire narrative is depressed to this 'low' level, despite the struggles of its characters to disengage themselves. There are no gods, as in Menippean satire, who discuss terrestrial problems; there are no divine councils, no meetings with great men in the Underworld, nor are the extreme questions of the human condition raised for discussion. Instead, there is a primary narrativity based on real events and centered on characters playing out their daily lives in their most sordid and thus, in a sense,

most authentic aspects. Nor is there any collapse: the level of action is low from the start. The ambitious acrobatics of the characters are not enough to raise them off the ground."

Appendix 2.   Boethius, *In de interpretatione*² 3.9, 221.27–227.12 Meiser

1. What Boethius does here is transpose the words "nor to do business" from their proper place in his translation (after "no one will be obliged to take counsel") to the end of the passage.

2. The two passages in parentheses are difficult: *si quid aliud fecerit* and *si hoc quod dixit faciat.* I take Boethius's point to be that a conjecture about the future does not influence the future if all things happen of necessity, even if the speakers of such conjectures act in a way that contradicts their conjectures.

3. "simple causes and effects of things": *simplices rerum ordines.*

4. "in the realm of free decision": *libero teneri iudicio.* The passive *teneri* was used above to mean "be considered to be," *tenentur*; this phrase might just mean "are thought (to be from) free decision." At any event, the phrase is not quite as strong as "are in the power of, or the grasp of, free will."

5. "rationale of our entire life": *totius vitae rationis,* in which *ratio* stands for λόγος.

6. "butts in": *interstrepit,* "interrupts with an unwelcome noise." Cf. Boethius *De interpretatione* 2, 87.17–18: *hoc loco Aspasius inconvenienter interstrepit.*

7. The example of the accidental discovery of the treasure chest, found in Aristotle (*Metaphysics* 4.30, 1025a15–19), appears at the beginning of book 5 of *Consolation* (5.1.11–19); Boethius follows there the explanation of such events that Aristotle gives in *Physics* 2.4–5. The example becomes a commonplace; Boethius's description of two separate causal chains is common to the Platonic exegesis of this passage (Aristotle speaks only of an unintended result of an action with a different primary purpose); Boethius further distinguishes himself by applying the example to a discussion of divine foreknowledge; further, see Sharples 1991, 214–15. I relate this to the parable of Matthew 13.44 (see here chapter 9, 133–35) as a key for the understanding of *Consolation* as a whole.

8. "each rules over all things": *omnium rerum et casus et voluntas et necessitas dominatur.* The singular verb with the staccato series of subjects emphasizes each individually.

9. "power": *potentia.* This and *potestas* in Boethius represent δύναμις, "possibility or capability; force," in Aristotle.

10. "the sequence of events leading to the completion": *perfectionis ordo.*

11. "fix": *constituerent,* Meiser's suggestion for ms. *restituerent.*

12. An objection raised by the prisoner at *Consolation* 5.3.30–32, and answered by Philosophy at 5.6.44. See here chapter 6, 90–91. Philosophy's response reflects the answer of Hierocles, from the tenth chapter of the third book of his work *On*

Providence (Photius 465a–466b, translated in Wilson 1994, 225–28). Aujoulat 1986, 427–28, draws a different parallel between Boethius and Hierocles, who is said to have accommodated his Neoplatonic studies to the realities of Alexandrian Christianity: "La clarté, la mesure, la maîtrise, la sérénité du *Commentaire sur les Vers d'Or* semblent déjà donner le ton du *De Consolatione Philosophiae.*"

13. "happen by necessity": *ex necessitate contingunt*, a seeming contradiction in terms, recurs at 225.12–13: *si omnia necessitate non contingunt;* so also at 226.19–20. At *Consolation* 5.4.1 ff., Philosophy speaks of divination as a topic thoroughly investigated by Boethius; this is the primary passage.

14. "be interrupted": *intercidi*, literally, "to be cut up"; the Basel edition of 1570 reads *interdici*, "be prohibited." The language is imprecise; Boethius is not talking about X becoming something else, but about causal chains in general.

15. "state the converse": *is profecto conversurus est.*

16. *nefas*, "blasphemous reasoning," above translates *impia ratione*.

17. An awkward sentence; I follow Meiser's suggestion and read *ne . . . contendat* for *quod . . . contendit.*

18. Deleting *se*, with Meiser.

19. Sharples (1991, 228–29) notes that in Boethius God knows future contingents as contingents, and that he knows definitely their outcomes; Boethius agrees here with Iamblichus and Proclus. Cf. *Consolation* 5.3.23; 5.6.24.

20. "by reasoning from the people themselves and their actions": *ex ipsorum hominum et actuum ratione*. It is important to understand the gulf between this position and that expounded in *Consolation*. As Kretzmann points out (Blank and Kretzmann 1998, 190 n. 50) Boethius's treatment of God's foreknowledge here is quite different from that of *Consolation*, which invokes the eternal aspect of God's knowledge: ". . . if God knows now both that John will freely sin tomorrow, *and* that John's freely sinning is of course not necessary but contingent, John's sinning tomorrow is nonetheless *ineluctable*—an outcome that *must* occur. Presumably Boethius himself would have disowned this earlier treatment of the problem when, near the end of his life, he came up with his solution in terms of the atemporality of God's knowledge (*Consolation* V, prose 6)." See also Lloyd 1990, 154–59: "Iamblichus' principle of knowing. Future contingents." Lloyd makes a neat formulation: it is not that "will be" does not have in the eternal now the character that it has in time; rather, "knowing" does not have in time the character that it has in the eternal now.

21. "good will": *benivolentiam*. Below, "generosity" translates *benignitas*, and "kindness" translates *benefacere*.

22. "so blasphemously wise": *tam impie sapiens.* See above, n. 16.

23. "the violence of that impossibility": *ista vis inposibilitatis.*

24. *quare ponendum in rebus est casu quaedam posse et voluntate effici [et] <nec> necessitate constringi et ratio, quae utrumvis horum subruit, inpossibilis iudicanda est.* A difficult sentence; *utrumque*, "either of the two," leads me to accept Meiser's suggested emendation.

25. "to this impossible reasoning": *ad inpossibilem rationem perducit*. An odd phrase: better would be *ad inpossibile* (Greek, εἰς τὸ ἀδύνατον) *rationem ducit*, "takes this line of reasoning to an impossible conclusion," the reading of ms. T.

26. Boethius is a little careless here; he means, "of pairs of contradictory statements about the future." The term "definitely," *definite*, is crucial here; Boethius adopts late antiquity's standard solution to this problem and will assert that, while it must be the case that one of such a pair is true and the other false, they are not definitely true or definitely false (Sharples 1991, 29).

27. "secretly banishes": *subiudicat*. Not to be found elsewhere in Boethius, the verb is noted in Souter, *Glossary of Later Latin*, as the equivalent of ὑπονοῶ, "surmise." But this can't be right, as the expected sense is "undermines," whence the manuscript readings *subripiat* and *subducat*. I take the *sub-* of the compound to imply a secret action; *iudicare*, "to condemn."

28. Boethius now continues with a translation of 18b36–19a6.

Appendix 3. Maximian, *Elegy 3*

1. "the maelstrom of the world": *uertigine rerum*. The Latin suggests revolutions both cosmic and mundane. The call to lift up the mind from the world to the heavens is generally Philosophy's as well.

2. Agozzino considers the text of this distich far from certain.

3. "to disguise the eagerness of our feet, to walk on tiptoe": *fallere sollicitos, suspensos ponere gressus*. Both Agozzino and Spaltenstein plausibly take *sollicitos* as a noun referring to the pedagogue and the mother: "to deceive our anxious guards." But I take *sollicitos* with *gressus* to make a chiastic line.

4. "intending to cure her wounds with still more wounds": *medicare parans uulnera uulneribus*. It is important to note that the mother, like Boethius later (v. 55), is presented here as a doctor; and that her attempt at a cure is similar, to give the patient a homoeopathic dose of what she already suffers from.

5. "and that's the way grief rages": *et sic . . . saeuit . . . dolor*. Spaltenstein takes *et sic* as the equivalent of *tum;* but I think that a more gnomic force is required.

6. "everywhere": *per totum*. I follow Spaltenstein in taking this as an anticipation of the French *partout;* Agozzino similarly translates *dovunque*.

7. "hot to the marrow": *uisceribus anhelis*. Literally, "with panting guts," too crude in context, but the erotic connotations of the visceral appeal should not be lost in translation.

8. "She's not ashamed to tell": *nec memorare pudet*, nor is she ashamed to tell at v. 37. Similarly, the poet is not ashamed to tell the story in retrospect at v. 1, though his *pudor* frequently silences him in the course of the story; cf. vv. 45, 57. The poem ends with a restitution of *pudor*; cf. vv. 84, 94.

9. She alludes not only to the wounds of her beating but to her hoped-for defloration. Similarly, in Maximian's *Fifth Elegy*, the Greek girl, addressing the

impotent poet's *mentula*, speaks of how happy the girl is to be wounded and bleed-ing (vv. 131-34): "sternitur icta tuo uotiuo uulnere uirgo / et perfusa nouo laeta cruore iacet. / fert tacitum ridetque suum laniata dolorem / et percussori plaudit amica suo."

10. "I went limp": *languebam*. The poet's reaction to stimuli is to cease to be stimulated; here too Boethius's effect on him is anticipated. Cf. v. 77: "permissum fit uile nefas, fit languidus ardor." The *Fifth Elegy* also turns on a matter of impo-tence, seen to have cosmic implications (5.109-10): "Illa furens: 'nescis, ut cerno, perfide, nescis: non fleo priuatum, sed generale chaos'" [In a rage, she said: "I see it now: you don't get it, you traitor, you just don't get it. I do not weep for a personal but for a universal chaos"]. The key punning word, "general" chaos, is both repro-ductive and universal.

11. The difference between the poet and Aquilina is his unwillingness to speak (though he is willing to speak after the fact, in recording the poem); like Boethi-us's prisoner, he has to find a voice. Boethius speaks to the poet twice before he finally speaks at vv. 61-62; his actual words are not recorded until Boethius speaks a third time at at v. 63, making the shocking suggestion that the poet proceed ac-cording to the girl's desires.

12. "shellshock and starvation were like a voice": *sed stupor et macies uocis habe-bat opus.* The silence of the poet is paralleled by the silence of Boethius's prisoner in the presence of Philosophy. *Consolation* 1.2.4-5: "'Agnoscisne me? Quid taces? Pudore an stupore siluisti? Mallem pudore, sed te, ut uideo, stupor oppressit.' Cumque me non modo tacitum sed elinguem prorsus mutum uidisset, ammouit pectori meo leniter manum" ["Do you know me? Why don't you say something? Is it from shame or from incomprehension that you have fallen silent? I'd prefer shame, but it's obvious to me that incomprehension has had its way with you." Be-cause she saw that I was not merely silent but dumb, completely without a tongue, she gently put her hand upon my chest].

13. "loftiest investigator of all lofty things": *magnarum scrutator maxime rerum.* Shanzer 1983, 189-90, points to an ironic distance between the exalted implications of the vocative *maxime* and the humble implications of *scrutator*, often used for one who grubs about in the dirt: the heavenly investigator here turns his eyes down-ward to "low busy body affairs." This irony would accord with the pun of *Boethi, fers . . . opem*, in which Boethius's name, despite the false quantity of the long *o*, is related to the Greek verb βοηθέω, "to bring aid." Barnish 1990, 27 n. 59, opposes Shanzer's interpretation only in saying that the phrase is "not obviously deroga-tory" (pointing to a phrase in Paulinus of Nola, *Carmina* 14. 7, *cordis taciti scrutator,* said of the blessed Saint Felix). But note that Philosophy in *Consolation* 1.m.2 similarly addresses the prisoner ironically as a heavenly investigator now forced to stare at the ground.

14. "in the grip of some silent disease": *tacita me peste teneri.* Agozzino points out that here and elsewhere in the elegy, the poet in his erotic distress is compared

to Vergil's Dido (*Aeneid* 4.90: *quam simul ac tali persensit peste teneri*). For the silence of the poet and of Boethius's prisoner, see above, notes 11 and 12.

15. "There is no cure for a disease that is not understood," *non intellecti nulla est
curatio morbi.* So too Philosophy at *Consolation* 1.4.1: "Quid fles, quid lacrimas
manas? Ἐξαύδα, μὴ κεῦθε νόῳ. Si operam medicantis expectas, oportet uulnus de-
tegas" [Why are you crying? Why do your cheeks run with tears? As Homer says,
"Oút with it, dón't keep it lócked in your mínd!" If you are anticipating the doctor's
attentions, you need to uncover your wound]. That Boethius needs to hear the poet
speak before judging the exact nature of the cure is paralleled at *Consolation* 1.6.1:
"Primum igitur paterisne me pauculis rogitationibus statum tuae mentis attingere
atque temptare, ut qui modus sit tuae curationis intellegam?" [So will you first
allow me, with just a few little questions, to take the pulse of your mental state, to
get the feel of it, so I can understand what is to be the manner of your cure?]. What
is lacking in Maximian is any suggestion of the levels of cure that Philosophy
speaks of in *Consolation* 1.5.11: "nondum te ualidiora remedia contingunt" [the more
caustic remedies are not yet appropriate]; 1.6.21: "Sed quoniam firmioribus remediis
nondum tempus est" [But as it is not yet the right time for stronger cures]; 3.1.2:
"Itaque remedia quae paulo acriora esse dicebas non modo non perhorresco, sed
audiendi auidus uehementer efflagito" [Accordingly, those remedies which you
said were more bitter-tasting—I'm not only not afraid of them, but I demand them
passionately, eager to hear more]. Given the equivalence of *cura* and passion in the
poem (v. 12, *amor . . . curaque*; v. 49, the poet is *intentum curis*; v. 81, the poet loses
his *uanas curas*), *curatio*, "healing," more specifically implies "the removal of *cura*."

16. Similarly, Aquilina's fires increased at vv. 31–36, and the poet's pent-up fires
are reminiscent of Aquilina's "panting guts" (*uisceribus anhelis*).

17. Again, the poet is too ashamed to speak; cf. vv. 45–46.

18. "a silent evil": *taciti . . . mali.* Cf. the silent disease at v. 51, and the hidden
plague at v. 59.

19. "betrayed": *prodita . . . est.* Boethius embarrasses the poet; the language reflects the poet-narrator's *prodere non ausus* at v. 45.

20. "Don't be afraid": *pone metum.* Cf. *Consolation* 1.6.20: "nihil igitur perti-
mescas, iam tibi ex hac minima scintillula uitalis calor illuxerit" [So you need
not be afraid; from this very tiny spark a life-giving heat shall soon burst into
flame]. In the subsequent poem, which ends book 1, Philosophy concludes by urg-
ing the true seeker to banish hope and fear, joy and grief, the four Stoic passions
(1.m.6.25–28).

21. Spaltenstein worries about the word "pardon," *ueniam*, because it violates
the context; Boethius does not upbraid the poet for his passion. He suggests that
the word may be used "automatically" in the clichéd language of erotic elegy. But
passion proves to be a sort of fault by the end of the poem.

22. "my shamefaced silence": *uerecunda silentia.* It was *uerecundia* that burst
through the couple's "delicate composure" at v. 23. The poet's encounter with Boethius recapitulates his encounter with Aquilina: when silence can no longer be

kept, confessions are made, and indulgence in passion leads to an abandonment of passion.

23. "the beauty that has so pleased you": *placitae . . . formae*. One could extend the parallels between the poet and Vergil's Dido by quoting Anna's words at *Aeneid* 4.38: "placitone etiam pugnabis amori?" [Will you even fight against a love that has met your approval?].

24. *pietas talia uelle fugit*. This proves prophetic: at v. 92 the poet will say that opportunity stole away his enthusiasm, and even his desire fled: *atque ipsum talia uelle fugit*.

25. "are fed": *pascuntur*. At v. 13 Aquilina did not know how to feed her fire; the two of them together come to discover tiptoeing to secret assignations; only after Aquilina is beaten by her mother does she begin to speak of the violence that will satisfy passion. Boethius tries to teach the poet what Aquilina's mother has already taught her.

26. "the shedding of blood": *uulnera*. As at vv. 30 and 40, *uulnera* suggests intercourse and defloration.

27. Boethius the pander is not so much the issue as Boethius the teacher, whose student learns moderation from the lesson of excess. Yet he seems comfortably placed in this context, and there is a tradition that Boethius was at some point in his life something of a sensualist. Ennodius's epigram, "On Boethius, wearing a sword" (*De Boethio spatha cincto, Carmina* 2.132), describes him as distinctly effeminate:

> Languescit rigidi tecum substantia ferri,
>> soluitur atque chalybs more fluentis aquae.
> emollit gladios inbellis dextra Boethi,
>> ensis erat dudum, credite, nunc colus est.
> in thyrsum migrat quod gestas, improbe, pilum.
>> in Venerem constans, linque Mauortis opus.

> In your hands, the substance of stiff iron droops; steel too dissolves like flowing water. (Boethius's cowardly right hand softens the swords of war; believe me, what was once a dagger is now the spinner's spindle.) The spear you carry, you bastard, turns into the bacchant's thyrsus. Abandon the business of Mars, you who stand firm only for Venus.

Part of the joke here, not noticed in Shanzer 1983, is that Boethius is here presented as a parody of Amor (the epithet *improbus* is the giveaway, I think: cf. *Aeneid*, 4.412).

28. It is curious that all of this will prove not to have led to sexual intercourse; in effect, Boethius's bribes and the parents' complicity lead only to that stage in their affair that the couple had achieved before they were found out by Aquilina's mother (vv. 25–28). Surely some irony is intended in the conjunction of "sins and secrets" (*dant uitiis furtisque locum*) and "holding hands."

29. "my wasted heart": *tabida corda*. To be taken as a poetic plural; a first reading would take this as "our hearts"; the next distich makes it clear that Aquilina's heart did not respond as the poet's did.

30. "her body intact": *illaeso corpore*. She had longed for *uulnera* (v. 42), and Boethius suggested he give them to her (v. 70). It is not quite clear just what cause she hates (she has several to choose from), but the *languidus ardor* of v. 77 suggests impotence. In the *Fifth Elegy* the Greek girl delivers two long apostrophes to the poet's *mentula* after he proves impotent (for the second, see above, note 10; the first is 5.61–70). Aquilina has no lament to parallel this, but departs depressed (v. 80, *tristis*); the word reappears significantly in the penultimate line.

31. "which was now healed": *sanato pectore*. *Consolation* never speaks of the prisoner as being cured or healed.

32. "empty anxieties": *uanas . . . curas*. He had been "bent over in worry" (v. 49, *curis intentum*) before Boethius's cure.

33. "learned": *didici*. Spaltenstein here as elsewhere loses the image, taking this as the equivalent of "realized," but this is a teacher-student relationship that is being dramatized, and Boethius is certainly the *praeceptor amoris*.

34. Agozzino draws our attention to Cicero, *Tusculans* 4.71–75, where it is stated that the appropriate cure for a man who loves to madness is to have the object of his desire revealed to him for the utterly contemptible thing that it is (*haec curatio adhibenda est*). Now it is true that the *Tusculans* have great influence on *Consolation*, but the point in Maximian is that the poet's own desiring, and not its object, is the problem. Like Augustine, the poet takes inability to perform sexually when one wants to as proof of the Fall; but the poet confuses lack of performance with positive virtue.

35. It is uncertain whether the poet addresses this to Aquilina or to himself. She seems to have left at v. 80, and this seems to inspire the realization of his lesson. He could address his own virginity, or Virginity as an abstraction—his actions keep Virginity on her throne, as it were; *salue* should introduce a prayer. If it is directed to Aquilina, he would claim to be responsible for her virtue, which would be exceptionally cruel. I take it that the poet is patting himself on the back, not mocking Aquilina. It is in any event excessive, and its exaggeration begins to prepare us for the ironic ending.

36. "the master of your own love": *proprii dominator amoris*. Again, the concern is purely with the poet's virtue, not with Aquilina's.

37. How ironic is Boethius? Very, according to Shanzer 1983, 191–92: why should the virgin warrior Minerva yield to the poet, who has overcome the enticements of love? For the goddess of wisdom to yield to the poet is to mock his wisdom. Here Maximian borrows from Horace, *Sermones* 1.2.31–35, telling the story of Cato's congratulating the young man who visits prostitutes instead of corrupting married women ("*macte uirtute esto*"). I think that Boethius's praise is at least as exaggerated as that of the poet at vv. 83–84.

38. As Barnish 1990, 23–24, puts it: "In the language of the *Consolation*, which his own recalls, Maximian, who had first the *uelle*, then also the *posse* for evil, loses the former, and so the *perficere*, regaining his *beatitudo*." The key parallels are *Consolation* 4.2.5–6 and 4.4.4–5.

39. "we both departed": *discessimus ambo*. Shanzer takes the pair to be the poet and Boethius, as Aquilina has already left the stage; Barnish presumes that they are Aquilina and the poet, as the previous distich seems to recapitulate the affair, and this distich seems to restate its outcome—*discidium* is certainly divorce, and *discessimus*, from *discedo*, can suggest *discessio*, a term for the separation of a married couple. Barnish also points to *Consolation* 3.7.3, Philosophy's words on the sad outcome of love affairs: "Quarum motus quid habeat iucunditatis ignoro; tristes uero esse uoluptatum exitus, quisquis reminisci libidinum suarum uolet intelleget" [I have no idea myself what delightfulness the excitement of these pleasures may possess; but any man willing to call his acts of lust to mind will understand that the end results of such pleasures are sorrowful]. But there has been no sexual satisfaction, and for the poet to be depressed (he is certainly one half of the pair in question) shows that even now he does not rejoice in having followed Boethius's advice. "We had not satisfied each other"—this is true of both pairs. Boethius has reason to laugh at Maximian's praise of his own virtue, and Maximian has cause to dislike Boethius's nasty, if effective, advice.

Appendix 4.   Agathias Scholasticus, *Greek Anthology*, 11.354

1. There are only typographic differences between this text and that in Paton's Loeb edition of the *Anthology* (4:236–38); similarly with the text in Viansino 1967, 152–53 (poem 95).

2. The most convenient discussion of this Nicostratus is provided in Dillon 1977, 233–36; passing references are in Glucker 1978; still fundamental is the article by von Fritz in the *Real-Encyclopädie*. He is known primarily through Simplicius's commentary on Aristotle's *Categories* as a "shameless" carper and a doubter of the validity of the categories. Cameron 1970, 101–2, discusses the acquaintance that Agathias had with, and the respect that he had for, such philosophers as Simplicius and Damascius; we may presume that Agathias was familiar with Simplicius's *Commentary* even if we do not view him as a philosophical adept.

3. Immediately implied is Nicostratus's belief in the agreement of Plato and Aristotle; this reappears explicitly in vv. 7–10. The young Boethius too insists that Plato and Aristotle are in fundamental agreement (though he adds that many would not agree) in his well-known plan to translate and comment on all of their works (*In de interpretatione*² 2.3, 79.9–80.9 Meiser). The neologism σκινδαλαμοφράστην, "speaker of splinters, splitter of words," certainly implies that Nicostratus is a comic figure, and that his mastery of Plato and Aristotle together has made him so.

4. "steepest wisdom": αἰπυτάτης σοφίης. Duffy 1983, 293 n. 23, notes that Aga-thias typically uses σοφίη with a bit of a sneer, to designate what we should call "book learning."

5. "of things stratospheric": τῶν μετεώρων. μετέωρος and its various con-geners are frequently used to disparage learning; it corresponds exactly to the En-glish phrase "head in the clouds," and if it makes us think of Aristotle's μετε-ωρολογικά, it is only in a comic sense. Examples are abundant in Aristophanes' *Clouds*: 228, 333 (μετεωροφένακας, "stratospheric quacks"), 360 (μετεωροσο-φιστῶν, "stratospheric sophists"), 404 (μετεωρισθείς, "raised up to the strato-sphere"), 490, 1284.

6. "loftiness": ὕψος. This participates in the same sort of humor as αἰπυτάτης σοφίης, "steepest wisdom," and τῶν μετεώρων, "things stratospheric"; similarly in the epigram of Callimachus that Agathias refers to (quoted below, note 12), Cleom-brotus leaps ἀφ' ὑψηλοῦ τείχεος, "from a lofty wall," to his death.

7. The poem depends upon a generalization: for Aristotle, a monist, the soul cannot be spoken of outside of the body; for Plato, the dualist, the soul exists out-side of the body. Thus they are portrayed as irreconcilable, a point made by the phrase "on every side with every accuracy." However, in his later dialogues Plato seems not to believe that the immortal soul that comes into the body can exist out-side of the body (see Ostenfeld 1987, 48); and even within *Phaedo* the nature of the soul outside of the body is defined in a number of different ways (see Bostock 1986, 25–30).

8. The theatricality of this gesture suggests a Cynic philosopher and a public performance. Diogenes Laertius 3.37 relates an anecdote told by Favorinus to the effect that when Plato first delivered *Phaedo*, Aristotle alone remained in the audi-ence, though everyone else stood up and left (see Riginos 1976, 180, Anecdote 131). The anecdote has it that *Phaedo* is so ill-conceived and so difficult that only Aris-totle can understand it; like Agathias's epigram, it too depicts a comic unity of Plato and Aristotle on the question of the soul, as people of normal intelligence go elsewhere.

9. "laid the solution out": ἐξέφερεν. The verb ἐκφέρω frequently means to "carry out" a body for burial, though it can also mean to "bring forth" an opinion.

10. στεγνοφυής, "constipated" ("of thick nature"), is unparalleled elsewhere. It therefore cannot be a Neoplatonic term of art for such discussions and should be a comic formation. στεγνόω and στέγνωσις frequently have the medical connota-tions that suggest "constipated" as a translation.

To parallel this inconclusive presentation of opposite opinions, one may com-pare Porphyry's introduction to the discussion of universals (*Isagoge* 1.9–14) and Boe-thius's second commentary on it (*In Isagogen Porphyrii*[2], 159.3–167.20 Brandt); Boe-thius decides that it is not appropriate for him to decide between the disagreements of Plato and Aristotle on this score. These texts are available in translation in Spade 1994, 20–25.

11. Other epigrams in the *Anthology* speak of Plato living now in the land of truth: his body is on earth, his soul in heaven is one way of putting it (7.61, 7.62,

7.363, 16.31); a less polite one is to say that Plato taught us to walk in the ether and forget our origins (10.45, Palladas). A more general parallel is afforded by Lucian, *Jupiter Confutatus* 17, in which Cyniscus reproves Zeus for speaking to him of the other world and its rewards and punishments in answer to his questions about the lack of justice here on earth: Ἅιδην μοι λέγεις καὶ Τιτυοὺς καὶ Ταντάλους. ἐγὼ δέ, εἰ μέν τι καὶ τοιοῦτόν ἐστιν, εἴσομαι τὸ σαφὲς ἐπειδὰν ἀποθανῶ [You're talking to me about Hades and characters like Tityus and Tantalus. But as for me, if there is anything to this, I will know it clearly when I die].

   12. Callimachus, Epigram 23 (25) Pfeiffer (*Greek Anthology* 7.471):

> Εἴπας ""Ἥλιε, χαῖρε" Κλεόμβροτος ὡμβρακιότης
> ἥλατ᾽ ἀφ᾽ ὑψηλοῦ τείχεος εἰς Ἀίδην,
> ἄξιον οὐδὲν ἰδὼν θανάτου κακόν, ἀλλὰ Πλάτωνος
> ἓν τὸ περὶ ψυχῆς γράμμ᾽ ἀναλεξάμενος.

> Cleombrotus of Ambracia shouted, "Farewell, O Sun!" and leapt from a lofty wall down into Hades; he had seen no evil worthy of death, but he had read Plato's one work on the soul from beginning to end.

Ammonius, *In Isagogen Porphyrii* 4.15 ff. Busse, cites Callimachus's epigram about Cleombrotus as an example of a misunderstanding of the precept φιλοσοφία ἐστὶ μελέτη θανάτου, "Philosophy is the practice of death." However, this epigram is not unparalleled in Callimachus. Sinko 1905, 9–10, speaks of epigrams 10 (12) and 13 (15) Pfeiffer as parallel to Agathias's poem. Epigram 10 (*Greek Anthology* 7.520): if you want to find Timarchus to learn about the soul or your posthumous fate, seek him among the blessed (in Hades); epigram 13 (*Greek Anthology* 7.524): a conversation with the dead Charidas at his tomb reveals that all of the stories about the underworld are a lie, but that if you want a pleasant story, things may be bought there at a low price. Of the late Neoplatonists who defend Plato from the charge of having encouraged this suicide (Ammonius, Elias, David, and Pseudo-Elias), none entertains the notion that the story was most likely just invented by Callimachus. After his defeat at Thapsus, Cato of Utica is said to have read *Phaedo* before committing suicide by pulling out his stitches; this is quite a different story.

   13. ἐπιγνοίης . . . σαυτόν surely calls to mind γνῶθι σαυτόν, "Know thyself." Courcelle 1974, 181–229, discusses the use of this precept in the fifth and sixth centuries, noting that it is frequently interpreted by both pagans and Christians to mean "live within yourself" so as to be fit for true revelation. See here chapter 6, 78.

   14. ὑπολειπόμενος: either "leaving behind" or "retaining." The latter is certainly possible; when he is dead, the student will have the thing that he is asking about. But were Nicostratus confident that the pupil would retain what he wants to find after death, he would know something for certain about the land of the dead, that there will be a soul to have there. I follow the first possibility, according to which Nicostratus says that the pupil will lose his life while trying to find it.

References

Ackrill, J. L., trans. 1963. *Aristotle:* Categories *and* On Interpretation. Rev. ed. Oxford: Oxford University Press.

Agozzino, Tullio, ed. 1970. *Massimiano: Elegie.* Bologna: Biblioteca Silva di Filologia.

Alfonsi, Luigi. 1942-43. "Sulla composizione della *Philosophiae Consolatio* boeziana." *Atti dell' Istituo Veneto di scienze, lettere e arti* 102:707-23.

———. 1955. "Storia interiore e storia cosmica nella 'Consolatio' boeziana." *Convivium* N. S. 3:513-21.

Anastasi, Rosario. 1948. "Boezio e Massimiano." *Miscellanea di Studi di Letteratura Antica* 2:1-20.

———. 1951. "La III elegia di Massimiano." *Miscellanea di Studi di Letteratura Christiana* 3:45-92.

Ashton-Gwatkin, Frank, trans. 1975. *Max: Poet of the Final Hour, Being the Elegies of Maximianus the Etruscan.* London: Paul Norbury Publications.

Astell, Ann W. 1994. *Job, Boethius, and Epic Truth.* Ithaca: Cornell University Press.

Asztalos, Monika. 1993. "Boethius as a Transmitter of Greek Logic to the Latin West: *The Categories.*" *Harvard Studies in Classical Philology* 95:367-407.

Aujoulat, Noël. 1986. *Le néo-platonisme Alexandrin: Hiéroclès d'Alexandrie. Filiations intellectuelles et spirituelles d'un néo-platonicien du Ve siècle.* Leiden: E. J. Brill.

Bakhtin, Mikhail. 1984. *Problems of Dostoevsky's Poetics.* Trans. Caryl Emerson. Theory and History of Literature 8. Minneapolis: University of Minnesota Press.

Barbour, John D. 1994. *Versions of Deconversion: Autobiography and the Loss of Faith.* Charlottesville: University Press of Virginia.

Barnish, S. J. B. 1990. "Maximian, Cassiodorus, Boethius, Theodahad: Literature, Philosophy and Politics in Ostrogothic Italy." *Nottingham Medieval Studies* 34:16-32.

Bell, Elizabeth S. 1988. "The Clash of World Views in John Kennedy Toole's *A Confederacy of Dunces.*" *Southern Literary Journal* 21:15-22.

Belsey, Andrew. 1991. "Boethius and *The Consolation of Philosophy,* or, How to Be a Good Philosopher." *Ratio* 4:1-15.

Bennett, Beth S. 1991. "The Rhetoric of Martianus Capella and Anselm de Besate in the Tradition of Menippean Satire." *Philosophy and Rhetoric* 24:128–42.

Bergant, Dianne. 1992. "The Perspective of Wisdom." In M. Jack Suggs et al., eds., *The Oxford Study Bible*. Oxford: Oxford University Press, 172–80.

Bieler, Ludwig. 1984. *Anicii Manlii Severini Boethii Philosophiae Consolatio*. 2d ed. Corpus Christianorum, Series Latina 94. Turnhout: Brepols.

Birley, Anthony. 1987. *Marcus Aurelius: A Biography*. Rev. ed. New Haven: Yale University Press.

Blanchard, W. Scott. 1995. *Scholars' Bedlam. Menippean Satire in the Renaissance.* Lewisburg, Pa.: Bucknell University Press.

Blank, David, and Norman Kretzmann, trans. 1999. *Ammonius:* On Aristotle's *On Interpretation 9; with Boethius,* On Aristotle's *On Interpretation 9*. Ithaca: Cornell University Press.

Bloom, Harold, ed. 1991. *Odysseus/Ulysses*. New York: Chelsea House Publishers.

Blumenthal, A. 1986. "New Muses: Poetry in Boethius' *Consolatio*." *Pacific Coast Philology* 21:25–29.

Boese, H., ed. 1960. *Procli Diadochi Tria Opuscula (De Providentia, Libertate, Malo)*. Berlin: De Gruyter.

Booker, M. Keith. 1995. *Flann O'Brien, Bakhtin, and Menippean Satire*. Syracuse: Syracuse University Press.

Bostock, David. 1986. *Plato's Phaedo*. Oxford: Oxford University Press.

Bower, Calvin M., trans. 1989. *Fundamentals of Music, Anicius Manlius Severinus Boethius*. New Haven: Yale University Press.

Brandt, Samuel, ed. 1906. *Anicii Manlii Severini Boethii In Isagogen Porphyrii Commenta*. Corpus Scriptorum Ecclesiasticorum Latinorum 48. Vienna: Tempsky.

Branham, R. Bracht, and Marie-Odile Goulet-Cazé, eds. 1996. *The Cynics: The Cynic Movement in Antiquity and Its Legacy*. Berkeley: University of California Press.

Branham, R. Bracht, and Daniel Kinney, trans. 1996. *Petronius: Satyrica*. Berkeley: University of California Press.

Brown, Peter. 1967. *Augustine of Hippo*. Berkeley: University of California Press.

———. 1971. *The World of Late Antiquity, AD 150–750*. London: Thames and Hudson.

———. 1987. "Late Antiquity." In Veyne 1987, 235–311.

———. 1988. *The Body and Society: Men, Women, and Sexual Renunciation in Early Christianity*. New York: Columbia University Press.

Buresch, C. 1886. "Consolationum a Graecis Romanisque scriptarum historia critica." *Leipziger Studien zur classischen Philologie* 9:1–170.

Cameron, A. 1970. *Agathias*. Oxford: Oxford University Press.

Cannata Fera, Maria. 1991. "La struttura delle consolationes plutarchee." In D'Ippolito and Gallo 1991, 315–26.

Chadwick, Henry. 1980. "Theta on Philosophy's Dress in Boethius." *Medium Aevum* 49:175–79.

————. 1981. *Boethius: The Consolations of Music, Logic, Theology, and Philosophy.* Oxford: Oxford University Press.

Cherniss, Michael D. 1987. *Boethian Apocalypse: Studies in Middle English Vision Poetry.* Norman, Okla.: Pilgrim Books.

Claassen, Jo-Marie. 1999. *Displaced Persons: The Literature of Exile from Cicero to Boethius.* Madison: University of Wisconsin Press.

————. 2007. "Literary *Anamnesis*: Boethius Reads Ovid." *Helios.* Forthcoming.

Cohoon, J. W., trans. 1939. *Dio Chrysostom.* Vol. 2. Loeb Classical Library. Cambridge: Harvard University Press.

Colish, Marcia. 2005. Review of Marenbon 2003. *Speculum* 80:272–74.

Conte, Gian Biagio. 1996. *The Hidden Author: An Interpretation of Petronius' Satyricon.* Trans. Elaine Fantham. Berkeley: University of California Press.

Corrigan, Kevin. 1996. "'Solitary' Mysticism in Plotinus, Proclus, Gregory of Nyssa, and Pseudo-Dionysius." *Journal of Religion* 76:28–42.

Courcelle, Pierre. 1948. *Les lettres grecques en occident de Macrobe à Cassiodore.* Bibliothèque des Écoles françaises d'Athènes et de Rome 159. Paris: de Boccard.

————. 1967. La Consolation de Philosophie *dans la tradition littéraire: Antécédents et postérité de Boèce.* Paris: Études Augustiniennes.

————. 1974. *Connais-toi toi-même de Socrate à Saint Bernard.* Vol. 1. Paris: Études Augustiniennes.

Crabbe, Anna. 1981. "Literary Design in the *De Consolatione Philosophiae.*" In Gibson 1981, 237–74.

Craig, W. L. 1988. "Boethius on Theological Fatalism." *Ephemerides Theologicae Lovanienses* 64:324–47.

Crossan, John Dominic. 1979. *Finding Is the First Act: Trove Folktales and Jesus' Treasure Parable.* Semeia Supplements 9. Philadelphia: Fortress Press.

Curley, Thomas F. 1986. "How to Read the *Consolation of Philosophy.*" *Interpretation* 14:211–63.

————. 1987. "The *Consolation of Philosophy* as a Work of Literature." *American Journal of Philology* 108:343–67.

Dalfen, Joachim, ed. 1979. *Marci Aurelii Antonini ad se ipsum libri XII.* Leipzig: Teubner.

Davies, Ioan. 1990. *Writers in Prison.* Oxford: Basil Blackwell.

Delabar, Walter. 1992. "Der Politiker als Philosoph, die Philosophie als Trösterin: Zur Rolle und Funktion der Philosophie in Boethius' *Trost der Philosophie.*" In Hardin and Jungmayr 1992, 1175–95.

Dillon, John. 1977. *The Middle Platonists.* Ithaca: Cornell University Press.

D'Ippolito, G., and I. Gallo, eds. 1991. *Strutture formali dei "Moralia" di Plutarco.* Proceedings of the Third Conference on Plutarch, Palermo, May 3–5, 1989.

Dougherty, M. V. 2004. "The Problem of *Humana Natura* in the *Consolatio Philosophiae* of Boethius." In Nash-Marshall 2004, 273–92.

Dronke, Peter. 1994. *Verse with Prose from Petronius to Dante: The Art and Scope of the Mixed Form.* Cambridge: Harvard University Press.

————, ed. 1978. *Bernardus Silvestris,* Cosmographia. Textus Minores 53. Leiden: E. J. Brill.

————, ed. 1988. *A History of Twelfth-Century Western Philosophy.* Cambridge: Cambridge University Press.

Duffy, John. 1983. "On an Epigram of Agathias (*AP* XI 382)." *American Journal of Philology* 104:287–94.

Dwyer, Richard A. 1976. *Boethian Fictions: Narratives in the Medieval French Versions of the* Consolatio Philosophiae. Cambridge: Harvard University Press.

Ebbesen, Sten. 1990. "Boethius as an Aristotelian Commentator." In Sorabji 1990, 373–91.

Evans, G. R. 1983. *Alan of Lille: The Frontiers of Theology in the Later Twelfth Century.* Cambridge: Cambridge University Press.

Favez, Charles. 1937. *La consolation latine chrétienne.* Paris: Librairie Philosophique J. Vrin.

————. 1976. "Consolatio (λόγος παραμυθητικός)." In N. G. L. Hammond and H. H. Scullard, eds., *Oxford Classical Dictionary.* 2d ed. Oxford: Oxford University Press, 279.

Fontaine, Jacques. 1965. "Isidore de Séville auteur 'ascétique': Les énigmes des *Synonyma.*" *Studi Medievali,* 3d ser., 6:163–95.

Fortin, John. 2004. "The Nature of Consolation in *The Consolation of Philosophy.*" In Nash-Marshall 2004, 293–307.

Fowden, Garth. 1993. *The Egyptian Hermes: A Historical Approach to the Late Pagan Mind.* 2d ed. Princeton: Princeton University Press.

Freudenburg, Kirk, ed. 2005. *The Cambridge Companion to Roman Satire.* Cambridge: Cambridge University Press.

Frye, Northrop. 1957. *Anatomy of Criticism: Four Essays.* Princeton: Princeton University Press.

————. 1976. *The Secular Scripture: A Study of the Structure of Romance.* Cambridge: Harvard University Press.

Fuhrmann, M., and Joachim Gruber, eds. 1984. *Boethius.* Wege der Forschung 483. Darmstadt: Wissenschaftliche Buchgesellschaft.

Gersh, Stephen. 1986. *Middle Platonism and Neoplatonism: The Latin Tradition.* 2 vols. Publications in Mediaeval Studies 23. Notre Dame: University of Notre Dame Press.

Gibson, Margaret, ed. 1981. *Boethius: His Life, Thought and Influence.* Oxford: Basil Blackwell.

Glucker, John. 1978. *Antiochus and the Late Academy.* Hypomnemata 56. Göttingen: Vandenhoeck & Ruprecht.

Green, Melissa. 1990. "The Consolation of Boethius." *Paris Review* 32:86–88.

Gregg, Robert C. 1975. *Consolation Philosophy: Greek and Christian Paideia in Basil and the Two Gregories.* Patristic Monograph Series, no. 3. Cambridge, Mass.: Philadelphia Patristic Foundation.

Griffin, Jasper, ed. 1995. *Homer:* Iliad Book IX. Oxford: Oxford University Press.

Grube, G. M. A., trans. 1963. *The Meditations of Marcus Aurelius*. Library of Liberal Arts. Indianapolis: Bobbs Merrill.

Gruber, Joachim. 1978. *Kommentar zu Boethius* De Consolatione Philosophiae. Vol. 9, Texte und Kommentare. Berlin: De Gruyter.

———. 1997–99. "Boethius 1925–1998." Parts 1–3. *Lustrum* 39:307–83; *Lustrum* 40: 199–259; *Lustrum* 41. Forthcoming.

Guthrie, W. K. C. 1969. *A History of Greek Philosophy*. Vol. 3. Cambridge: Cambridge University Press.

Haarberg, Jon. 1998. *Parody and the* Praise of Folly. Acta Humaniora 42. Oslo: Scandinavian University Press.

Habinek, Thomas. 2005. "Satire as Aristocratic Play." In Freudenburg 2005, 177–91.

Hadot, Pierre. 1993. *Plotinus, or the Simplicity of Vision*. Trans. Michael Chase. Chicago: University of Chicago Press.

Hardin, James, and Jörg Jungmayr, eds. 1992. *"Der Buchstab tödt—der Geist macht lebendig": Festschrift zum 60. Geburtstag von Hans-Gert Roloff.* Bern: Peter Lang.

Häring, Nikolaus M., ed. 1978. "Alan of Lille, 'De planctu naturae.'" *Studi Medievali*, 3d ser., 19:797–879.

Hays, Bradford Gregory. 1996. *Fulgentius the Mythographer*. Ph.D. diss., Cornell University.

———. 2006. "Further Notes on Fulgentius." *Harvard Studies in Classical Philology* 13. Forthcoming.

Heise, William E. 1996. *Aristotle and the Allegorical Aesthetic: Poetry and the Limits of Philosophy from Alan of Lille to Edmund Spenser*. Ph.D. diss., University of Illinois.

Hillas, Roger S. 1987. *Elias of Thriplow*, Serium Senectutis: *An Edition and Translation*. Ph.D. diss., University of Virginia.

Howlett, David. 1995. *The Celtic Latin Tradition of Biblical Style*. Dublin: Four Courts Press.

———. 2006. *Pillars of Wisdom in Ireland and England*. Dublin: Four Courts Press. Forthcoming.

Hudry, Françoise. 1989. "Prologus Alani *De Planctu Naturae*." *Archives d'Histoire Doctrinale et Littéraire du Moyen Age* 63:169–85.

Humphries, Michael L. 1997. "Michel Foucault on Writing and the Self in the *Meditations* of Marcus Aurelius and *Confessions* of St. Augustine." *Arethusa* 30: 125–38.

Johann, H.-T. 1968. *Trauer und Trost: Eine quellen- und strukturanalytische Untersuchung der philosophischen Trostschriften über den Tod*. Studia et Testimonia Antiqua 5. Munich: Fink.

Kane, George, and E. Talbot Donaldson, eds. 1975. Piers Plowman: *The B Version*. London: Athlone Press.

Kaplan, Carter. 2000. *Critical Synoptics: Menippean Satire and the Analysis of Intellectual Mythology*. Madison: Fairleigh Dickinson University Press.

Kassel, Rudolf. 1958. *Untersuchungen zur griechischen und römischen Konsolationsliteratur.* Zetemata, no. 18. Munich: C. H. Beck'sche Verlagsbuchhandlung.

———. 1965. "Trostliteratur." In *Lexikon der Alten Welt,* col. 3135–3137. Zürich and Stuttgart: Artemis Verlag.

Kaylor, Noel Harold, Jr. 1992. *The Medieval Consolation of Philosophy: An Annotated Bibliography.* Garland Medieval Bibliographies 7. New York: Garland.

Kennedy, George A. 1980. *Classical Rhetoric and Its Christian and Secular Tradition from Ancient to Modern Times.* Chapel Hill: University of North Carolina Press.

Kirk, Eugene. 1980. *Menippean Satire: An Annotated Catalogue of Texts and Criticism.* Garland Reference Library of the Humanities 191. New York: Garland.

———. 1982. "Boethius, Lucian, and Menippean Satire." *Helios* 9:59–71.

Klingner, F. 1921. *De Boethii* Consolatione Philosophiae. Philologische Untersuchungen 27. Berlin: Weidmann.

Könsgen, Ewald, ed. 1990. *Arbor amoena comis: 25 Jahre: Mittellateinisches Seminar in Bonn.* Stuttgart: Franz Steiner Verlag.

LaChance, Paul J. 2004. "Boethius on Human Freedom." In Nash-Marshall 2004, 309–27.

Laín Entralgo, Pedro. 1970. *The Therapy of the Word in Classical Antiquity.* Trans. L. J. Rather and John M. Sharp. New Haven: Yale University Press.

Lamberton, Robert. 1986. *Homer the Theologian: Neoplatonist Allegorical Reading and the Growth of the Epic Tradition.* Berkeley: University of California Press.

Langlois, Ernest, ed. 1914–24. *Guillaume de Lorris and Jean de Meun: Le Roman de la Rose.* 5 vols. New York: Johnson Reprints, 1965.

Leftow, Brian. 1990. "Boethius on Eternity." *History of Philosophy Quarterly* 7:123–42.

LeMoine, Fannie J. 1991. "Parental Gifts: Father-Son Dedications and Dialogues in Roman Didactic Literature." *Illinois Classical Studies* 16:337–66.

Lerer, Seth. 1985. *Boethius and Dialogue: Literary Method in* The Consolation of Philosophy. Princeton: Princeton University Press.

Lewis, C. S. 1964. *The Discarded Image. An Introduction to Medieval and Renaissance Literature.* Cambridge: Cambridge University Press.

Lind, L. R., trans. 1988. *Gabriele Zerbi,* Gerontocomia: *On the Care of the Aged and Maximianus, Elegies on Old Age and Love.* Memoirs of the American Philosophical Society 182. Philadelphia: American Philosophical Society.

Lloyd, A. C. 1990. *The Anatomy of Neoplatonism.* Oxford: Oxford University Press.

Magee, John. 1988. "Note on Boethius, *Consolatio* I. 1, 5; 3, 7: A New Biblical Parallel." *Vigiliae Christianae* 42:79–82.

Mann, Jill. "Jean de Meun and the Castration of Saturn." In Marenbon 2001, 309–26.

Marenbon, John. 2002. Review of Relihan 2001. *Medieval Review* 02.09.22.

———. 2003. *Boethius.* Great Medieval Thinkers. Oxford: Oxford University Press.

————. 2004. "Boethius and the Problem of Paganism." In Nash-Marshall 2004, 329–48.

————. *The Middle Ages and the Problem of Paganism.* Forthcoming.

————, ed. 2001. *Poetry and Philosophy in the Middle Ages.* Mittelalterliche Studien und Texte 29. Leiden: Brill.

Martindale, Charles. 1993. *Redeeming the Text: Latin Poetry and the Hermeneutics of Reception.* Cambridge: Cambridge University Press.

Maurach, G., ed. 1976. *Römische Philosophie.* Wege der Forschung 193. Darmstadt: Wissenschaftliche Buchgesellschaft.

McEvoy, James T. 1992. "Neoplatonism and Christianity: Influence, Syncretism or Discernment?" In Thomas Finan and Vincent Twomey, eds., *The Relationship between Neoplatonism and Christianity,* 155–70. Dublin: Four Courts Press.

McMahon, Robert. 1994. "The Structural Articulation of Boethius's *Consolation of Philosophy.*" *Medievalia and Humanistica* 21:55–72.

————. 2006. *Understanding the Medieval Meditative Ascent: Augustine, Anselm, Boethius, and Dante.* Washington, D.C.: Catholic University of America Press.

Meiser, Karl. 1877. *Anicii Manlii Severini Boetii commentarii in librum Aristotelis περὶ ἑρμηνείας.* Vol. 1. Leipzig: Teubner.

————. 1880. *Anicii Manlii Severini Boetii commentarii in librum Aristotelis περὶ ἑρμηνείας.* Vol. 2. Leipzig: Teubner.

Micaelli, Claudio. 2004. "Boethian Reflections on God: Between Logic and Metaphysics." In Nash-Marshall 2004, 181–202.

Mignucci, Mario. 1987. "Boezio e il problema dei futuri contingenti." *Medioevo* 13:1–50.

Minio-Paluello, Lorenzo. 1970. "Boethius, Anicius Manlius Severinus." In Charles Coulston Gillispie, ed., *Dictionary of Scientific Biography,* 2:228–36. New York: Charles Scribner's Sons.

Mitchell, J. Allen. 2003. "Boethius and Pandarus: A Source in Maximian's 'Elegies.'" *Notes and Queries* 50:377–80.

Mitchell, Stephen, trans. 1987. *The Book of Job.* Reprint, New York: Harper Perennial, 1992.

Mohrmann, C. 1976. "Some Remarks on the Language of Boethius, *Consolatio Philosophiae.*" In J. J. O'Meara and B. Naumann 1976, 54–61.

Moorhead, John. 1992. *Theoderic in Italy.* Oxford: Oxford University Press.

Moreschini, Claudio, ed. 2000. *Boethius: De Consolatione Philosophiae, Opuscula Theologica.* Bibliotheca Teubneriana. Munich: K. G. Saur.

Muecke, Frances. 2005. "Rome's First 'Satirists': Themes and Genre in Ennius and Lucilius." In Freudenburg 2005, 33–47.

Nash-Marshall, Siobhan, ed. 2004. *Boethius.* Special issue. *American Catholic Philosophical Quarterly* 78(2).

Newman, Robert J. 1988. "Rediscovering the *De Remediis Fortuitorum.*" *American Journal of Philology* 109:92–107.

Nitzsche, Jane Chance. 1975. *The Genius Figure in Antiquity and the Middle Ages.* New York: Columbia University Press.

O'Daly, Gerard. 1991. *The Poetry of Boethius.* Chapel Hill: University of North Carolina Press.

O'Donnell, James J. 1993. Review of Moorhead 1992. *Bryn Mawr Classical Review* 04.04.10.

———, ed. 1984. *Boethius,* Consolatio Philosophiae. Bryn Mawr: Bryn Mawr Commentaries.

O'Gorman, Ellen. 2005. "Citation and Authority in Seneca's *Apocolocyntosis.*" In Freudenburg 2005, 95–108.

Olmstead, Wendy Raudenbush. 1989. "Philosophical Inquiry and Religious Transformation in Boethius' *The Consolation of Philosophy* and Augustine's *Confessions.*" *Journal of Religion* 69:14–35.

O'Meara, J. J., and B. Naumann, eds. 1976. *Latin Script and Letters 400–900: Festschrift for Ludwig Bieler.* Leiden: E. J. Brill.

Ostenfeld, Erik. 1987. *Ancient Greek Psychology and the Modern Mind-Body Debate.* Aarhus: Aarhus University Press.

Pabst, Bernhard. 1994. *Prosimetrum: Tradition und Wandel einer Literaturform zwischen Spätantike und Spätmittelalter.* 2 vols. Ordo: Studien zur Literatur und Gesellschaft des Mittelalters und der frühen Neuzeit 4. Cologne: Böhlau.

Patch, Howard Rollin. 1970. *The Tradition of Boethius: A Study of His Importance in Medieval Culture.* New York: Russell & Russell.

Payne, F. Anne. 1981. *Chaucer and Menippean Satire.* Madison: The University of Wisconsin Press.

Pépin, Jean. 1991. "The Platonic and Christian Ulysses." In Bloom 1991, 228–48.

Quacquarelli, Antonio. 1989. "Il sogno di Boezio." *Invigilata lucernis* 11:485–90.

Quandt, Kenneth. 1982. "Socratic Consolation: Rhetoric and Philosophy in Plato's *Crito.*" *Philosophy and Rhetoric* 15:238–56.

Ratkowitsch, Christine. 1986. *Maximianus amat: Zu Datierung und Interpretation des Elegikers Maximian.* Österreichische Akademie der Wissenschaften, philosophisch-historische Klasse, Sitzungsberichte, 463. Vienna.

———. 1990. "Weitere Argumente zur Datierung und Interpretation Maximians (zu vorliegenden Rezensionen)." *Wiener Studien* 103:207–39.

Reichenberger, Kurt. 1954. *Untersuchungen zur literarischen Stellung der* Consolatio Philosophiae. Kölner Romanistische Arbeiten, n.s., no. 3. Cologne: Romanisches Seminar der Universität Köln.

Reiss, Edmund. 1981. "The Fall of Boethius and the Fiction of the *Consolatio Philosophiae.*" *Classical Journal* 77:37–47.

Reitz, Christiane. 1990. "Beobachtungen zum fünften Buch der *Consolatio Philosophiae* des Boethius." *Würzburger Jahrbücher für die Altertumswissenschaft* 16:239–46.

Relihan, Joel C. 1984. "Ovid *Metamorphoses* I.1–4 and Fulgentius' *Mitologiae.*" *American Journal of Philology* 105:87–90.

———. 1987. "Vainglorious Menippus in the *Dialogues of the Dead.*" *Illinois Classical Studies* 12:185–206.

———. 1989. "The Confessions of Persius." *Illinois Classical Studies* 14:145–67.

———. 1990a. "Agathias Scholasticus (*A.P.* II.354), the Philosopher Nicostratus, and Boethius' *Consolation.*" *Classica et Mediaevalia* 41:119–29.

———. 1990b. "Menippus, the Cur from Crete." *Prometheus* 16:217–24.

———. 1990c. "Old Comedy, Menippean Satire, and Philosophy's Tattered Robes in Boethius' *Consolation.*" *Illinois Classical Studies* 15:183–94.

———. 1993. *Ancient Menippean Satire.* Baltimore: Johns Hopkins University Press.

———. 1995. Review of Martindale 1993. *Classical Review* 89:73.

———. 1996. "Menippus from Antiquity to the Renaissance." In Branham and Goulet-Cazé, 265–93.

———. 2004. Review of Dronke 1994. *Carmina Philosophiae* 13:86–90.

———. 2005. "Late Arrivals: Julian and Boethius." In Freudenburg 2005, 109–22.

———, trans. 2001. *Boethius:* Consolation of Philosophy. Indianapolis: Hackett Publishers. 2d printing, revised, 2003.

Riginos, Alice Swift. 1976. *Platonica: The Anecdotes Concerning the Life and Writings of Plato.* Columbia Studies in the Classical Tradition 3. Leiden: E. J. Brill.

Riikonen, H. K. *Menippean Satire as a Literary Genre with Special Reference to Seneca's* Apocolocyntosis. Commentationes Humanarum Litterarum 83. Helsinki: Societas Scientiarum Fennica.

Robertson, D. W., Jr. 1962. *A Preface to Chaucer: Studies in Medieval Perspectives.* Princeton: Princeton University Press.

Schmid, Wolfgang. 1976. "Philosophisches und Medizinisches in der 'Consolatio Philosophiae' des Boethius." In Maurach 1976, 341–84.

Schrenk, Lawrence P., ed. 1994. *Aristotle in Late Antiquity.* Studies in Philosophy and the History of Philosophy 27. Washington, D.C.: Catholic University of America Press.

Scott, Jamie. 1995. Christians and Tyrants: The Prison Testimonies of Boethius, Thomas More, and Dietrich Bonhoeffer. New York: Peter Lang.

Scourfield, J. H. D. 1993. *Consoling Heliodorus: A Commentary on Jerome,* Letter 60. Oxford: Clarendon Press.

———. 1996. "Consolation." In Simon Hornblower and Anthony Spawforth, eds., *Oxford Classical Dictionary.* 3d ed. Oxford: Oxford University Press, 378.

Shanzer, Danuta. 1983. "Ennodius, Boethius, and the Date and Interpretation of Maximianus's *Elegia III.*" *Rivista di Filologia e di Istruzione Classica* III:183–95.

———. 1984. "The Death of Boethius and the *Consolation of Philosophy.*" *Hermes* 112:352–66.

———. 1988. Review of Ratkowitsch 1986. *Gnomon* 60:259–61.

———. 1989. "Alan of Lille, Contemporary Annoyances, and Dante." *Classica et Medievalia* 40:251–69.

———. 1990. "A New Prologue for the 'De Planctu Nature'?" In Könsgen 1990, 163–72.

————. 1991. "Parturition through the Nostrils? Thirty-Three Textual Problems in Alan of Lille's 'De Planctu Nature.'" *Mittellateinisches Jahrbuch* 26:140–49.

————. 1996. Review of Pabst 1994. *Speculum* 71:749–52.

Sharples, R. W. ed., and trans. 1991. *Cicero:* On Fate (De Fato) *and Boethius:* The Consolation of Philosophy (Philosophiae Consolationis) *IV. 5–7, V.* Warminster: Aris & Phillips.

Sheridan, James J., trans. 1980. *Alan of Lille:* The Plaint of Nature. Medieval Sources in Translation 26. Toronto: Pontifical Institute of Mediaeval Studies.

Shiel, James. 1990. "Boethius' Commentaries on Aristotle." In Sorabji 1990, 349–72.

Simon, John Keller. 1994. "John Kennedy Toole and Walker Percy: Fiction and Repetition in *A Confederacy of Dunces.*" *Texas Studies in Literature and Language* 36:99–116.

Singleton, Charles S., trans. 1970. *Dante Alighieri: The Divine Comedy.* 3 vols. Bollingen Series 80. Princeton: Princeton University Press.

Sinko, T. 1905. "De Callimachi epigr. XXIII. W." *Eos* 11:1–10.

Sorabji, Richard. 1980. *Necessity, Cause, and Blame: Perspectives on Aristotle's Theory.* Ithaca: Cornell University Press.

————. 1983. *Time, Creation, and the Continuum: Theories in Antiquity and the Early Middle Ages.* Ithaca: Cornell University Press.

————. 1990. *Aristotle Transformed: The Ancient Commentators and Their Influence.* Ithaca: Cornell University Press.

Spade, Paul Vincent. 1994. *Five Texts on the Mediaeval Problem of Universals: Porphyry, Boethius, Abelard, Duns Scotus, Ockham.* Indianapolis: Hackett.

Spaltenstein, François. 1983. *Commentaire des Élégies de Maximien.* Bibliotheca Helvetica Romana 20. Rome: Institut Suisse de Rome.

Stewart, H. F., E. K. Rand, and S. J. Tester, trans. 1973. *Boethius: The Theological Tractates and* The Consolation of Philosophy. Loeb Classical Library. Cambridge: Harvard University Press.

Stock, Brian. 1972. *Myth and Science in the Twelfth Century: A Study of Bernard Silvester.* Princeton: Princeton University Press.

————. 1996. *Augustine the Reader: Meditation, Self-Knowledge, and the Ethics of Interpretation.* Cambridge: Harvard University Press.

Strange, Steven K. 1994. "Plotinus on Eternity and Time." In Schrenk 1994, 22–53.

Sutherland, Robert. 1992. "Eternity in *Darkness at Noon* and the *Consolation of Philosophy.*" *Classical and Modern Literature* 13:31–43.

Synan, Edward A. 1992. "Boethius, Valla, and Gibbon." *The Modern Schoolman* 69:475–91.

Szövérffy, Joseph. 1967. "Maximianus a Satirist?" *Harvard Studies in Classical Philology* 72:351–67.

Taylor, Thomas. 1823. *Select Works of Porphyry.* Reprint, Lawrence, Kan.: Selene Books, 1988.

Theiler, Willy. 1966. "Antike und christliche Rückkehr zu Gott." In his *Forschung zum Neuplatonismus*. Quellen und Studien zur Geschichte der Philosophie 10. Berlin: De Gruyter, 313–25.

Toohey, Peter. 1990. "Some Ancient Histories of Literary Melancholia." *Illinois Classical Studies* 15:143–61.

Toole, John Kennedy. 1980. *A Confederacy of Dunces*. Reprint 1987. New York: Grove Press.

Tränkle, H. 1984. "Ist die 'Philosophiae Consolatio' des Boethius zum vorgesehenen Abschluss gelangt?" In Fuhrmann and Gruber 1984, 311–19.

van Straaten, Modestus. 1946. *Panétius: Sa vie, ses écrits et sa doctrine, avec une édition des fragments*. Amsterdam: H. J. Paris.

Varvis, Stephen L. 1986. *The Consolation of Boethius*. Ph.D. diss., Claremont Graduate School, 1986. Abstract in *Dissertation Abstracts International* 47:2 (1986): 628A.

Veyne, Paul, ed. 1987. *A History of Private Life: From Pagan Rome to Byzantium*. Vol. 1. Trans. Arthur Goldhammer. Cambridge: Harvard University Press.

Viansino, G., ed. 1967. *Agazia Scolastico: Epigrammi*. Milan: Trevisini.

von Fritz, Kurt. 1937. "Nikostratos (26)." In *Realencyclopädie*, 17:547–51. Stuttgart: J. B. Metzler.

von Moos, Peter. 1971–72. *Consolatio: Studien zur mittellateinischen Trostliteratur über den Tod und zum Problem der christlichen Trauer*. Münstersche Mittelalter-Schriften. Vol. 3, books 1–4. München: Wilhelm Fink.

Walsh, P. G., trans. 1999. *Boethius:* The Consolation of Philosophy. Oxford: Oxford University Press.

Waterfield, Robin, trans. 1987. *Plato:* Theaetetus. Harmondsworth: Penguin Books.

Waterfield, Robin, trans., and Ian Kidd. 1992. *Plutarch: Essays*. Harmondsworth: Penguin Books.

Weinbrot, Howard D. 2002. "Bakhtin and Menippean Satire: Soviet Whiggery, Bion, Varro, Horace, and the Eighteenth Century." *Classical and Modern Literature* 22:33–56.

———. 2005. *Menippean Satire Reconsidered: From Antiquity to the Eighteenth Century*. Baltimore: Johns Hopkins.

Wetherbee, Winthrop. 1972. *Platonism and Poetry in the Twelfth Century: The Literary Influence of the School of Chartres*. Princeton: Princeton University Press.

———, trans. 1973. *The* Cosmographia *of Bernardus Silvestris*. Records of Civilization: Sources and Studies 89. New York: Columbia University Press.

Wilson, N. G. 1994. *Photius'* Bibliotheca: A Selection, Translated with Notes. London: Duckworth.

Wright, Thomas, ed. 1872. *Anglo-Latin Satirical Poets of the Twelfth Century*. Vol. 2. London: Longman & Co.

Ziolkowski, Eric. 1996. Review of Barbour 1994. *Journal of Religion* 76:165–66.

Ziolkowski, Jan. 1985. *Alan of Lille's Grammar of Sex: The Meaning of Grammar to a Twelfth-Century Intellectual*. Speculum Anniversary Monographs 10. Cambridge: The Medieval Academy of America.

Index

JOEL C. RELIHAN

is professor of classics at Wheaton College, Norton, Massachusetts.

His translation of Boethius's *Consolation of Philosophy*

was published in 2001 by Hackett Publishing Company.

www.ingramcontent.com/pod-product-compliance
Lightning Source LLC
Chambersburg PA
CBHW070359100426
42812CB00005B/1567